CITY TRENCHES

Urban Politics and the Patterning of Class in the United States

Ira Katznelson

 PANTHEON BOOKS · NEW YORK

LIBRARY OF CONGRESS CATALOGING IN PUBLICATION DATA
KATZNELSON, IRA.
CITY TRENCHES.
INCLUDES INDEX.
1. WASHINGTON HEIGHTS (NEW YORK, N.Y.)—POLITICS AND GOVERNMENT.
2. WASHINGTON HEIGHTS (NEW YORK, N.Y.)—SOCIAL CONDITIONS.
3. NEIGHBORHOOD GOVERNMENT—UNITED STATES—CASE STUDIES.
I. TITLE.
JS1240.W37K37   320.8'09747'1   81-47197
ISBN 0-394-50075-X   AACR2

CITY TRENCHES

For Deborah, and her bounty

"... 'civil society' has become a very complex structure and one which is resistant to the catastrophic 'incursions' of the immediate economic element (crises, depressions, etc.). The superstructures of civil society are like the trench-systems of modern warfare."

ANTONIO GRAMSCI, *Selections from the Prison Notebooks*

"Around the idea of settlement, nevertheless, a real structure of values has grown. It draws on many deep and persistent feelings: an identification with the people among whom we grew up; an attachment to the place, the landscape, in which we first lived and learned to see ... the strength of the idea of settlement, old and new, is then positive and unquestioned. But the problem has always been, for most people, how to go on living where they are. .... So that I then see the idealisation of settlement, in its ordinary literary-historical version, as an insolent indifference to most people's needs."

RAYMOND WILLIAMS, *The Country and the City*

"With economic life we will emerge from the routine, from the unconscious daily round. ... Higher still on the top floor we will place capitalism and its vast ramifications. ... What, we will be asked, has this sophistication to do with the humble lives at the bottom of the ladder? Everything perhaps, because it involves them in its gamble."

FERNAND BRAUDEL, *Capitalism and Material Life*

CONTENTS

PERSONAL ACKNOWLEDGMENTS

There is a famous folk tale about the wise men of Chelm. Needing wood for the construction of a synagogue, they felled a large hilltop forest and carried the logs, one by one, to their village below. When they were nearly done, a passing stranger asked why they had not rolled the logs down the hill. A community meeting decided to heed this sensible advice. Chelm's citizens carried each of the logs back up the hill, and, this time, rolled them down, one by one.

Writing this book has had more in common with this tale than I like to admit. When I arrived at the University of Chicago in 1974, I thought it was nearly done, since I had accomplished most of what I had initially set out to do. I had begun some three years earlier, under the funding auspices of the "New York Neighborhood Study" of the Bureau of Applied Social Research at Columbia University, directed by Allan Barton and managed on a daily basis by Nathalie Friedman, to study the programs in neighborhood government initiated by the administration of Mayor John Lindsay. Program evaluation was the *raison d'être* of the bureau's project, funded by grant GI-32437 of the Advanced Productivity Research and Technology Division of the Research Applied to National Needs Directorate (RANN) of the National Science Foundation. Barton and Friedman graciously allowed me to craft a component of this project that would focus exclusively on northern Manhattan, and which would inquire about the relationship between the policy responses of city hall and the character of the movements and demands that had called them forth. Above all, I was interested in exploring what had happened to the radical energies and mobilizations of the period of the "urban crisis" of the 1960s. My initial hunch was that simple incantations about cooptation would not do, but that at least part of the story had to be told in terms of the institutional responses by local officials that were similar in many respects of language and orientation to the thrust for community control by the insurgents of the 1960s. I set out, quite directly, to tell the tale of innovation and reform and of its impact on the period's urban movements and aspirations. Assisted by a first-rate research staff of Perry Davis, Sharman Mather, and especially Henry Wells and Arnold Zable, I was convinced I had answers to my questions, as well as a

reasonable working draft of a manuscript, by the end of 1974. Much of this material, in revised form, can be found in the later chapters of this volume.

But as I reflected on what I had accomplished from the distance of Chicago and under the stimulation of an extraordinary group of colleagues, I realized that I had raised as many questions as I had found answers. If, as I argued, the programs created in the late 1960s and early 1970s reduced uncertainties and restored order by absorbing the period's discontents in substantively ineffectual ways, then why did movement activists find them institutionally attractive? Why did they join and participate in activities that deflected their demands for fundamental changes in the social structure and that treated each issue they raised as if it were separate from all the others? Above all, why did the insurgents share with authorities an understanding of the content and limits of urban politics that made them able, in spite of the anger and adversary quality that marked their relationship, to avoid questions of economic investment, employment, and the discontents associated with work? Why was class absent from their mutual discourse? Why, instead, did they share a language of community, ethnicity, territoriality, and race? I began to feel like Stupid Boy in the Javanese folktale, "who, having been counseled by his mother to seek a quiet wife, returned with a corpse."*

To answer the questions my previous answers had generated, I tried to define the distinctive features of the rules of American urban politics that all the players adhered to, and to find, ultimately in the antebellum period, the origins of this pattern. The somewhat peculiar mix of macrohistorical, case-study, and policy analysis that characterizes *City Trenches* is the result of this personal history of self-clarification.

Along the way, like most authors (but perhaps more than most) I acquired many intellectual debts. My largest is to two women who shaped my work and this manuscript. It is very rare to be held to high standards in the demanding but supportive way of Deborah Socolow Katznelson, whose sustained intelligence and good sense were invaluable. Susan Gyarmati, my editor at Pantheon Books, taught me many lessons, some painful, about organization and clarity, and in the process helped me reformulate my ideas. Many colleagues read portions of the manuscript, talked formulations through, wrote me comments, or suggested alternative ways of considering my themes. They include Gordon Adams, Robert Alford, Demetrios Caraley, Manuel Castells, Stephen Elkin, Norman Fainstein, Susan Fainstein, Richard Fogelsong, Kenneth Fox, Ester Fuchs, J. David Greenstone, Charles Hamilton, Mark Kesselman, Margaret Levi, Michael Lipsky, Steven Lukes, Margit Mayer, Paul

*Clifford Geertz, *The Interpretation of Cultures* (New York: Basic Books, 1973), p. 196.

Peterson, Frances Fox Piven, Kenneth Prewitt, Adam Przeworski, Philippe Schmitter, Martin Shefter, Theda Skocpol, James Q. Wilson, William J. Wilson, Alan Wolfe, Aristide Zolberg, and Amy Bridges. I place Amy out of alphabetical order not only because her work on the antebellum period breaks major new ground, but because the footnotes in the text leave me in considerable arrears. The Chicago phase of my research and writing was helped by the committed work of research assistants Kevin Gleason, James Greer, and James Johnson. Judith Philips and Faye Lewis were sympathetic and efficient typists, who managed to be insistent editors along the way.

When I started to carry my logs down the hill, only Jessica had arrived on the scene. She has been joined by Zachary, who saw me roll them, and by Emma and Leah, who have just begun to see and have still to learn the lesson that buildings and books are not constructed without hauling, carrying, labor, and thought.

CITY TRENCHES

CHAPTER 1

Introduction

I

Most people live on the margin of history. They experience its flux, their lives are shaped by inherited and shifting limits, and their daily behavior testifies to the constraints on their lives. And yet, people are never merely passive agents of structural imperatives. Within lives whose definitions and possibilities are largely created for them, they create—families, symbols, solidary ties, beliefs, friendships, institutions, rebellions. In short, people create a culture, which in all its dimensions composes a set of resources for living in society and for affecting the contours of society.

Ordinarily, the cultural patterns of most working and poor people are hidden from view. They neither control nor find themselves recognized by the society's mechanisms of communication and schooling. Their neighborhoods are theirs alone. Only fragments of their lives appear in the public domain, often as the stuff of human-interest tales. So long as they are politically quiet (political scientists have seen their apathy as a bulwark of stability) and do not disturb the regular routines of other people, they can be absent from the calculations of middle- and upper-class America.

In the early 1960s such calculations were made with much confidence for the future. The slump of the 1930s receded as a distant aberration after the phenomenal boom of the postwar years. American global economic, political, and military dominance was unquestioned, even after Sputnik and the Bay of Pigs. The most important social challenges were associated with the bounty of a surplus of goods, money, and government largesse. Scarcity had been overcome. Social problems of race and poverty

could be identified and dealt with on their own terms. Civil rights, long denied, were legislated. For a time it even seemed that a major war and a program of major national social reform could be sustained simultaneously.[1]

America's older cities in the East, especially New York, were located spatially and ideologically at the core of this vision. Their bustling commerce, their diversified manufacturing, their explosive rates of downtown construction, and even their attempts at political reform placed the cities in the midstream of the period's complacent assumptions.

Yet in this urban core the very processes that had sustained the postwar boom—including, most important, uneven economic investment and development—came to undermine the security of the dominant and middle classes. By the middle of the decade, from the vantage point of its older cities, American society was under the threat of rebellions that might swamp the social order. Discourse about older American cities in the media, in political confrontations, in corporate boardrooms, and in countless private conversations came to be conducted in a language of "crisis." An extraordinary range of phenomena were understood in these terms. The "urban crisis" was about physical and social threats, revenue problems, housing abandonment, skewed economic development, poverty, disorder, dirt, welfare cheating, unionization, and uses of space. The total fabric of city life suddenly appeared uncertain and indeterminate—hence for many people very threatening, and for others (for the very same reason) a source of hope.

Students of urbanism have too often assumed that the city is a bounded "container with ill-defined, heterogeneous, and sometimes indiscriminate contents."[2] This way of thinking about cities is not new. On the eve of capitalist industrialization, Raymond Williams recently reminded us, English literature maintained a rigid distinction between the processes of rural exploitation—which were dissolved in idyllic portraits of landscapes and green fields—and urban wickedness. The country was innocent and sublime; the city was the dwelling place of iniquity of all kinds, including moral and material cupidity. This portrait was a mystification, of course, though for the dominant classes a useful one; the English town of the seventeenth and eighteenth centuries was the agent and the reflection of the patterns of the society as a whole.

Recourse to this artificial divide was the first, almost reflexive,

response to the dramatic forms of popular agitation that began in the early and middle 1960s in the older cities of the United States: the remarkable black political ferment above all; the rediscovery of white ethnicity; municipal employee militancy; and the formation of angry coalitions to resist public works that threatened the neighborhoods of the working class and the poor. The city was portrayed as the locale of a myriad of social ills, as if these shortcomings were uniquely or inherently urban, and as if cities and their problems were not condensed versions of the relations that characterize the society as a whole.

Attempts to domesticate urban problems by treating them as special, even technical, phenomena were overwhelmed by the sheer density of the turmoil, by its location in those cities that were the command posts of the political economy, and by its visibility. Riots from Watts to Newark, transit shutdowns, garbage strikes, and massive disobedience transported the daily lives of the usually invisible into the homes of most Americans. The confidence of middle- and upper-class America was severely shaken (a process abetted, of course, by the catastrophic war in Indochina). Old arrangements no longer cohered, or at least seemed not to; alternate configurations remained to be discerned.

It is remarkably difficult to recapture the degree of uncertainty, the fears and the hopes, of this period. Writing from a position of privileged access, Daniel Patrick Moynihan noted that "in retrospect, the domestic turbulence of the United States in the late 1960s may come to appear as something less than cataclysmic." But, he hastened to add, "this was not the view of the men then in office." The very expressive, often anomic character of the daily challenges to the social fabric—including attacks on property and police—created a mood of despair at the top of the social order that mirrored the heightened expectations of those at the bottom. The responses that were fashioned ranged from overt repression to attempts at appeasement.[3]

The targets of these public policies were not objects of compassion, but of fear born of uncertainty. The most fundamental practices and tenets of property and authority appeared insecure. Suddenly, because much was uncertain, much seemed possible. Such perceptions underlay the period's mass disruptions. Indeed, as students of organization remind us often, since the mobilization of large numbers of people to act in risky and potentially costly ways on behalf of shared ends is so difficult to achieve,[4] a common

sense that dramatic alterations in deeply rooted racial and distri-
butional practices were possible was the requisite for translating
a common thread of mass *ressentiment* into a willingness to engage
in irregular political activity.

The turmoil in American cities, in short, displayed a strong
resemblance to those "moments of madness" when all seemed
possible that Aristide Zolberg identifies in the French past.[5] Like
1848, 1871, and 1968 in Paris, the 1960s in America were times
of heightened sensibilities, of intoxicating alternatives, and of the
erosion of boundaries between the political and the private, the
expected and unexpected, the routine and the irregular. The
bursting of bounds—of segregation, deference, demarcated space,
and on and on, it seemed—produced for many the spirit of a
liberating party.

This party is over. From today's vantage point it is clear that
this particular era of urban crisis has come to a close. Neither the
fears nor the promises of radical or fundamental change have
been redeemed. Political language provides a striking indicator.
In the middle and late 1960s, it was commonplace to speak
dramatically of power and powerlessness, internal colonialism,
repression, poverty, racial and ethnic discrimination, participatory
democracy, and community control. For a short period, these
terms defined debated alternatives, and the political noise of the
city was deafening. The political language in the same cities only
a decade later is quite different. Concerned principally with
managerial and fiscal matters, the new terminology defines action
in terms of balancing budgets, bondholder confidence, service
cutbacks, wage freezes, municipal employee layoffs, the erosion
of the tax base, and making do with less. The pluralist language
of group conciliation that was replaced by a discourse of conflict
and redistribution of the 1960s today concentrates on fiscal
requirements in terms unthinkable just a few years ago. "The
main job of municipal government," Edward Koch stated two
months after his inauguration as mayor of New York, "is to create
a climate in which private business can expand in the city to
provide jobs and profit. It's not the function of government to
create jobs on the public payroll."[6]

Having passed not only through the social turbulence of the
1960s, of the "babel of voices and the multiplication of claimants,"[7]
but now also through its termination, we are still, remarkably,
without adequate analyses—and even historical, theoretical, and

political criteria—for making reasonable assessments of what happened. Just a little more than two decades ago, it was fashionable for social scientists to lament the "lost world" of urban politics. American cities, which had been the locales for many studies in the early decades of the century, had ceased to excite scholarly and popular imaginations, or so it seemed.[8] But no longer. There has been an outpouring of work that has searched for convincing interpretations of the urban turmoil of the 1960s. But a reading of this literature brings to mind Lévi-Strauss's report on his quest in Brazil for a people "spared the agitations of history." Penetrating the interior, he discovered the Tupi-Kawahib, totally untouched by European civilization. But since he and they lacked a common system of signs, he found their culture unintelligible. Having found them, he could not know them.

The ways we usually talk about urban politics make it impossible to know what has happened and why. The urban crisis has often been understood as the sum of discrete microcrises of housing, transport, finance, and the like, and new public policies are proposed to deal with each of the diagnosed "social problems." The language of analysis is clinical, not political; diagnostic, not historical. Far too much remains hidden from view. Institutionalized inequalities, overall patterns of capitalist development, and the nature of the contemporary state are not seen as part of the crisis. Quite the contrary. Technical solutions to the microcrises are posed as possible within the existing political economy.[9] It remains stubbornly the case, however, that the technical and social problems of the 1960s have persisted, and in many respects been aggravated, in the 1970s. Yet the "crisis" of the 1960s was "resolved." The technocratic approach has nothing to say about the crucial political dimensions of the crisis and its resolution.

There exist, of course, many treatments of political conflicts in large American cities. To the extent that these works have been more than merely descriptive, their main theoretical interest has been to support or to contradict the propositions of various academic analysts of community power who differ about whether urban America is governed by cohesive elites or by more fluid and permeable sets of overlapping, even competing, groups. These treatments have quite rightly underscored that city politics has been a *contest* whose main participants have been bureaucrats, politicians, and ethnic, racial, and community groups that have

struggled, often bitterly, about the scope, governance, and delivery of municipal services. The massive literature about these conflicts is not so much wrong as it is too narrow. Quite unlike Lévi-Strauss in his investigation of the Tupi-Kawahib, most analysts of urban politics share too completely and unreflectively the tacit cultural assumptions of those whose behavior they wish to understand. In describing the "play" of city politics, they take its boundaries and rules as a given.

Analyses of games or contests, political or otherwise, must do more than describe the players and their adversary play. They must also say something about the boundaries of the contest, which define its limits prior to the playing of the game itself. Such boundaries are an integral part of the rules of the game: they determine who may participate, what identities participants may assume, what they may legitimately do, and so on. Such rules preclude certain outcomes and make others improbable.

American urban politics has been governed by boundaries and rules that stress ethnicity, race, and territoriality, rather than class, and that emphasize the distribution of goods and services, while excluding questions of production or workplace relations. *The centerpiece of these rules has been the radical separation in people's consciousness, speech, and activity of the politics of work from the politics of community.* This subjective division has been such a powerful feature of American urban life that it has been operative even in situations where blue-collar workers live in immediate proximity to their factories. In South Chicago, for example, mammoth steel mills loom over the surrounding communities that house their workers. In the mills, these workers see themselves as labor (in opposition to the steel companies and, on occasion, to capital more generally); and as labor they are quite militant. The ordinary idiom of plant life is that of class. There, clear majorities vote for radical insurgencies within their union. Yet as soon as these workers pack up and go home, they cease to see themselves primarily as workers. On the East Side and Hegewisch, in Irondale and Slag Valley, they are Croatians, Mexicans, Poles. Here the Tenth Ward organization of the Chicago Democratic party machine, whose language is ethnicity, patronage, and services, is political king.[10]

This division between work and community has been constitutive of American urban politics for a very long time. Participants in city politics avail themselves of the set of abilities, opportunities,

and limitations presented by this cultural system of language and activity.[11] Yet, curiously, urbanists have paid little attention to the rules of this game, to their origins, persistence, and consequences. If we are to understand recent urban history, we must tackle these questions, for if we do not we will not be able to understand why the events of the 1960s constituted a "crisis," or how so energetic a challenge was resolved so quickly and without the kinds of changes that authorities had feared so much. We thus have two tasks—to account for the distinctive linguistic, ideological, and organizational conventions of American urban politics, and to show how these traditions of thought, expression, and practice informed the behavior of city residents during the period of the urban crisis and its resolution.

II

The first of these tasks is the subject of Part One. I argue that what is special about American big-city politics and what is distinctive about the American class experience constitute two aspects of a single pattern of historical development. This marriage of urban studies and questions usually treated under the rubric "American exceptionalism" is not a familiar one, but it is a natural match. Industrialization and working-class history throughout the West have been mainly urban phenomena. Workers have experienced industrial capitalism as dwellers in the cities where they have labored and where they have lived. To a very large degree differences in the national histories of working classes reflect the different ways in which workers have understood the relationship between urban workplaces and residential communities.

If the boundaries and rules of U.S. urban politics have rarely been scrutinized in comparative perspective by urbanists, the same cannot be said for class relations more generally. Most European and American observers have thought American cultural and political understandings of class to be rather peculiar, considered within the universe of the capitalist societies of the West. When the Dutch historian Johan Huizinga, best known as a student of the cultural life of the Low Countries and northern France in the Middle Ages, undertook to teach a course in American history at the University of Leiden during the First World War, for example, he felt like a person who is "accustomed to the strict, transparent forms of classical music . . . hearing a

modern composition for the first time. He does not immediately perceive the form that controls it . . .; instead, he is merely confused at first by the overpowering masses of sound and the unfamiliar harmonies." A central source of his difficulty was the apparent inappropriateness of Continental patterns of class and group association for an understanding of the American experience. The contrapuntal relations of individualism and association seemed to be distinctive in the United States, as were the bases of group conflict: "We see exaggerated movements, passionate conflicts, and flagrant contradictions of words and deeds, but the reasons for the conflicts and the causes of the movements are not immediately clear."[12] Class relations did not seem as simple or as transparent as elsewhere in the industrial capitalist world. The links between categories of individuals and their behavior were more remote, or at least less obvious.

This set of puzzles and concerns was not Huizinga's alone, of course, but has been the centerpiece of virtually all varieties of American historiography and social science. To what extent, and in what way, is the American experience distinctive? What are the peculiar features of American social relations in general, and of class relations in particular? And how, given these relations, many of which are pregnant with conflict, does American society cohere? These questions imply a comparative reference. Sometimes, as in Werner Sombart's query, "Why is there no socialism in the United States?"[13] the comparative frame is clearly stated. But even when it has not been made explicit, what appeared to be the relative absence of class-based politics in the United States has been the central focus of treatments of American exceptionalism.

This immense literature, whose main themes I will review briefly in a moment, lacks a systematic explanation of exactly what has been peculiar in the American class experience, except for a general agreement about the relative unimportance of class as an element of political life. The term "American exceptionalism" has too often been used as if it provided a self-evident explanation, yet its meaning is hardly obvious.

If the issue is as Sombart stated it, there was nonetheless a significant socialist movement in America, in the period in which he wrote. It was by no means clear in the first few years of the twentieth century that mass socialist or labor parties had a more promising future in some European countries than they appeared to have in the United States. Sombart himself concluded his volume with the prediction that "in the next generation Socialism

in America will very probably experience the greatest possible expansion of its appeal."[14] If it is held that the issue of American exceptionalism is why the United States has not become a socialist society, as a very simpleminded reading of Marx might have led one to expect, then it must be noted the United States hardly stands alone in not having achieved the predictions of the teleological theorists. No Western society has ever been socialist in the usual sense of the public ownership and command of investment and industrial capital, though the size and nature of welfare-state expenditures and the ability of governments to regulate business and even to own some share of capital have, of course, varied from state to state. If it is argued that the issue of American exceptionalism hinges on Lenin's distinction between revolutionary and trade-union consciousness—that is, between the willingness of workers to overthrow capitalism as opposed to their willingness to fight for more goods and services within capitalism—then it must again be pointed out that the United States is quite typical. Nowhere in the West has the proletariat lived up to Lenin's revolutionary standard. At least to date, the most revolutionary activities of the working classes in Europe and North America were their earliest ones, their resistance to the creation of the capitalist order itself. Once inside the capitalist epoch, as E. P. Thompson argues, the epochal characteristics "recede into unimportance beside the local particularities. What mattered to people was not whether it was a capitalism but whether it was a ruthless or a tolerable capitalism."[15] Nor is the issue of American exceptionalism one of the absence of class-related conflicts. American history is littered with the passion of extraordinary resistance and struggle. Labor-organizing disputes, violent strikes, indirect resistance to the authority of capital (as in sabotage, absenteeism, and shop-floor crime), community-based land use and school conflicts, and struggles against the state have been regular characteristics of class conflict and disequilibrium in American capitalism. In all of these ways the United States does not seem qualitatively different from other Western capitalist societies.

And yet the issue of American exceptionalism cannot be summarily dismissed. References to the absence of socialism or revolutionary currents elsewhere or to class conflicts in the United States notwithstanding, the American experience of class *has* been special, but it remains to specify how and in what ways.

Attempts to make sense of what is special about class in America

have ordinarily proceeded without this specification. They have most frequently focused on one of three conditions of American life—the racial and ethnic fragmentation of the working class itself, the unusual economic rewards of the economy, or the values that integrate American society—and they have generally argued that these conditions have made virtually impossible the development of class-based politics.[16]

America's working class was not created once and for all, but has been fashioned and refashioned in the past century and a half as members of national, ethnic, or religious groups that had been outside of the frame of capitalist labor relations have entered the "free" labor market. The composition of the working class has thus been determined by three population movements—from country to city, from east to west and south to north, and from Europe and Asia and the Caribbean. The result has been an incredibly polyglot working class, differentiated culturally, racially, economically and spatially. Rowland Berthoff notes,

We expect to find a certain coincidence in the South, for example, of British ancestry, Protestant religion, and well-defined class distinctions; or in a northern coal mining town of people of Slavic descent, Catholic or Orthodox religion, and the working class. While there have no doubt been individuals who incorporated in themselves every conceivable regional, ethnic, and social mixture, still our history has made some combinations of ancestry and religion, locale, and class more likely than others.[17]

The prevalence of such combinations, it is argued, makes class solidarity difficult, if not impossible. The workers of virtually each successive generation since the 1830s have been recruited from a new pool of people. Torn by the traumas of migration and proletarianization, ethnic and racial groups have tended to enclose themselves within spatially as well as culturally specific communities. Writing in 1893, Engels explained why there was "No Large Socialist Party in America" in just these terms:

Then, and more especially, immigration, which divides the workers into two groups: the native born and the foreigners, and the latter into (1) the Irish, (2) the Germans, (3) the many small groups, each of which understands only itself: Czechs, Poles, Italians, Scandinavians, etc. And then the Negroes. To form a single party out of these requires quite unusually powerful incentives. Often there is a sudden violent *élan*, but the bourgeoisie need only wait passively and the dissimilar elements of the working class fall apart again.[18]

More recently, as American society has been torn by racial conflicts and assertions of ethnic identity, this explanation has appeared still more compelling. It is thus not surprising that numerous studies echo the claim that "it was the divisions within the working class that constituted the critical deterrent to the development of a unified working class social and political movement."[19]

This argument is only partially convincing. Much of the history of the American labor movement suggests otherwise. As one analyst has put it, "If mechanics of the 1830's and 1840's saw the Irish as the cause of their declining economic status, workers after 1880 were less confused about who their antagonist was. With the exception of non-whites, the organization of the Knights of Labor, the IWW and the CIO could hardly be said to have been significantly impeded by ethnic hostility within the working class."[20] To be sure, there was much suspicion of and hostility toward new immigrants and blacks in these and other working-class organizations. Nevertheless, generation after generation of immigrants joined unions in disproportionate numbers, organized some of the country's most militant labor struggles, and strongly resisted the erosion of working-class wages and conditions that accompanied the growth of large capital.

Under some circumstances, ethnic and racial ties may actually stimulate collective class activity. Writing about Polish activists in the CIO of the 1930s, David Greenstone suggests that their ethnic ties may have provided the necessary affect, trust, and shared experience for overcoming the barriers to militancy in a situation where the potential costs were high.[21] Likewise, Herbert Gutman has found that the process of industrializing native and immigrant rural and artisan cultures in the United States, which has regularly recurred, has repeatedly provoked the kinds of class-forming collisions that E. P. Thompson found to be the core elements in the making of the English working class. At different historical moments, to be sure, virtually all new, first-generation members of the American working class have *shared* this wrenching transformation. Different though their particularistic pasts may be, most American workers share a heritage of material and cultural trauma, as well as common experiences in their present labors, which provide the *potential* for collaboration. Indeed, as Gutman shows, the highly differentiated community lives of ethnic workers often served as separate but reinforcing sources of refuge and energy for rebellion.[22]

The "character of the working class" explanation thus cuts two ways. It obviously delineates potential divisions within the working class. With respect to race, especially, as opposed to ethnic divisions among white workers, the distinctive character of the black experience—at once economic, cultural, and political—has created fissures in American society that are as deep as, and often deeper than, those of class. But with this one immense exception (and even here the matter is not one of absolutes), ethnic divisions within the working class do not automatically cause a diminution of class collaboration; indeed, as we have seen, quite the contrary may be the case. By itself, therefore, an analysis of American exceptionalism based on these divisions alone is unconvincing.

A second account of American exceptionalism stresses the bountiful nature of American capitalism. Since individuals and groups have over time been able to achieve upward mobility that is comparatively unusual, they are likely either to find individualistic solutions to economic problems or to use mobility as a benchmark of success. The classic statement of this position is Werner Sombart's. Writing in 1906, he compared the incomes and life-styles of American and German workers, and found the American standard significantly higher. Noting that a mass socialist movement existed in Germany that linked the workplace and the community dimensions of class, while in the United States most workers voted for the two major political parties, he argued that "all socialist utopias have come to grief on roast beef and apple pie."[23] A complementary argument has been made by a number of scholars in the United States, the most important of whom is Stephan Thernstrom. In an essay based on research in Newburyport, Massachusetts, and in Boston, he argues that residential, occupational, and intergenerational mobility have been higher in the United States than elsewhere and "that this distinctiveness did have a good deal to do with another fairly distinctive aspect of the American historical record—the failure of working-class-based protest movements to attract a mass following."[24]

Underpinning this kind of analysis are the assumptions that economic growth creates social order and that there is a rather mechanical relationship between high mobility and a low degree of threat to the social order. These assumptions are problematical. Growth and mobility are often basic causes of dislocations, tensions, and crises of order. But even at the more elementary level

of facts, the comparative-mobility explanation is highly suspect. Thernstrom argues that some 25 to 30 percent of the blue-collar workers in Boston from 1880 to 1963 moved to the middle class in their lifetimes and that "fully 40 percent of the working-class sons in Boston held middle-class jobs of some kind by the end of their own careers. The comparable figure for mid-nineteenth-century Marseille . . . was a mere 11 percent. . . . certainly here was evidence which challenged the socialist critic's assumption that the dream of individual mobility was illusory and that collective advance was the only realistic hope for the worker."[25] That these figures do indicate that the ideology of mobility had some basis in fact is not in doubt. But the extent and the meaning of mobility surely are.

Mobility rates are artifacts of boundary definitions. By including *all* white-collar workers in the middle class, Thernstrom found high mobility rates within and between generations. But, as Edward Greer has recently pointed out, if he had more compellingly drawn his upper line of the working class between lower-tier white-collar workers and other white-collar workers, he would have found a very different portrait emerging: "Except for those on the margin of this class divide, the rate of upward social mobility for male workers (measured either within or between generations) is rather low: well below ten per cent. On the other hand, those with substantial wealth or high level jobs are very likely to be able to pass along their class position to their sons."[26]

Even if Thernstrom's own categories are used, his comparative assertions (which echo Sombart and much conventional wisdom) remain problematical. In a rejoinder to Thernstrom, Seymour Martin Lipset has drawn on his own research and that of other scholars to argue that American mobility rates are not distinctive: "A number of students of social mobility in comparative perspective (Sorokin, Glass, Lipset and Bendix, Miller, Blau and Duncan, and Boudon) have concluded from an examination of mobility data collected in various countries that the American rate of mass social mobility is not uniquely high, and that a number of European countries have had comparable rates."[27] Although such data are more impressive for the twentieth century than the nineteenth, recent scholarship, like the work of Tom Rishøj on Copenhagen from 1850 to 1950, finds mobility rates comparable to those that Thernstrom found in Boston or that other scholars have found in different American cities.[28]

Following Pitirim Sorokin's pathbreaking 1927 study of mobility,[29] Lipset argues that this finding is hardly surprising, since mobility rates may most fundamentally be explained by structural causes, not by uniquely national causes such as ideologies or belief systems about opportunity. Mobility rates are the consequence of the relationship of empty occupational places created by economic development and the numbers of people available to fill these places. Thus most cross-national studies have found that countries with a higher proportion of the population in industry (and a lower proportion of the labor force in agriculture) have the higher rates of social mobility. Class barriers are surmountable in this limited way because they must be if the reproduction of the class structure is to occur.

The last of the leading conventional explanations of American exceptionalism—the national-character tradition—asserts that a shared value system, created well before industrialization, fashioned the people of the United States into *a people* resistant to class interpretations. The search for this overarching national character has produced a litany of now familiar phrases: individualism, absence of a feudal past, the frontier, equality *and* achievement, diversity, practicality, consensus. In the most sophisticated treatments, as in Michael Kammen's, the American character is most or even all of these features jumbled into a stable set of apparently contradictory meanings. For Louis Hartz, Daniel Boorstin, and other leading interpreters of the American character, the United States is distinguished by a durable cultural configuration of values and ideas shaped in the crucible of the colonial and early-postcolonial periods. The structuring principle of American history is precisely that combination of values that reflect what the nation was not (feudal, urbanized, or crowded), as well as what it was (property owning, institutionally British, and socially pluralist), at a time of the vigorous development of Lockean liberal theory.[30]

The criticisms of this dominant vision are well known. Immigrants imported a feudal past. The frontier offered less opportunity than Turner claimed for it. Fundamental divisions of class and race mock portraits of a homogeneous social structure in early America.[31] Consensual interpretations usually treat conflict and its sources with patronizing afterthought. These criticisms, which are largely correct, do not puncture the central assertion of the national-character interpretation, however, which claims

that the structuring die of the American experience was cast early, and that it has informed and canalized subsequent events. Struggles can be accommodated in this view (even though they are usually not), because it holds that their direction, ideological claims, and relative chances of success have been shaped by the defining elements of American character, values, and style. Hartz himself stressed that the dichotomy between conflict and consensus is a false one:

One cannot say of the liberal society analysis that by concentrating on national unities it rules out the meaning of domestic conflict. Actually it discovers that meaning, which is obscured by the very Progressive analysis that presumably concentrates on conflict. You do not get closer to the significance of an earthquake by ignoring the terrain on which it takes place. On the contrary, that is one of the best ways of making sure you will miss its significance. The argument over whether we should stress solidarity or conflict in American politics misleads us by advancing a false set of alternatives.[32]

Indeed, as he later wrote, it is the character of their interrelationship that defines what is distinctive about the United States: "American history contains both of these elements in the proportions which make it, in relation to other national histories, explicable."[33]

Much the same may be said about the other well-known critique of the national-character tradition—that it accurately describes the United States in the early-nineteenth century, perhaps even to the beginning of the twentieth century. With the rise of large-scale capital and the Progressive state, it is rightly said, America underwent fundamental changes. A society of independent property owners became a society divided between capital and labor. Radical changes in the character of immigration, first from Europe, and in this century from the South, have transformed the relations of culture, class, race, and space. The new America is urban, not rural; its continent settled, not largely empty. The United States has become a global power. The liberal America of the national-character consensus tradition, in short, ceased to exist long ago. Indeed, by the 1880s, under the impact of capitalist industrialization, many Americans bemoaned the Europeanization of the United States: "We are now an *old country*"; "The Golden Age is indeed over—the Age of Iron has taken its place."[34]

Correct as this assessment is, it too misses the central point of the national-character tradition. Values, ideologies, and cultural

practices may long outlast the destruction of their formative environments. This claim cannot be rebutted by describing vast alterations in the economy and the state.

The basic problems of the national-character school thus have little to do with America's history of conflict or with the fact that the country has changed very much. The character of the origins and the early decades of the United States undeniably shaped the structures of meaning that provided motivation and interpretation for subsequent events. Unlike modern France or England, the United States was born, in Daniel Boorstin's phrase, without having experienced conception. The absence of a genuine ancien régime ruled out a social revolutionary birth, and thus also ruled out a European-style counterrevolution. As a result American politics took place within narrower bounds than did the politics of other Western societies, within what Hartz calls "this fixed, dogmatic liberalism of a liberal way of life. It is the secret root from which have sprung many of the most puzzling of American cultural phenomena."[35]

Hartz argues that the antagonisms of American political life, which have mainly presented themselves in a group politics lacking in class identification, have been contained within the limits of liberal possibility. But to the extent that this is a claim that a liberal tradition rules out a politics of class—to that extent it is wrong. Individualist and instrumentalist orientations to political life by individual workers are quite compatible with collectivist behavior based on class affiliations. Privatized aims may promote the adoption of collective means—in trade unions, or in socialist or labor parties. Indeed, John Goldthorpe and David Lockwood coined the term "instrumental collectivism" to capture just such features of the English working-class experience.[36] As we shall see in Chapter 3, the idiom of class was an ordinary feature of antebellum politics in the United States. *What needs to be explained is not the absence of class in American politics but its limitation to the arena of work.*

We shall see, too, that the arguments of this school, particularly those that concern the power of liberal thought, *are* germane to that task, but not in the overly simple form in which they are usually presented. Our challenge will be to connect explanations about the liberal national character of the United States to the ways in which governmental forms and policies affected people's thoughts and actions regarding the separation of work and home.

Lacking a coherent vision of the relationship between values and the social structure, the national-character tradition has been incapable of explaining how liberal values have affected American history at specific moments. In the work of the tradition's leading figures, the "liberal tradition" has become a sponge term, soaking up all kinds of meaning. American values hover over American history at a level too remote to account convincingly for specific behavior and events. The value structure of the American experience appears fixed and without challenge.

Yet no system of values, however powerful, is automatically self-reproducing. If values persist, then their persistence must be explained. Such explanations are notably lacking in the work of the national-character school. It is instructive to note that with the exception of Daniel Boorstin, who thinks that the absence of coherent thought and ideology is the basis of consensus, most of the school's scholars devote rather little space to post–Civil War American history. Any interpretation that stresses, as mine will, the importance of early American cultural patterns for subsequent developments must account not only for the origins but also for the reproduction of these values and practices. Such questions, Richard Hofstadter has observed, "must be a matter of behavior as well as thought, or of institutions as well as theories."[37] A cultural system is not an immutable set of ideas or values, but a prescription for making sense of the experiences of living in society and for affecting society.[38]

III

What each of these schools of explanation lacks is a clear statement about which aspects of living in society have been mapped in a unique way by the working classes in America, compared with those in other countries. The analytical marriage between urbanism and American exceptionalism may produce the progeny needed to remedy this deficiency. Part One, the product of weaving these connubial ties, will argue that the main elements of explanation for the boundaries and rules of American urban politics, *and* for what has been special about class relations in the United States, may be found in the ways in which workers understood the objective separation of work and home in early industrial cities and acted on that understanding. The major societies of the West have shared a very similar history of the

spatial patterning of workplaces and communities from the development of feudal towns to modern industrial cities. I trace this common heritage in Chapter 2, and I contend that differences between these societies in the ways their working classes have interpreted the growing division between work and community date from the period of rapid industrial urbanization—roughly from the beginning of the nineteenth century to the 1870s. At that time modern working classes (characterized by their situation as people who work in exchange for a wage, and who neither own nor control investments, capital, or the labor of others), modern cities (characterized by the separation of work and community, in space and by role, for all social classes), and modern politics (characterized by the duties and rights of citizenship, including the possibility of the vote) all made their simultaneous appearance. How workers mapped this new and problematical situation, and why, are questions of comparative history.

I shift the focus in Chapter 3 from what the industrializing societies had in common in spite of their differences to how they differed in spite of what they held in common. The objective separation of work and home in the antebellum city presented American workers with three logical and empirical choices. They might have come to see themselves (as workers did in England, for example) as workers not only at work but also at home; or (as in the "plural societies" of Belgium and Holland) as ethnics at work and ethnics at home. Although these two configurations were in fact lively possibilities at the time, they gave way to a third, and distinctively American, pattern. The two main European definitions of work and home used the same coordinates for both realms. In the United States, by contrast, they were quite separate: most members of the working class thought of themselves as workers at work but as ethnics (and residents of this or that residential community) at home. To borrow Amy Bridges's phrase, the American working class was formed as labor; outside of work, nonclass identifications and institutions predominated.

Some of the distinctive features of American political and social history have been noticed so often that their very familiarity has been a barrier to systematic understanding. They include (in relative, comparative terms) the failure of attempts to create socialist and labor parties on the various Continental and European models, and an ordinary political language that treats class

as only one of a larger number of competing bases of affiliation. I argue below that these commonly observed realities are aspects of a sharply divided consciousness about class in American society that finds many Americans acting on the basis of the shared solidarities of class at work, but on that of ethnic and territorial affinities in their residential communities. The links between work and community-based conflicts have been unusually tenuous. Each kind of conflict has had its own separate vocabulary and set of institutions: work, class, and trade unions; community, ethnicity, local parties, churches, and voluntary associations. Class, in short, has been lived and fought as a *series of partial* relationships, and it has therefore been experienced and talked about as only one of a number of competing bases of social life. *What is distinctive about the American experience is that the linguistic, cultural, and institutional meaning given to the differentiation of work and community, a characteristic of all industrial capitalist societies, has taken a sharply divided form, and that it has done so for a very long time.*

This system of values and customary practices, elaborated over time, has provided the main political formula of ideas, organizations, and activities that has protected the core arrangements of capitalism in the United States from challenge. Writing in a prison cell in Fascist Italy, Antonio Gramsci, this century's most original Marxist thinker, argued that in the advanced industrial societies such clusters of ideas and behaviors "are like the trench systems of modern warfare."[39] In wars of position—like World War One—the system of trenches defines the terrain of battle and thus imparts a logic to the war itself. Because each system of trenches is distinctive, it defines both the place and the content of conflict.

Gramsci's metaphor for what he called "the superstructures of civil society" is apt. All of the capitalist democracies of western Europe and North America are defined politically by their country-specific systems of political and social "trenches," which delineate what is special about class and politics in each society and which help shape the country's rules of conflict. In the United States the most important set of rules has been urban. This American urban-class system of "city trenches" has defined what is exceptional about class (and race) in the United States, and it has made very difficult the emergence of socialist, social democratic, or labor parties on the European model of the late-nineteenth and early-twentieth centuries.

Elsewhere in the West, mass-membership party and union organizations have succeeded, at least much of the time and in varying degrees, in connecting the segmented dimensions of class, even if usually in distributive, reformist ways. As both a cause and a reflection of this comparative success, ordinary politics in virtually all the European democracies is defined by institutionalized class-based party competition, in which social democratic, socialist, and communist parties use, with different degrees of intensity, a *global* rhetoric and analysis of class, and mobilizing strategies that join economics and politics, and link together the struggles of workers where they labor and where they live. Such parties or movements require that supporters see themselves as workers not only at work but also at home. The separate consciousness of early American industrialization thus impeded a global class politics in later industrialization. And once such a politics was ruled out, a great many other political questions and formulations became inaccessible. Huizinga's puzzles are explicable in these terms.

Although Chapters 2 and 3 propose solutions to these often bewildering features of class in the United States, they do no more than allow us to begin to investigate the central questions of this volume: what kind of crisis was the urban crisis of the 1960s, and how was it resolved? The unruly skirmishes against local authorities in the 1960s represented a limited, but powerful, revolt against some of the most basic features of the system of "city trenches." The story of this challenge, and of the reactions to it, is, of course, a tale of many cities and communities. Nevertheless, I have chosen the strategy of a community study to explain in close detail how the traditional urban system worked, how it was challenged, and how it was ultimately reconstituted.

The locale I have selected is Washington Heights–Inwood, a heterogeneous working-class community of approximately 200,000 in Manhattan north of Harlem. Unlike many community studies, the portrait of northern Manhattan is not an ethnographic miniature. "Anthropologists," Clifford Geertz reminds us, "don't study villages (tribes, towns, neighborhoods); they study *in* villages."[40] I make no claim that northern Manhattan is American society *writ small* or that it is representative of all city neighborhoods. Indeed, no such simple microcosm exists. For the purposes of examining the main questions of this book, however, a study of this territory commends itself for a number of reasons. As the

last area of Manhattan to be settled by large numbers of people, the community came into being only in the 1920s. Consequently it is possible to see with unusual clarity how inherited cultural ideas and activities concerning class, ethnicity, and politics were incorporated into the built form and institutions of an area created *de novo,* and how the economic changes, population shifts, and political reforms that have been at work in all the older large Eastern and Midwestern cities for the past four decades affected these relationships to produce the crisis of the 1960s. In this community we can also look closely at how the authorities responded to the disorderly politics of the urban crisis.

This analysis is conceived, much as Harry Eckstein thought of his well-known study of Norway, as a "tentative case study."[41] By itself, no study of one place over time can constitute "proof" of the many assertions in this book. But such is not my intent. I do not claim that the case study is a test of my arguments about American exceptionalism. Rather, the treatment of northern Manhattan grapples with the consequences of the American urban system and presents, with Part One, what I take to be a highly plausible set of claims. *City Trenches* as a whole should be read as an extended argument. And like any argument, it is presented in order to be argued with. Indeed, the book concludes by contending with the theoretical and strategic arguments of other students of urbanism and class in the United States and by suggesting alternate directions for research and political practice.

PART ONE

American Patterns of Urbanism and Class

Community, Capitalist Development, and the Emergence of Class

What has been the relationship between work and home in the development of cities in the West? To take the central issue of this chapter, why have there been times when most people worked in their communities, and times when they did not? Historical changes of this sort cannot be understood in isolation from the rest of society; they must be viewed in terms of changes in the economy, political authority, and uses of space.[1]

In its broadest terms the gradual separation of work and home is part of the story of capitalist development, from its earliest nascent forms within feudalism to the present. Like the long and varied history of capitalist development itself, the history of urban communities and their transformations is "not a movement proceeding along a straight line, but has been marked, rather, by a series of separate impulses not forming continuations one of another, but interrupted by crises. . . . This history resembles a staircase, every step of which rises abruptly above that which precedes it. We do not find ourselves in the presence of a gentle and regular ascent, but of a series of lifts."[2] What is the nature of these "lifts"?

I

Visions of the high-medieval town perform an important ideological function for those who wish to distinguish a more satisfactory past from the present. Distinctions such as those between *Gemeinschaft* and *Gesellschaft,* folk and urban, and tradition and modernity are used to distinguish a lost (but retrievable?) past

from contemporary society. In this usage, the term "community," Raymond Williams notes, "never seems to be used unfavourably, and never to be given any positive distinguishing term."[3] As a warmly persuasive symbol, "community" is the alternative to negative labels for the present: mass society, capitalism, the acquisitive society, industrialism, the modern age. The strongest empirical warrants for this approach have been provided by the medieval town. "The commune," Murray Bookchin argues,

provided not only security to its populace but also a deep sense of community. It offered not only protection but the comfort of sociality and a human scale the burgher could comprehend and in which he could find a uniquely individual space. The commune was home—not merely an environment that surrounded the home. The concrete nature of the labor process, the directness, indeed, familiar character, of nearly all social relations, and the human scale of civic life which fostered a high degree of personal participation in urban affairs—all combined to retain a natural core to social life which the cosmopolises of the ancient world had dissolved with the passing of the *polis*. . . . Contrast this mentality with that of bourgeois society—a society that dissolves the natural basis of civic life by transmuting the fraternal relations of the medieval commune into harsh commodity relations. . . .[4]

As in Lewis Mumford's work, this contrast hinges on the distinction between organic wholeness and unnatural fragmentation.[5] Although the principal function of the town in feudal society was the exchange of agricultural and handicraft production, within the town the vast majority of the population were artisans. The town's legally free residents were joined in two bases of fellowship, "common work and a common faith." The guilds and the Church integrated the city-community symbolically and institutionally. The Church, in Mumford's terms, universalized the monastery. Spending the compulsory and voluntary contributions of the population as a whole, it built hospitals, almshouses, and other municipal institutions. It was impossible to draw a clear distinction between the sacred and the secular.

The towns were enclosed by walls, which served more than one function. They provided for defense. But more important, like the boundaries of modern nation-states, they provided for the control of exit and entry during peacetime—of people and goods. Within these walls (unlike those of Roman towns, where a central market square was part of a planned design), "all spaces, narrow or wide within the medieval town, were 'markets' of some kind

or degree." As a result, places "of production and market were usually identical."[6] Cities expanded when settlers established new spaces of production and market outside the established walls; their ability to avoid gate taxes and their growing economic power usually forced the inclusion of such faubourgs within an expanded ring of city walls.

The integration of market and production spaces within the walls of the town was accompanied by a commingling of private and public spaces, and of residences and places of economic activity. A typical well-to-do burgher's home in mid-thirteenth-century Troyes, Joseph and Frances Gies report, occupied "all four stories of its house, with business premises on the ground floor, living quarters on the second and third, servants' quarters in the attic, stables and storehouses in the rear."[7] Poorer artisans lived much more modestly, often crowded into a single room. Yet they too worked where they lived. Indeed, spatial and family identities came to be identified with distinctive crafts:

Related crafts tend to congregate, often giving their name to a street. Crafts also give their names to craftsmen—Thomas le Potier ("Potter"), Richarte le Barbier ("Barber"), Benoît le Peletier ("Skinner"), Henri Taillebois ("Woodman"), Jehan Taille-Fer ("Smith"). With the rise of the towns, surnames are becoming important; the tax collector must be able to draw up a list.[8]

The guilds of these craftsmen joined the various households, the units of production, together: the workshop was an extended family, and the family composed a workshop. "With their craft as a center," Mumford writes, "they fabricated a whole life" of work, social association, public works, and municipal construction.[9]

The organization of urban space made tangible the unity of the whole. The curves of the town usually conformed to the topography of the land, not to the exigencies of buying or selling, as in a grid. Streets converged on markets and cathedrals. This combination of interlacing streets and their convergence at the town's symbolic and functional centers expressed the community's interdependence: "every necessary institution, every friend, relative, associate, was in effect a close neighbor, within easy walking distance. So one was bound every day to encounter many people by coincidence whom one could not meet except by pre-arrangement and effort in a bigger city."[10]

The city was a social whole precisely because its *Gesellschaft* relations were so intimately bound to those of *Gemeinschaft*. The

city was divided into neighborhood units that were also functional production and exchange spaces. The "integration into primary residential units, composed of families and neighbors," Mumford observes, "was complemented by another kind of division, into precincts based on vocation and interest: thus both primary and secondary groups, both *Gemeinschaft* and *Gesellschaft,* took on the same urban pattern."[11] The community, as place of residence, provided for the total existence of its residents—for relations of affect and of the marketplace, for production as well as for politics.

This portrait, especially as it concerns the mixed uses of space, is not simply an ideological myth. But it is misleading in two respects. The townspeople were sharply demarcated from those outside their walls—peasants, princes, and other noncitizens—but they were also deeply divided within their own ranks. Braudel took note of their "class struggles":

Because if the towns were "communities" as has been said, they were also "societies" in the modern sense of the word, with their pressures and civil wars: nobles against bourgeois, poor against rich ("thin people," *popolo magro,* against "fat people," *popolo grasso*). The struggles in Florence were already more deeply akin to those of the French industrial early nineteenth century than conflicts of the Roman type (classical Rome of course).[12]

Second, and more important, Mumford fails to place the high-medieval town in its context—the changing milieu of feudalism as a whole. Implicit in Mumford's portrayal is the view associated with M. M. Postan that the towns of the medieval epoch were "non-feudal islands in the feudal seas."[13] The seats of free citizenship and market relations, the cities appeared as negations of the immobile patron-client ties of the countryside.[14] Long the conventional wisdom, this kind of treatment stresses the integrated social relations within the walls of the towns, seeing the towns as whole communities to themselves.[15]

To be sure, social relations in the towns were distinguished from those of the countryside, where a complex series of ordered engagements between inferior and superior defined ties of obedience, protection, and obligation. "In feudal society the characteristic human bond," Marc Bloch wrote, "was the subordinate's link with a nearby chief. From one level to another the ties thus formed—like so many chains branching out indefinitely—joined

the smallest to the greatest." From the vantage point of these relations, it is possible to see the town "as a foreign body in feudal society."[16] Yet this perspective allows only a partial view, for these characteristic human bonds of feudalism made the towns possible, perhaps even necessary, and bound the fate and character of the towns to the dynamics of the countryside, at least for most of the history of feudalism. The relationship between town and countryside was not one of external agent to a dominant mode of production. Rather the town, *as part of that mode,* was located in a state of reciprocal need and tension with the countryside that defined its "relative autonomy."

Braudel has stressed that the most original feature of medieval cities was not their independence from agrarian relations, but their "unparalleled freedom" from the territorial state:

In fact the miracle in the West was not so much that everything sprang up again from the eleventh century after having first been almost annihilated with the disaster of the fifth. History is full of those slow secular up and down movements, urban expansion, birth and rebirth: Greece from the fifth to the second century B.C.; Rome too; Islam from the ninth century; China under the Songs. But these revivals always featured two runners, the state and the town. The state usually won and the town then remained subject and under a heavy yoke. The miracle of the first great urban centuries in Europe was that the town won entirely, at least in Italy, Flanders and Germany. It was able to try the experiment of leading a completely separate life for quite a long time. This was a colossal event. . . . the main, the unpredictable, thing was that certain towns made themselves into autonomous worlds, city-states, buttressed with privileges (acquired or extorted) like so many juridical ramparts.[17]

This freedom from the state, however, did not make the town an unusual or external element within feudalism, for one of the defining features of feudalism taken as a whole was the absence of powerful, unitary state sovereignties. The uniqueness of Western towns was truly the uniqueness of Western feudalism itself.

This point is a centerpiece of Perry Anderson's treatment of feudalism. "Political sovereignty was never focused in a single centre. The functions of the State were disintegrated in a vertical allocation downwards, at each level of which political and economic relations were, on the other hand, integrated. This parcellization of sovereignty was constitutive of the whole feudal mode of production."[18] In *both* the country and the city, the integrated

character of daily life stemmed from this process. It was precisely this parcelization of political authority that permitted, and in many ways promoted, the genesis of medieval cities. Whereas Braudel stresses the towns' distinctive freedom from state domination, Anderson emphasizes that the feudal mode of production was the "*first* to permit cities an *autonomous development* within a natural-agrarian economy." The autonomy of the towns was a reflection of the autonomy of all the distinctive units of sovereignty within feudal society *writ large*.[19] Furthermore, both the manor and the town shared another basic characteristic of feudal relations—the fusion of economy and polity. Each locus of economic activity was also a political jurisdiction.

Because medieval towns were dependent parts of the complicated economic, political, and spatial patterns of feudalism more generally, it is a mistake to treat them in isolation. Such towns were not paradigmatic of a lost premodern utopia, nor were they typical of precapitalist relationships. Even within the various feudal societies of western Europe, the importance of urbanization and the social uses of town space varied considerably from place to place. Furthermore, the kinds of integrated, well-demarcated urban communities that Mumford portrays simply did not exist until the late-thirteenth and the fourteenth centuries. In early feudalism the town economies were devoted far more to commerce than to artisan production. The merchants who established themselves in the towns treated them as bases of operation, living "there but little, save in winter."[20] The more self-contained character of the fourteenth-century town depended on the development of a more sophisticated commerce that permitted merchants to stay at home and on the increasing dependence of the countryside on goods produced by artisans in the towns.

While some cities produced these goods for local or immediately regional markets, others, usually those most favored by geographic location, became the nodal points for a new and far-reaching long-distance commerce. And alongside this trade in goods there developed a new expanded trade in money and in such instruments of money as letters of credit. These new forms of commerce heralded future mercantile patterns:

Documents abound which attest the existence in the great cities of men of affairs who hold the most extended relations with the outside world, who export and import sacks of wool, bales of cloth, tuns of wine, by the hundred, who have under their orders a whole corps of factors or "sergents" (*servientes, valets*, etc.), whose letters of credit are negotiated

in the fairs of Champagne, and who make loans amounting to several thousands of livres to princes, monastaries, and cities in need of money.[21]

What distinguished these new forms of urban production and commerce most of all was their incipiently mercantile character. More and more, the town became an integrated unit of economic activity, much as the nation-state was to become centuries later. The towns, through municipal legislation and the regulation of citizenship, became protected economic units. Municipal statutes and guild regulations increasingly came to regulate terms of exchange, access to artisanal and merchant positions, and conditions of work. *The city, in short, became in this period a self-contained and self-reproducing unit of action within the parcelized framework of feudalism.* Its walls defined a corporate monopoly. "Towns became distinctive economic and social units," Hibbert has written, "just when and because certain places were set apart and defended by laws and privileges making them market or production centres and denying some or all such rights to the countryside around." Trade was "strictly reserved to those who had joined the trading community of a given town."[22] In a significant article, John Merrington has taken up this point. Pirenne, he argues, was mistaken in seeing this restrictive character of the town as an unnatural obstacle to the free movement of merchant capital. Quite the reverse was true: "the exclusivism of the towns must be seen as precisely the *precondition* for the development of merchant capital at this stage."[23] This early "capitalism" was inherently feudal, in its dependence on its slot in the parcelized world of medieval Europe. The units of market competition were not individual merchants, but towns that sought to enforce their monopolistic privileges against the countryside and against rival towns. Trade did not establish feudal relations; it existed in their interstices and thus depended on "the town's success in securing a favoured position as middleman by means of staple policies, concentrating and diverting exchange transactions to its market, enforcing sale and excluding foreigners from direct access by means of 'hosting laws,' etc."[24]

As this configuration of economics and politics changed in late feudalism, so, not surprisingly, did the towns. The countryside in late feudalism was wracked by a series of increasingly explosive conflicts, which exacerbated a structural crisis already at hand. Prices fell and wages rose. One response by beleaguered nobles was the commutation of dues into money rents; another was the attempt to regulate wages and prices by legislation, which caused

further conflict between nobles and peasants. The very existence
of cities hastened the spread of the rural crisis. Discontented
peasants could flee to the cities; commutation accelerated the
process. In turn, "the presence of these towns put constant
pressure on the embattled nobles to realize their incomes in
monetary form."[25] This imperative produced further relaxations
of servile ties on the land.[26]

The very existence of towns implies a differentiation between
town and country, but the character of this relation may take
many forms. Early feudal cities were dependent on the countryside
for food, yet the country was self-sufficient. By the fourteenth
century the towns had emerged as autonomous collective sei-
gneurs, able to defend and supply themselves, and capable of
producing metal and cloth goods that the rural nobility and
peasantry came to depend on. From 1300 to 1500 this relation
changed further to the advantage of the cities, as "town wealth
grew relative to that of the countryside,"[27] a harbinger of the
long-term process by which the cities conquered the countryside.
With the development of merchant and industrial capitalism in
the centuries to follow, this pattern of change accelerated, as
urbanization and ruralization (the loss of nonagricultural activities)
of the countryside were the "opposite sides of the same process
of the capitalist division of labor."[28]

Within late-medieval cities the position of local merchants was
eroded by two roughly concurrent processes. First, the dynamics
of national and international commerce changed. The system of
parcelized sovereignties that had made the "organic" medieval
community possible was being replaced almost everywhere in
western Europe by a new national economic and political order
characterized by the rise of absolutist states and a new, and
unprecedented, global market of exchange.[29]

The political outcome of the crisis of late feudalism was the
absolutist state. "With the generalized commutation of dues into
money rents," Anderson writes,

the cultural unity of political and economic oppression of the peasantry
was gravely weakened, and threatened to become dissociated (the end
of this road was "free labor" and the "wage contract"). The class power
of the feudal lords was thus directly at stake with the gradual disap-
pearance of serfdom. The result was a *displacement* of politico-legal
coercion upwards towards a centralized, militarized summit—the Absolutist State.[30]

The immediate consequences of this development were three-fold. First, political authority weakened at the local level in town and country. Second, property rights became more absolute, as they lost the conditional political character they had had in high feudalism. Third, the state as a new actor, though brought into being largely to preserve feudal social relations, had the capacity to act against members of the nobility and to protect the development of technical, merchant, and preindustrial manufacturing ventures that undermined traditional feudal patterns. "The political order remained feudal, while society became more and more bourgeois," Engels wrote.[31] The paradox of absolutism, Anderson comments, "was that it fundamentally represented an apparatus for the protection of aristocratic property and privileges, yet at the same time the means whereby this protection was promoted could *simultaneously* ensure the basic interests of the nascent mercantile and manufacturing classes."[32] The nobility welcomed the central imposition of order by Henry VII, Ferdinand of Aragon and Isabella, and Louis XI only because they were "in a weakened condition in which they found it more difficult to resist the claims of central authority and more ready to welcome the benefits of imposed order."[33] With this acceptance the coincidence of dominant-class interests was promoted by the separation of property and political authority, and by their *independent* concentration.

Order, Wallerstein has stressed, was not only the product of new state forms that had expanded armies, bureaucracies, and powers to tax, but it also depended on an expansion of "the economic pie to be shared, a solution which required, given the technology of the time, an expansion of the land area and population base to exploit."[34] Nation-states became the crucial units of a global stratification system. The dominant core states of western Europe (principally Britain and the Netherlands) pioneered in the development of commercialized agriculture and new forms of industrial production. The intermediate, or semi-peripheral, states were somewhat less diversified in their economies and, as in the case of Polish wheat production, became increasingly dependent on core-state markets. At the bottom of this new international order were the peripheral regions that specialized in the export of primary materials, largely to western Europe. The towns of western Europe now nestled in a much wider context of absolutism and mercantilism.

II

There have been two major breaks or discontinuities in the history of postfeudal cities. The first coincided with the growth of capital cities in the new absolutist states, the second with the growth of factory cities of early industrial capitalism.

In the sixteenth century, most established towns were growing at roughly similar rates. In the seventeenth century, by contrast, *political* capitals, the centers of royal authority and of the organization of national and international patterns of commerce, developed a tempo of growth that left other urban centers far behind:

After the sixteenth century . . . the cities that increased most rapidly in population and area and wealth were those that harbored a royal court: the fountainhead of economic power. About a dozen towns quickly reached a size not attained in the Middle Ages even by a bare handful: in a little while London had 250,000 inhabitants, Naples 240,000, Milan over 200,000, Palermo and Rome, 100,000, Lisbon, port of a great monarchy, over 100,000; similarly Seville, Antwerp, and Amsterdam; while Paris in 1594 had 180,000.[35]

These cities were the most visible products and achievements of absolutism and mercantilism, and also in crucial ways a part of their cause and means of reproduction. "The centralization of authority," Mumford stresses, "necessitated the creation of the capital city, while the capital city, commanding the main routes of trade and military movement, was a powerful contribution to the unification of the state."[36] The decentralized days of parcelized sovereignty were at an end. "The state grew at the expense of the component parts: the capital city grew out of all proportion to the provincial cities, and in no small measure at their expense."[37] The multiplication of cities in western Europe ceased, and the city became an agency for consolidating political and economic power.[38]

Power and population grew centralized, accelerating the expansion of both. Increases in the size of capitals increased the rent paid to the central exchequer, and this money was used with other funds to expand the capacities of the state. Within each city the state's presence and power were executed and confirmed by new construction, especially of office buildings, that symbolized the "permanence" of the state's courts, archives, tax powers, and bureaucracy. State functions were carried out in new places of

work, usually centrally located. For those whose power and wealth stemmed most directly from these sources of authority, place of work and residence became separated. For wealthy merchants and leading state officials, the character of the household was altered in decisive ways "by the gradual divorce of the home, henceforth a place for eating, for entertaining, and in a secondary way for rearing children, from the workplace." The private house came into existence in the sense of *"private from business,* and spatially separated from any visible means of support." For these families the household became exclusively a place of consumption, and the "housewife lost her touch with the affairs of the outside world: she became either a specialist in domesticity or a specialist in sex, something of a drudge, something of a courtesan, more often perhaps a little of both."[39]

The wealthy created new kinds of enclosed residence communities, seen most graphically in the character of the residential square. Heretofore, open space had never been entirely residential. "But now, beginning, it would seem, with the establishment of Gray's Inn in London in 1600, a new kind of square was formed: an open space surrounded solely by dwelling houses, without shops or public buildings, except perhaps a church."[40] These residential squares created residence areas that were homogeneous in class for the first time in modern cities; they were paradigms of more generalized community patterns to come. Such residence communities were not only private from business; they also demarcated the new realm of private life physically and symbolically.

Like the late-feudal town, but on a vastly enlarged canvas, the new capital cities were essentially composed of three classes: wealthy merchants and political authorities, property-holding artisans, and the poor and the marginal. But the first and especially the third of these classes were relatively much larger than their counterparts in the late-feudal town. Hogarth, Defoe, Gay, Fielding, and other chroniclers of the period captured the contrasts of the new complex urbanity of the city and its poverty, crime, vice, and squalor: "The 'insolent rabble,' the 'insolence of the mob,' the 'idle, profligate and debauched' workmen are commonplaces of middle class observation." Unlike the medieval town, where "the upper and lower classes had jostled together on the street, in the marketplace, as they did in the cathedral," in the capital city *"the dissociation of the upper and lower classes achieves form*

in the city itself. The rich drive, the poor walk. The rich roll down the axis of the grand avenue; the poor are off-center, in the gutter; and eventually a special strip is provided for the ordinary pedestrian, the sidewalk."[41] The introduction of wheeled vehicles on the avenues of the city made possible not only the separation of work and community for the wealthy, but the increasingly clear lines of demarcation for patterns of contact between the classes. The majority became less and less visible. Fielding observed of London in 1751:

Whoever considers the Cities of London and Westminster, with the late vast increases of their suburbs, the great irregularity of their buildings, the immense numbers of lanes, alleys, courts and bye-places, must think that they had been intended for the very purpose of concealment, they could not have been better contrived.[42]

The residence communities of the artisanal and marginal classes—still integrated jumbles of work and home—were cut off from the newer residence communities of the dominant classes.[43] An urban mosaic, whose parts were distinguished by class and by function, had begun to emerge, altering the meaning, place, and nature of "community." One result was a new kind of political conflict about urban space, as members of the dominant class sought to capture the benefits of city life without having to deal with the consequences:

It is then ironic to reflect that much of the physical squalor and complexity of eighteenth century London was a consequence not simply of rapid expansion but of attempts to control that expansion. For complex reasons, ranging from fear of the plague to fear of social disorder—itself a transference and concentration in London of the disturbances of the rural economy—there had been repeated attempts to limit the city's growth. From the first phase of its rapid expansion, in the late sixteenth century, when a proclamation of 1580 came out against new buildings, . . . to as late as 1709, when a Bill against new houses was attempted, there was a prolonged struggle, by ruling-class interests, to restrain the growth of London, and in particular to prevent the poor from settling there. . . . Yet the general changes were of an order which made exclusion impossible. Not only the retinues of servants but many thousands of others flooded in, and the main consequence of the limitations was a long-continued wave of overcrowded and insecure speculative building and adaptation within the legal limits: forced labyrinths and alleys of the poor. And this was happening as part of *the same process as the building of town mansions, the laying out of squares and*

fashionable terraces: the "Georgian" London now so often abstracted. As indeed so often, a ruling class wanted the benefits of a change it was itself promoting, but the control or suppression of its less welcome but inseparable consequences.[44]

The commercial, political, and artisanal character of the great capital cities was sustained even after the zenith of absolutism and mercantilism passed, and as their populations grew rapidly in the first half of the nineteenth century (in this period Paris doubled and London nearly tripled in size) to number in the millions. Their social structures contained three distinct classes: administrators, public officials, merchants, rentiers, and a few industrial capitalists at the top; artisans, small shopkeepers and employers, and lower-level government workers in the middle; and a variegated working class at the bottom. The vast majority of the population, including most workers, considered that they had an occupation and identified themselves with a single craft or trade. In her comparison of mid-nineteenth-century Paris and London, Lynn Lees observes that both

were centers of artisanal production before the Industrial Revolution and remained so long afterward. Despite the general shift to a machine dominated technology, the transition to factory production was a slow process in both cities. But each was an important center of craft production. . . . In both places, the tradition of skilled handlabor remained strong. Therefore, artisans and journeymen—tailors, shoe-makers, printers, butchers, and bakers— . . . formed the major part of the urban working class.[45]

Small workshops remained prototypical well into the century. "In 1851, only 21 per cent of all industrial establishments in London employed over four workers, and a mere 14 per cent had ten or more employees."[46] The comparable figure for Paris was 18 percent. Indeed, for both cities a major impact of industrialization was the displacement of much of whatever large-scale production they had to the new factory cities.

The rapid growth of these cities, while not subversive of their basic features, contributed to an acceleration of the spatial trends noted above. By midcentury there had occurred a net population loss in the central city, as public and private office construction caused the razing of residential areas; patterns of growth came to be defined by a centrifugal movement, which had the effect of further intensifying the residential separation of the cities' three

main classes. As more and more of the population at the top and in the middle of the social structure were able to create class-homogeneous residence communities on the outskirts of the capital cities, the housing they left "trickled down" in a now familiar pattern:

Many in the London middle class had deserted the center of town for the villas and wide streets of Kensington or Camberwell, and the Parisian bourgeoisie marked out for its own the expanding quarters that flanked the Seine in the west. The much lauded Parisian system of mixed housing, where class divisions operated in vertical rather than horizontal space, broke down during the July Monarchy and the Second Empire. The whirlwind of renewal that changed the city geographically also changed it socially, destroying the older pattern of settlement along with the houses that had maintained it. As in London, areas in the east became much more exclusively inhabited by workers, while the middle and upper classes settled in the west.[47]

Growth thus achieved what earlier legislation on building restrictions had tried in vain to accomplish—the pressing from view of the working class. "The circle that closed over much of the labouring mass," Dyos and Reeder have observed, "was a spring for the middle classes. The wealth that was created in the commercial metropolis benefited them first, and they used it quite literally to put a distance between themselves and the workers.[48] Street widening, slum razing, and the building of new houses and public buildings were not only immensely profitable but contributed to the uneven rewards, in space, that economic development produced for the city's different classes.

For the lower-class majority, work and residence remained closely joined. The separation of work and community was essentially a mark of class privilege. The imperatives of casual labor for the propertyless and unskilled—people with no fixed job, who earned their living on a daily or even hourly basis in a wildly fluctuating labor market—made it necessary to live near work. In the docks or in such trades as textiles or shoemaking it was important for casual labor to be on call; the spatial interlacing of slum residences and places of insecure, poorly paid, and sweated labor was the result. Yet even in these capital cities the pressures pointing to the growing separation of work and community were clearly felt. As the city grew at the periphery, more and more of the relatively well-off could move to class-homogeneous residence neighborhoods away from their work places.

Artisan production declined in relative importance within the city, and craft production in small shops increasingly "separated into different streets and different parts of the city."[49] And as city cores were "improved" to make way for new banks, department stores, and offices, much of the manufacturing that had taken place in those areas was shifted away from the residential streets.

III

The second major discontinuity in the history of postfeudal cities was the very rapid growth of industrial cities, especially in the nineteenth century. Although, as we have seen, the absolutist state aimed in the first instance at recreating feudal patterns of order, the merchant capitalism to which it was fused acted as a solvent on feudal restrictions on production. Strong guild regulation of manufacturing had inhibited possibilities for industrial advances, and as a consequence forced industrial activity such as the English woolen industry "to seek out locations in rural areas away from urban influence and regulation." The putting-out system, and later the creation of large factories, confirmed this tendency for new cities to develop in the countryside as sites of industrial production. Thus David Harvey notes that the "industrialization that ultimately subdued merchant capital was not an urban phenomenon, but one which led to the creation of a new form of urbanism—a process in which Manchester, Leeds, and Birmingham were transformed from insignificant villages or minor trading centres, to industrial cities of great productive might."[50] These cities, it should be noted, not only grew apart spatially from the great mercantile political capitals, but grew rapidly in the age of classic liberalism, individualism, and laissez faire. "The dominance of the town," Merrington writes, "is no longer externally imposed: it is now reproduced as part of the accumulation process."[51] In the era of rapid industrialization, capitalist imperatives defined the tempo and character of city growth directly, relatively unmediated by state intervention.

Urban space now expressed two separations—of the classes and of work and community. Consider England's leading textile city, Manchester, studied by Engels in 1844. In The *Condition of the Working Class in England,* he presents the city as symbolic and tangible space, and as a vantage point from which to capture the larger social whole. By charting the connections between the new

class structure and the topography of the city (an analytical social topography that both presages and is more trenchant than the Chicago school's ecological analysis), he indicates how, on the one hand, the city's spatial arrangements visibly reveal capitalist social relations and how, on the other hand, the segmentation of the city into distinctive class and functional areas masks and mystifies the relational nature of class patterns:

The whole of this built up area is commonly called Manchester, and contains about 400,000 people. . . . Owing to the curious layout of the town it is quite possible for someone to live for years in Manchester and to travel daily to and from work without ever seeing a working class quarter or coming into contact with an artisan. . . . The upper classes enjoy healthy country air and live in luxurious and comfortable dwellings which are linked to the center of Manchester by omnibuses which run every fifteen or thirty minutes. To such an extent has the convenience of the rich been considered in the planning of Manchester that these plutocrats can travel from their houses to their places of business in the center of the town by the shortest routes which run entirely through working-class districts, without even realizing how close they are to the misery and filth which lie on both sides of the road. This is because the main streets which run from the Exchange in all directions out of the town are occupied almost uninterruptedly by shops, which are kept by members of the lower middle classes.[52]

Engels saw Manchester as a dynamic whole. Each of its communities—class-homogeneous residential spaces—had a history, an archeology, a set of meanings, symbols, institutions, relationships of its own. Like the working class itself in a capitalist order, the new communities "were at the very center of things yet out of sight. To say that they were at once central and peripheral is to describe their contradictory existence in the structure of social consciousness of the time."[53]

It is important to stress that this spatial differentiation occurred at precisely the moment when the characteristic features and requirements of a system of industrial capitalism achieved national expression. Thus in England in the period of Manchester's early growth, capital was becoming impersonal and highly mobile, and "a single, increasingly sensitive, market for labor" overtook earlier patterns of separate, more imperfect local markets.[54] Indeed, the dynamic of differentiation and the simplification of the social structure into the antinomy of capital and labor were products of the same process of capitalist development, suspended in the same network of dependencies. Max Weber has argued that the

functional and class segmentations of space, given modern legal meanings, were essential conditions of sustained capital accumulation. He notes that it is not the ecological factor per se that is decisive for capital, since

the spatial differentiation or separation of the household from the workshop and the store . . . is rather typical of the bazaar system of the Islamic cities in the orient, which rests throughout on the separation of the castle (*kasbah*), bazaar (*suk*), and residences. What is crucial is the separation of household and business for accounting and legal purposes, and the development of a suitable body of laws, such as the commercial register, elimination of the dependence of the association and the firm upon the family, separate property of the private firm or limited partnership, and appropriate laws on bankruptcy. . . . This is one of the many phenomena characterizing most clearly the qualitative uniqueness of the development of modern capitalism.[55]

The counterpart of these features of differentiation for workers was the dual nature of their postfeudal freedom: free *from* property (and thus compelled to work for others for a wage), and free *to* create social lives in families and communities outside of the immediate imperatives of production. Since the worker "only sells a temporary disposition over his labouring capacity," Marx wrote, "the worker is thereby posited as a person who is something for himself *apart from his labor.*" These communal relations are not survivals of a precapitalist *Gemeinschaft,* but are creations of the development of capital itself. In Marx's terms, they are the product of the "historic process of the divorce of elements which up until then were bound together."[56] With this divorce it is possible to describe the social world for the first time in the Marxist rhetoric of capital, wage labor, and exploitation; in Weber's language of class, status, and party; and in the new political slogans of "liberty, equality, fraternity."[57]

The forms and content of collective activity "in pursuit of common grievances and aspirations," Charles Tilly has suggested, have changed since the sixteenth century in roughly sequential ways. In the very earliest part of the modern capitalist era, most social relationships still had a precapitalist character. Conflicts took largely ritualized, competitive forms—brawls between detachments of soldiers, between soldiers and civilians, village fights, the custom of the charivari, struggles between groups of artisans. People sharing an identity that was a compound of work and residence fashioned the units of such conflicts. With the growing penetration of the state and the market, these traditional forms

of action were overtaken by collective *reactions* in resistance to the claims of the new order and in defense of established routines. Peasants rebelled against taxation and military service; artisans against the devaluation of their labor. Overall, of course, the story of such reactive struggles is one of defeat. Once people were incorporated in the characteristic work and community relations of modern industrial capitalism, the expression of their discontents took new forms, which Tilly calls proactive. Strikes for higher wages, demands for inclusion in the liberal franchise, and participation in mass politics, among other kinds of collective activities, were used to assert claims.[58]

At this historical moment two new kinds of links were forged between a developing working class and the dominant class: between capital and labor at work, and between the state and workers where they lived. These links framed much of the class activity for generations to come.

In the period preceding rapid industrialization and the separation of work and community, capitalist development was sustained by methods of social control that depended on very close and direct relations between the classes. The most typical of the transitional forms of organizing production in both capital and nascently industrial cities was what Foster calls the employer-dominated household:

Two main problems of social control seem to have brought it into existence. The first was the actual coexistence of capitalist and precapitalist forms. At a time when the craft worker and small farmer maintained at least formal control over the use to which their labour was put, the capitalist worker—whether hired by the hour or on piecework—visibly did not. Moreover, in the new conditions he had little hope of becoming a master. The class division now ran through (and not round) the production unit. So on top of the problem of imposing work discipline there was the constant danger of subversive "levelling" comparisons. This seems to have been the *source* of the tensions. The other constituent was the social context within which it had to be met. Early capitalist production involved immediate face-to-face contact between employer and employed. Even out-work manufacturing was intensely local, with the working cottagers living round the employer family and known to them over the years. Somehow a working relationship had to be maintained. . . . *The essence of the solution seems to have been an attempt to gloss over the class split by binding the worker into the larger household of the employer and then asserting the moral priority of the overall group.*[59]

The ecological and ideological relations of the household continued to bind the worker tightly into the cultural group of the employer. Similarities between employer and employee were emphasized, as they still worked together and as their neighborhoods were not yet segregated. The authority systems of the state (which regulated food prices and supply), and the church (including those of the new evangelical sects) reinforced this interlaced pattern of control. These arrangements were complemented by the beginnings of a network of individuals subject to state controls who penetrated the relatively few institutions where laborers could constitute a partially autonomous culture, thus presaging future patterns. Alehouse keepers, teachers, and friendly societies in late-eighteenth-century England were all licensed by the state, a procedure that helped insure their loyalist orientation.

This dual system of traditional work-home institutions and tied loyalism could not survive the spatial and social pressures of industrial capitalism. One of the central features of the new order was a new kind of social crisis that was associated with the emergence of a cycle of boom and bust. The basic source of conflict in preindustrial capitalism had been rising prices, and food riots had been the characteristic form of expression. With the first appearance of the modern business cycle in England in the 1790s, sharp increases in food prices were accompanied by cuts in wages. For more than a decade most protest still centered on prices, but after the turn of the century, wage conflicts supplanted more traditional forms. These early conflicts over wages, however, bore little resemblance to modern union-management disputes. Workers did not so much challenge the ownership of the means of production, or fight for larger wages, as resist the new modes of capitalist labor control.[60]

The separation of work and community was an integral part of this bitter, protracted process. The rapid growth of factories and industrial cities commanded the breakup of the cross-class household, and with it, the demise of preindustrial capitalist patterns of social control. The massive transformation of economic and social life was experienced and resisted at the workplace and in workers' neighborhoods in distinctive, but often related, ways. A radically new kind of solidarity led to the creation of autonomous workers' institutions—unions, clubs, secret societies, protest groups, churches, and schools—which became potent agencies of

reactive struggle. As a result, the agenda and imperatives of social control changed radically, in ways common to the process of capitalist industrialization.

Everywhere in the West the state responded in pursuit of order in unprecedented ways. These responses were hardly identical from place to place, but they did always have three constituent elements: the attempt to regulate, and often to proscribe, combinations of workers at the point of production; the use of the franchise to incorporate workers and their leaders into the polity in ways that least threatened social cohesion; and the development of a new nexus of political relationships linking residence communities to government. Collectively, these responses by the state replaced traditional "private" forms of social control with public authoritative activity. One consequence was the displacement of much of the emerging dynamics of conflict between capital and labor into relations between the state and citizen.

The ways in which this process of displacement occurred, the connections between the elements of state control activities, and the character of newly created intermediary party, union, church, and voluntary associations shaped the distinctive character of class in each of the industrializing capitalist countries. These elements, the hallmarks of modern liberal democratic political life, were initially fashioned in the period of transition from "reactive" to "proactive" conflicts. The period of their emergence was a critical one, in that it provided the initial basis for subsequent patterns of class expression. That is why analyses of the distinctive elements of class in any single capitalist society must look first at this formative period.

CHAPTER 3

City Trenches

It is hard to find the right words to discuss politics and the American working class without reaching for the clinical language of schizophrenia. The main element of what Raymond Williams calls the "selective tradition"[1] of the working class in the United States has been a stark split between the ways workers in the major industrial cities think, talk, and act when they are at work and when they are away from work in their communities. When was this disconnected pattern first formed? How did it differ from the ways working classes developed in other Western societies at comparable moments? What were the main causes of the political dissociation between work and home?[2]

I

The eighteenth-century northern mercantile port cities of Boston, Philadelphia, and New York were urban enclaves in a rural world. Their internal organizations of space; the character of production; class relations between merchants, the property-owning middle classes, and a small but growing group of propertyless unskilled laborers and some artisans; their rates of growth; their economic prosperity; and their relations to other units of government—all these were determined largely by the commercial and transport functions they performed by linking internal and external markets for the agrarian economy. Three kinds of economic activities were predominant: trade with Britain, the Continent, Africa, and the West Indies (furs, tobacco, rice, lumber, wheat, fish, indigo, and livestock for export, and the importation of manufactured goods, sugar, immigrants, and slaves); production in industries like flour milling and shipbuilding (sails, ropes, and barrels) that

45

directly supported this commerce; and crafts of baking, carpentry, weaving, and tailoring, among others, which provided goods and services for the local population. "The prevailing mode of production in the colonial towns was the workshop craft, employing generally one or two journeymen and a like number of apprentices." Most frequently the household provided the place of production.[3]

In the forty years from 1820 to the outbreak of the Civil War, the economic context within which these cities functioned changed radically. In the 1830s and 1850s especially, there was an extraordinary increase in the tempo of investment in canals, roads, and railways, the internal improvements that created an extended domestic market and provided the infrastructure for subsequent industrial development. A recognizably modern business cycle of boom and bust, closely tied to the pattern of these expenditures, replaced oscillations of food prices as the dominant feature of economic life. The labor force that was engaged in manufacturing grew from 3 percent in 1810 to 14 percent by 1860.[4]

Economic historians differ about whether the United States experienced an industrial revolution in the antebellum years. Douglass North's view that the period 1820–1860 constituted the "era of industrialization" and Rostow's dating of the "take-off" stage in the decades before the Civil War are sharply disputed by Louis Hacker, Alfred Chandler, and other analysts who locate the divide between a traditional and modern industrial America in the 1870s and beyond.[5] For our purposes these debates are beyond the point, for it is indisputable that the antebellum years were an era of major economic change, rapid urbanization, and political democratization. By 1860 the older port cities had been transformed in ways that are familiar to us today.

To be sure, the U.S. economy remained chiefly agrarian and commercial throughout the antebellum period. But the explosive expansion in commerce, domestic and overseas, qualitatively transformed economic patterns of exchange. After the conclusion of the War of 1812, domestic trade displaced foreign trade in importance. Allan Pred has carefully documented the consequences of the "great turnabout" of 1810–1820. In 1810 approximately two tons were shipped abroad for every one that was carried on vessels engaged in domestic trade. By 1820 parity had been reached, and by 1840 the ratio of 1810 had nearly been reversed. Commodities were exchanged in growing volume be-

tween Northeast and South, between the major northeastern cities of New York, Boston, Philadelphia, and Baltimore, and between these cities and the newer lake and river cities west of the Allegheny Mountains.[6] The geographic points of exchange were cities; the expanded pattern of trade was interurban. Rapid urbanization and commerical expansion went hand in hand.[7]

Until the 1840s manufacturing clearly had a subsidiary role in the older port cities. Local markets were too small and the national transportation system too primitive to support large-scale manufacturing independent of mercantile imperatives. Rather, the urban economy was characterized by highly diversified industrial production in small handicraft and unmechanized firms that had relatively low output. "An overwhelming portion," Pred observes, "perhaps virtually all, of the industrial activities located within the confines of New York, Boston, Philadelphia, and Baltimore were either directly or indirectly linked to the mercantile functions of those cities." Tobacco milling, tanning and leather processing, and sugar refining were among the largest industries in these cities. Only in Philadelphia was manufacturing on a significant scale divorced from either direct or indirect dependence on merchants' requirements and commercial capital. Its cotton, locomotive, and iron works were atypical.[8]

Although virtually all the major industries of the mercantile cities had roots that reached back at least a century or more, their growth in number produced major alterations. Chandler observes that in the first four decades of the nineteenth century the traditional enterprise in commerce changed under the impact of economic expansion and business specialization. General merchants presided over the colonial and early-postcolonial economy. The family was the basic unit of commerce. The general merchant was a "grand distributor," who "bought and sold all types of products and carried out all the basic commercial functions. He was an exporter, wholesaler, importer, retailer, shipowner, banker, insurer." He presided not only over overseas and domestic intercity trade, but over the local distribution and marketing of the products of the city's many small enterprises. "In all these activities, the colonial merchant knew personally most of the individuals involved." By 1840 the general merchant had virtually disappeared. The earliest distinction was between shopkeepers and merchants; then the merchant was replaced by the "impersonal world of the jobber, importer, factor, broker, and the

commission agent." Commercial enterprises grew increasingly specialized, as they came to deal exclusively in a specific genre of goods—china, glass, hardware, dry goods, watches, wines, clothing. Market forces replaced personal contact in the management of the growing volume and complexity of trade. And in finance and transportation the joint-stock finance company superseded more traditional family and partnership forms of ownership. These enterprises came to cluster more and more in specialized portions of the city, divorced from residence communities.[9]

Change came more slowly to the traditional organization of production, but it came nevertheless. Victor Clark's classic study of manufacturing in early America documents at some length the family basis of manufacturing; at the turn of the century, manufacturers were skilled artisans who lived at, or very near, the premises where they worked at highly specialized trades. Before 1840 urban production expanded in three distinctive ways. First, traditional shops were enlarged, as "craftsmen added more apprentices and journeymen to their work force." Work was still performed in or near the home of the master, though more and more laborers lived away from the workplace. Second, work was distributed for processing in the homes of nearby families. Third, large industrial factor establishments wholly divorced from the home were created; before 1840 factories employing more than fifty workers were common only in the textiles.[10]

After 1840, in the last two antebellum decades, the factory system began to expand. By the late 1850s foreign observers regularly took note of the "American system of manufacturing." Primarily, but not exclusively, in southern New England,

in the light metalworking industries, notably in firearms, clocks, watches, locks, and tools of various kinds, and then spreading into neighboring states and a broadening range of industries, there came into being the basic elements and patterns of modern mass manufacturing; that is, the principles and practice of quantity manufacture of standardized products characterized by interchangeable parts and the use of a growing array of machine tools and specialized jigs and fixtures, along with power, to substitute simplified, and as far as possible, mechanized operations for craftsman's arts.[11]

In this period, Mohl notes, "commerce began to give way to manufacturing in eastern cities. New York and Philadelphia led the way. Factories . . . proliferated and became typical places of work for urban laborers."[12] After the 1840s what Pred calls an

"industrial threshold" was reached in cities, as accumulated capital came to be invested more and more in large-scale urban manufacturing, rather than in the traditional wholesaling-trading complex.[13] In these ways the economic base of the major cities before the Civil War was transformed. By the outbreak of hostilities, they had developed a mix of manufacturing and nonmanufacturing employment that remained roughly stable, in spite of continuing city growth, for the subsequent century. Thus, Williamson stresses that we should take note of

the general similarity in the economic structure of cities between 1860, 1870, and 1950. Especially for those in the northeastern tier of states . . . the ratio of manufacturing employment to total employment is not very different from that of the "industrial" cities of 1950. . . . Even relative to their industrial maturity in 1950, by 1860 most of the cities in the Northeast and many in the Midwest fully qualified as industrial-urban complexes.[14]

Interpreting the precise extent to which the social and spatial structures of these industrializing cities differed from the prevailing patterns of the late-eighteenth century is made difficult by disputes about the character of the mercantile city. Recent scholarship indicates that in the port cities of the Revolutionary era, workplaces and residence spaces had begun to segment; small neighborhoods became increasingly segregated by class; inequality between the classes may have become more acute.[15] In his study of New York, Carl Abbott argues that the mercantile city was not an integrated jumble of work and residence with little differentiation of neighborhoods. Rather, a new built form was being created in which different kinds of functional spaces could be distinguished:

Proceeding on the basis of economic function, one can discover a commercial district along the lower East River, a sector devoted to light manufacturing and retailing in the middle part of town, and a heavier manufacturing sector on its northern edge. The city was similarly split into residential neighborhoods of different status and characteristics. Its upper classes lived within the commercial district and adjacent to it west of Broad Street. Artisans and tradesmen . . . lived as well as worked in a broad band across the center of the city. Areas with the poorest housing, worst physical conditions, and most undesirable and transient population were found on the fringes.[16]

Nevertheless, in spite of these emerging divisions in space, the mercantile cities in the Revolutionary era stood, from the vantage

point of 1860, rather closer to the level of differentiation characteristic of medieval cities than to that typical of the modern commercial-industrial city. The incipient divisions—which Abbott, among others, rightly emphasizes and sets against overromanticized notions of the mercantile city—were more in the nature of a combination of emerging tendencies and traditional patterns. The cities were very compact and crowded. A complete, or even a terribly well-defined, separation of land uses and activities was virtually impossible, given the ecology and topography of the cities. The latter developed close to their shores (their "hinge" to the world market) and hugged the coast. Philadelphia in 1780 was nine blocks square and had a population of 16,500. New York's 22,000 residents lived and worked in a triangle only four thousand feet wide and six thousand feet from apex to base.[17] This crowding expressed and helped reproduce the ideology and reality of an integrated community. Thus, Warner has insisted that late-eighteenth-century Philadelphia

was a community. Graded by wealth and divided by distinctions of class though it was, it functioned as a single community. The community had been created out of a remarkably inclusive network of business and economic relationships and it was maintained by the daily interactions of trade and sociability . . . every man and occupation lived jumbled together in a narrow compass.[18]

By the time of Civil War, the ambiguous status of "community" in the older port cities had been resolved, by the impact of capitalist development. Between 1800 and 1850 Philadelphia grew in population from 69,000 to 340,000; and New York City from 60,000 to 516,000.[19] The cities were becoming unmistakably divided into distinctive districts of work and home.[20] The "unity of everyday life, from tavern to street, to workplace, to housing," of the late-eighteenth-century city shattered; Philadelphia was by 1860 "a city of closed social cells." One manufacturing worker in four labored in the principal downtown ward (the sixth) in a city of twenty-four wards:

The garment industry in all its branches, boot and shoe makers, bookbinders, printers, and paper box fabricators, glass manufacturers, machinists, coopers, sugar refiners, brewers, and cigar makers especially concentrated here. Thousands of workers walked to the downtown every day, while omnibuses, and just before the Civil War, horse-drawn streetcars brought shopkeepers and customers. No tall office buildings

yet outlined the downtown, no manufacturing lofts filled entire blocks, but the basic manufacturing-wholesale-retail-financial elements had already been assembled by 1860 for the future metropolis.[21]

New manufacturing clusters radiated "out from the original urban core like a crude spiderweb spun through the blocks of little houses." Although the incompleteness of street directories and census data makes it very difficult to know precisely how many workers left their homes to labor, documented commutation patterns for Philadelphia and New York indicate unmistakably that "work began to be separated from home neighborhood."[22] Even before the rapid industrial development of the 1840s, there were "significant alterations in the propensity to commute and in the average length of commutation that did occur." Pred very conservatively estimates that in New York City in 1840 approximately one-fourth of the *industrial* workers were already working outside their homes.[23] The increasing separation of work and home was matched by the growing segregation of residence communities by class, ethnicity, and race. New York City in this era, Robert Ernst reports, became increasingly differentiated in these ways:

Whether in shanty towns or in the commercial districts, whether along the waterfront or in the Five Points, immigrant settlers drew to their area others having the same nationality, language, religion, or race. Once a nucleus was established toward which later arrivals were attracted, the cohesive bond resulting from consciousness of similarity tended to replace the magnetic forces of cheap shelter and ready employment. Native prejudice against foreigners furthered the isolation of these communities, and white prejudice against Negroes similarly produced well-defined colored settlements.[24]

This organization of the city's social landscape altered the class composition of local associations and clubs. The membership of lodges, benefit associations, parish churches, gangs, athletic clubs, fire companies, and political clubs no longer cut across the class divisions of the social structure. The new working classes of the antebellum city borrowed many of the organizational forms of the mercantile city. But in their increasingly segregated communities, separated not only from their workplaces but also from merchants and industrial capitalists, workers controlled these institutions. They were free to develop new organizations as they saw fit, and those they did create belonged exclusively to them.

Together with the labor organizations that workers were beginning to devise at work, these neighborhood institutions provided the possibility for the development of an independent working-class culture. Paradoxically, just at the moment when the development of industrial capitalism undercut the skill levels and control over work that artisans had exercised, the working class became capable of developing and controlling the institutions of daily neighborhood life.

For this reason, many social historians see this period of the history of the working class, not only in the United States, but also in England, France, Prussia, and other industrializing areas of western Europe, as the era of the development of an autonomous working-class culture.[25] This period's structural developments—the split between work and residence and the growth of workingmen's social clubs, gangs, and other institutions—were not unique to the United States. What was different, and what therefore requires explanation, was the distinctive response of American workers to the separation of work and home, and the social and political use that they made of the local institutions they controlled.

By the Civil War the connections between conflicts at work and conflicts in residence communities became increasingly tenuous. This separation between the politics of work and the politics of community was much more stark in the United States than elsewhere. The patterns of consciousness, speech, and organization at work and away from work grew increasingly distinctive. Away from work, ethnic and territorial identifications became dominant. They were acted out through community groups and through local political parties, churches, and secondary associations. At work, workers were class conscious, but with a difference, for the awareness narrowed down to labor concerns and to unions that established few ties to political parties.

These essential elements of the early system of American "city trenches" continue to define the idiom of U.S. politics to such an extent that we forget how special they were. In England a modern working class, although sharing the structural attributes of the American working class, was "made" in a very different way. The English drew from a similar experience of industrialization and urbanization to arrive at a coherent presocialist interpretation of class that saw the new society divided along a single class cleavage at work, in politics, and in community life.[26] In other societies,

including those of Belgium and Holland, ethnicity rather than class came to frame political conflicts both at work and in residential areas.[27] The rigid separation of the American pattern was thus by no means inevitably dictated by capitalist industrialization.

Indeed, in the U.S. experience two main alternatives presented themselves, logically, and to some extent empirically, to the system of city trenches that developed. First, the labor unions and parties that were formed in the early part of the period by a declining artisan class might have succeeded in defining the experience of industrialization wholly in class terms. Or, second, territorially based movements and parties of old settlers and new immigrants might have accomplished their aim of interpreting industrialization in ethnic terms. Neither of these holistic alternatives joining the labor and community parts of working-class lives emerged from the antebellum period—this in spite of considerable workingmen's agitation in the late 1820s and early 1830s, and in spite of the power of nativist ideas and organizations in the latter part of the period.

Yet holistic outcomes were real possibilities in antebellum America. An important political force—the workingmen's parties in the older cities of the East—had a class perspective of the new order. Utilizing the available tools of eighteenth-century republicanism (of the very sort that undergirded the making of the English working class), these mass parties sought to create a politics of class that cut across the work-community divide. The workingmen's parties were led and supported principally by artisans, who had experienced the world in traditional integrated terms and whose very existence as a class was threatened by industrialization and the separation of work and home. Workingmen were broadly defined to include virtually the whole population; their adversaries were speculators and wealthy merchants and businessmen. The central argument of the workingmen's movement was that "contravening the principles of equal rights and equal protection, government had been acting to benefit some citizens at the expense of others. . . . Once in office, working men would be able to eliminate those policies that enabled one class to oppress another and that violated the maxim of equal protection."[28] To this end they called for the elimination of charters that gave unfair competitive advantages to some businessmen, for the abolition of the caucus system, for the compen-

sation of legislators, jurors, and witnesses, for the direct election of mayors, for mass public education, and for a fairer system of taxation. This ideology, Martin Shefter observes, "was anything but socialistic," especially in its support for free competition.[29] This observation does not remove the fact that these parties sought to interpret and to influence the world in class ways and that they joined the concerns of labor and of community. By contrast to the experience in England, however, where the lead was also taken by artisans who used a nonsocialist (indeed, presocialist) republican ideology, the workingmen's vision did not become the dominant one in the United States.

Neither did an alternative possibility, proposed most strongly by the nativist movements and parties of the antebellum years, that saw the new industrial world primarily divided between Catholic, mostly Irish, immigrants and native American Protestants. Ethnic, cultural, and religious differences were in this vision the appropriate ways of distinguishing between groups both at home and at work. The American Republicans and the Know-Nothings treated the immigrants as both the tangible symbols and the cause of the problems associated with the growing dominance of industrial capital. Whereas the workingmen's parties had sought to broaden and equalize political participation, the nativists campaigned on platforms that promised to exclude illiterates and paupers from the franchise.[30] But like the workingmen, the nativists ultimately failed to impose their holistic vision on American politics.

The workingmen's parties were short-lived affairs. Their successes were confined to isolated victories in the late 1820s and 1830s. The nativists likewise did not survive very long as a significant political force. They reached their peak in the 1840s and had lost their political potential by the Civil War. We have long known that the core support for the workingmen's parties was drawn from artisan voters. Bridges has recently demonstrated that this declining class also provided the bulk of nativist backing.[31] Neither the workingmen nor the nativists made much headway in organizing the votes of the new industrial working class. Instead, members of this class were mobilized into politics principally by political machines where they lived and by labor unions where they worked. This split pattern became the unmistakably dominant one in the post–Civil War decades, but it was already apparent in a more primitive form in the thirty years before the Civil War.

This new urban system of "city trenches" had three main elements: trade unions at the workplace; a quite separate decentralized party system; and an array of new government services that were delivered to citizens in their residential communities.

The trade unions that developed at the workplace in the antebellum period sought to protect the traditional prerogatives of skilled workers, struggled for better working conditions, and, above all, fought for higher wages. These unions were prepared to be quite militant, especially in periods of prosperity and labor scarcity. Urban unions called many strikes, which were notably successful in raising pay scales. Between 1850 and 1857 skilled unionized workers in New York secured a 25 percent increase in wages. The unions of the 1850s collected dues systematically and accumulated strike funds. Their most important progressive achievement was their ability "to apply the principles of collective bargaining to the whole trade in order to establish a uniform wage scale for all workers."[32] More than any other institution of the period, the trade unions overcame the differences between native and immigrant workers to forge a common consciousness of class. Many unions, including those of the bakers, smiths, and wheelwrights, actively recruited immigrants. "Quite often," Foner writes,

several nationalities united within the same labor organization, as in the Upholsterers Union in New York which had among its membership in 1850 German-American, Irish-American, French-Canadian, English, and native American workers. The Tailors Union of New York was made up of native American and German-American workers. At first they were not on the best of terms, but police brutality, impartial as to a worker's national origin, during a strike made for greater understanding.[33]

Although most of these unions were shattered by the economic crisis of 1857, they left a legacy of a class-conscious labor movement and of the familiar paraphernalia of the union shop, strike funds, and collective bargaining. They also left the legacy of restricting their attention to immediate trade-union demands and eschewing party activity and political action outside the workplace.

The antebellum party system complemented the limited focus of the unions because it was grounded exclusively in the residence community. The main political parties in the three decades before the Civil War were less interested in ideology than in mobilizing voters. Their attempts to garner votes in the big cities were

organized on the geographical basis of the ward by professional politicians who used new kinds of patronage to woo supporters.

Although the parties competed in national presidential elections, party organizations were intensely *local* territorial institutions. Seen from the bottom of party hierarchies, party life in this period, especially with respect to local offices, gave the overwhelming impression of factional fluidity, individual initiative, clientalistic ties between leaders and followers, and the isolation of organizations in one ward from those in other parts of the large cities. The centralized urban machines date from the 1870s and beyond. In the antebellum years the urban party structures especially were decentralized and enmeshed in the organizational life of neighborhoods—their gangs, firehouses, secret societies, saloons.[34] The ward, as community and as the juridical unit of politics, was the core of the political community.

In these wards, indeed at all levels of the political system, the professional politician (whose prototype can be found in the Albany Regency of the 1820s)[35] superseded the older governing elite of patrician merchants. The sheer number of elections and the organizational skills and time required "put a premium on the efforts of men who were willing to devote all, or almost all, of their time to politics, and who did not expect leadership to fall to them as a matter of deference, celebrity, or wealth."[36] For these new organizers the perpetuation of the party took precedence over ideological commitments. They sought to prosper by organizing political life. And they reflected in their diverse social backgrounds and ties to neighborhood institutions the increasingly heterogeneous class and ethnic character of the urban mosaic. Not all these politicians, of course, came from working-class wards. But those who did were, from the vantage point of working-class neighborhoods, a part of "us," not "them."[37]

The new political organizations that they led bound voters to the party by distributing patronage. Traditional patron-client forms of patronage, in which family and personal ties determined job distribution, came to be replaced by more instrumental bases of distribution. At the national level this transformation was achieved most importantly by the Jacksonians who "established a party system and built a system of public administration which were independent of the informal social hierarchies upon which the Jeffersonians had relied." Locally, too, patronage became the principal instrument of party cohesion. In his important work on

the subject, Shefter notes the shift in the character of patronage in New York City in the antebellum years. In the early decades of the nineteenth century, local politics was a politics of low participation. The Tammany elite that governed in close association with the merchant elite pursued a politics "centered chiefly around the competitive quest for patronage and mercantile privileges—charter franchises, supply contracts—and these leaders had no incentive to distribute the fruits of power more widely." When, under the impact of the franchise extension and the appeals of the Workingmen's party, new voters without ties to Tammany were brought into the electorate, Tammany responded by soliciting support on the basis of a new kind of patronage network. Patronage was distributed to leaders of indigenous working-class associations in the wards who could utilize these new resources to secure and expand their followings.[38]

The party system's decentralized and intensely community-based character reflected the necessary parallelism between government structure and party organization. Its distributive character hinged on the development of political control over public bureaucracies. In important recent treatments of administrative developments at the national level, Crenson and Shefter stress how the Jacksonians created the rudiments of modern bureaucratic structures by divorcing job descriptions and duties from the characteristics of individual persons. In this way "the Jacksonians sought to sever the ties between the bureaucracy and these traditional social structures; and by reorganizing the bureaucracy, they sought to subject it to the control of the office-holders whom they had elected, the institutions (especially the party organizations) which they commanded, and the social groups for whom they spoke."[39] Once these reforms had been accomplished, substantial patronage became available for distribution through the new mass-party structures.

These national changes were paralleled and reinforced by patronage developments at the local level. In the antebellum years a new kind of political system was created there; at its center were municipal *services.* The systematic organization of disciplined professional policemen at the city level was unknown in the West before the creation of a police force in London in 1829. The London system was introduced in the major cities of the United States in the three decades before the Civil War. This period is also characterized by the bureaucratization of municipal charity

and poor relief and by the establishment of modern mass public school systems. These organizations, together with the massive expansion in the budgets and the capacities of local governments to license, award contracts, and shape the tempo and spatial direction of city growth, put unprecedented distributive resources in the hands of local government and party officials.[40] These tangible resources provided the largesse needed to organize the world's first mass urban political parties that were working-class based. By the 1850s, it is important to stress, local political parties at the community level were genuinely working-class institutions, rooted deeply in the local institutions and cultural life made possible by the development of class-homogeneous neighborhoods separate from workplaces.

Significantly, however, these parties at the neighborhood-ward level organized workers not as workers, but as residents of this or that ward, as members of this or that ethnic group; and they did not intrude on workplace concerns. Although throughout the antebellum period such class-related economic issues as banking, tariffs, internal improvements, and slavery dominated the national and state political agendas, votes were increasingly solicited on the basis of ethnic and religious affiliations. It is striking that in a society undergoing very rapid change, and offering many possible points of conflict between groups and classes, the party system exploited locality-based ethnic divisions in the older cities more than anything else.

II

What accounts for the failures of the workingmen and the nativists to create a global politics of class or ethnicity, and for the divided character of urban political development and class consciousness in the antebellum period? The most important answers are to be found in key constitutional and political characteristics of the American system. The federal constitutional order and a relatively weak central government were hallmarks of a state that was very different from the states of Europe. In this context, and in a Jacksonian climate of toleration for the pursuit of interest, the early mass political parties and trade unions emerged as separate institutions. These two clusters of institutions—whose equivalents were unavailable to workers in England in the comparable period of economic development—crucially shaped the ways American workers in the older port cities interpreted and acted out the

objective separation of the workplace from the residence community.

The relative tolerance of the courts for trade unions, as compared to the English and French experiences, made it possible for workplace grievances to be organized around the workplace itself. To be sure, "the onset of industrialization was marked by increased repression of collective labor actions" in the United States. Still, the preindustrial statutory regulation of labor found in England and on the Continent was simply absent in the colonies. Richard Morris has documented the labor activities of journeymen in colonial America, and has found no record of prosecution. Such toleration continued after independence. New York's shoemakers struck for higher wages in 1785, and Philadelphia's printers did so in 1786; in neither case did the authorities intervene. Workers were prosecuted and convicted in 1806 for the first time for combining to raise their wages. Over the next three and a half decades, seventeen conspiracy convictions were obtained, curtailing union activity.[41]

The weight of repression was thus comparatively mild. French restrictions on strikes that antedated industrialization stayed on the books until 1864, when a law was passed that introduced new penalties for committing violence or intimidation, and which sanctioned an increase in state surveillance of worker activity. The 1864 law did not grant workers the freedom to organize. The prohibition of combinations was abolished only in 1884.[42] The English pattern was similar. The Combination Acts of 1799 and 1800, E. P. Thompson observes, "forced the trade unions into an illegal world in which secrecy and hostility to the authorities were intrinsic to their very existence."[43] Although these acts were repealed in 1824, new legislation in 1824 and 1825 did not "establish any collective rights. The orientation was toward the individual's right of contract, not the rights of organizations." Unions were within the boundary of the law only when they did not move beyond actions that were an individual's right. Interpreted by generally hostile courts, these laws made it virtually impossible for unions to strike. Strikes themselves were not illegal, the courts usually found, but since they involved intimidation and coercion, they were not permitted in case after case. As a result, until "the passage of the 1871 Trade Union Act, the unions were still looked upon by the courts as illegal entities at common law, except as specifically exempted by the 1825 Act."[44]

In this universe, U.S. practices have to be regarded as compar-

atively tolerant, even in the period of the conspiracy convictions. No national legislation and only isolated instances of state legislation restricted the rights of workers. Conspiracy convictions were obtained in the courts on the basis of English common law. Generally, only very light sentences were given on conviction, and these in any event did not deter considerable union activity, especially in the 1830s. And in 1842 the chief justice of Massachusetts, in *Commonwealth* v. *Hunt,* recognized the right of workers to organize and to bargain collectively.[45]

Especially after, but also before, this decision, American workers shared little of the "vigorous traditions of illicit trade unionism"[46] of their English counterparts. Rather, labor activity was robust and open. In spite of the legal limitations and the opposition of employers, organized labor was very active in the 1830s. More than 150 unions were organized between 1833 and 1837 in Philadelphia, New York, and Baltimore. More than two-thirds of New York City's workers were said to be unionized:

Wage earners who had never before been organized, including plasterers, cigarmakers, seamstresses, handloom weavers, and milliners, now formed unions and went on strike. In the four years from 1833 to 1837, in the country as a whole, there were one hundred and sixty eight strikes. Of these, one hundred and three were for higher wages, twenty-six for a ten hour day, and four for the closed shop.[47]

The depression of 1837 brought this brief period of union activity to a close, mainly because of the surplus of labor it produced. But before the collapse the legal climate had been significantly improved. In 1829 the New York State legislature had passed a statute, not originally aimed at workers, that made it a conspiracy "to commit any act injurious to public morals or to trade or commerce."[48] When shoemakers in the upstate town of Geneva struck in 1835, the statute was successfully applied to them. In the following year twenty journeymen tailors were found guilty of conspiracy in New York City. A week after sentence was pronounced, a mass rally of over 27,000 workers met outside City Hall, where the judge in the case was burned in effigy.[49] This reaction, and the failure of unions to desist from strike activity— justifying their resistance in the Painean rhetoric of liberty— changed the climate surrounding judicial action. Three weeks after the decision in the tailors' case, a group of shoemakers who had been enforcing a closed shop was found not guilty of conspiracy. *Commonwealth* v. *Hunt* followed six years later.

The revival of union activity in the late 1840s and early 1850s thus took place in a benign climate. Although the flurry of activity was brought to a close by the panic of 1857, this period of worker organization had a distinctively modern cast. Thanks largely to the efforts of skilled workers, most of the crafts in New York were unionized. Craftsmen were now chiefly wage workers, and they fought primarily for the bread-and-butter issues of higher wages, a minimum wage, shorter hours, collective-bargaining rights, and the closed shop. Their activity was not part of a larger working-class movement; indeed, they excluded common laborers and did not involve their unions in attempts to build a workers' political party. They acted directly at the workplace, their main weapon being the strike.[50] Their rhetoric was unmistakably a rhetoric of class, but class understood as labor—no less, but no more.

These limitations continued into the post–Civil War era. They had not been characteristic of the agitation of artisans in the period 1827–1833. At that time this declining class had organized politically on older, if no longer wholly relevant, understandings of the connections between work, community, and political life. Stressing the ten-hour day, free public education, and opposition to the banks and imprisonment for debt, the workingmen's parties had real, though ephemeral, successes, especially in Philadelphia and New York. Their failure to last as the main organizational vehicles of the urban working classes has been explained largely by their internal dissension and inexperience, by the cooption of their demands by the mainstream parties, and by the fact that they represented a declining social force. All these explanations have merit, but they are partial at best.[51] For the inability of the workingmen's parties to survive and grow was intimately related both to the possibilities for independent trade-union activity and to the ability of the party system to organize the emerging modern working classes where they lived on the basis of nonclass ethnic and territorial affiliations.

If a relatively benign legal climate made possible the development of autonomous trade unions, the early franchise for the white adult male facilitated the creation of such a party system. On the Continent and in Britain, workers were excluded from the franchise on an explicit class basis. Consequently, their demands for the franchise were demands made *against* the state. In the United States, by contrast, white workers quickly entered the world of citizens; the state, by belonging to them too, at least

formally, was not available as an agency against which workers as a class could be mobilized.

The story of nineteenth-century European politics is largely a tale of class divisions, at work and in residence communities, that were exacerbated as well as held in check by debates over the size of the political community that was to be included in the franchise. The franchise was expanded in fits and starts. Expansion was accompanied into the twentieth century by elaborate household, property, and residence criteria.[52] This political experience located class at the heart of the political process, and it thus helped create and perpetuate working classes that had the capacity to act politically.

In the United States, by contrast, the franchise was not extended quite so gradually. Rather, the universalization of white male suffrage came early and quickly in the life of the nation. Recent research, moreover, indicates that access to the franchise was more widespread by the 1780s than has conventionally been believed.[53] In late-eighteenth-century America generally, and in its mercantile cities in particular, participation was restricted as much by nonvoting as by property qualifications. The reality and ideology of a single community, ruled and integrated by general merchants, powerfully inhibited the development of a mass politics. This society, Hofstadter writes, was

one in which large masses of the people, many of them technically eligible, did not normally and regularly take part in politics, and in which, out of their regard for and acceptance of the role of leading men and leading *families*, drawn from or at least linked to the ruling elite, the common people did not usually clamor for a great deal more participation.[54]

With the decline of this tightly governed old order, clamor they did. Extension of the franchise in the period after the War of 1812 was principally effected by social groups excluded from the Jeffersonian coalition. "The Jeffersonian political economy," Shefter writes,

had excluded, or at least disadvantaged, a rather heterogeneous collection of social groups. Chief among these were businessmen seeking to break into the existing order of limited mercantile privilege . . . ; farmers who faced competition in the local markets they once had monopolized from grain transported on government-subsidized canals; master mechanics being squeezed out by merchant-capitalists who were able to

obtain credit from publicly chartered banks; and marginal farmers and laborers hurt by the price inflation caused, at least in their view, by the issue of currency by those banks.[55]

The expansion of the franchise and other democratizing reforms—including an increase in the number of elective public offices, the introduction of the direct election of mayors, an increase in the regularity and frequency of elections, the introduction of the uniform ballot, and the development of nominating conventions by political parties—would make possible laissez-faire government policies favored by these groups. The Jacksonians who benefitted from these procedural reforms, not surprisingly, were prepared to extend them.

But it was not only the new Jacksonian "democratic" coalition that so quickly opened up the political system to all white adult males. Widely shared assumptions about representation and popular sovereignty left no ideological basis for resistance to democratic claims. Here Louis Hartz undoubtedly is right: post-independence conflicts about political citizenship were fought on the shared ground of liberal assumptions. Moreover, the dominant Jeffersonian and Jacksonian ideologies of the period both proclaimed the sovereignty of private interests and goals, so long as political behavior conformed to the constitutional rules of a framework of ordered competition.

This world view was intimately bound up with the elusive qualities of the American state. Indeed, from its founding, the very term "state" has had an odd ring in the United States. Whereas "a large part of the point of the word 'state' in Europe is that it is the only concept that effectively joins government, bureaucracy, and the legislature into one collectivity," the division and separation of powers in the United States impels us to speak of the federal government and not the state. Federalism has had a direct impact on common-sense understandings and the language of politics. "In Italy and France," Nettl writes,

the state is instantly recognizable as an area of autonomous action, parallel to other spheres of economy, religion, family, and so on. In Germany, too, there is some of this autonomy, though, as we have seen, it is, as in France, strongly linked to notions of supremacy and superordination. In England, it would be on the whole difficult to find an agreed definition at all, *while in the United States, the word has a precise but totally different meaning in contradistinction to its European meaning—namely,*

the residual area of regional government and territory. Insofar as there is any salient notion of autonomy in the area of central government, there it is sometimes characterized by the term "United States."[56]

The diffuse character of the state in America took much of the charge out of the issue of franchise extension. For there was no unitary state to defend or transform; rather, calculations made at multiple levels of the federal system and based on a rather broad agreement about the nature of the regime produced the world's first mass democracy. The effect of this democratization, moreover, was to reinforce the "low stateness" of the polity. In Europe the franchise expanded as a result of movements against the state; in the United States "the expansion of participation was linked with the dispersion of power and the maintenance of established units of government. Thus, the institutional pluralism inherited from the past first encouraged the expansion of political participation and then was strengthened by it."[57] By 1824 signif- icant restrictions on adult white male suffrage still obtained outside of the South only in Rhode Island. Modern industrial society in the United States, with its distinctive patterns of class interaction, was forged in the crucible of democracy. Workers as citizens did not feel they needed to battle the state, for they were included in its embrace.

The modern political party was invented in the United States in order to structure mass political participation. It is by no means clear that the Federalist and the Jeffersonian Republican parties deserve the modern label "party." Without question, U.S. politics before the 1790s could not be described in terms of party, but only of faction. Factions have an unstable, ad hoc, issue-specific character. Parties, by contrast, are more durable and less tied to specific issues than to a general world view. In the 1790s first the Federalists and then the Republicans coordinated groups of local and national notables who developed consistent appeals and methods of organization, nomination, and electioneering. They provided ambitious men with structured political careers.[58] Yet Walter Dean Burnham, with good reason, has described the period 1789–1820 as the era of an experimental system: "In a real sense, the first American party system was a bridge between a pre-party phase in American political development and the recognizably modern parties found in the second and succeeding party systems." He stresses the narrow base of an active public, the primitive communications and transport facilities of the time,

which inhibited party penetration, and the organization of both of the party coalitions "from the center outward toward the periphery," rather than the reverse, which was later the case.[59] Indeed, the very idea of a party system, in which each party accepts the legitimacy of the opposition and the regular alternation in power, was still absent. "Men remained largely rooted in older politics," Formisano notes, "one that remained hostile to the idea of party as 'legitimate opposition.' . . . Public officials and electorates did not believe that virtue demanded adherence to party norms. Rather, many thought party at best a necessary evil and some activists did not come to revere party as a positive good until 1840 and beyond. Resistance subsided unevenly to the idea of party as an *enduring institution commanding a separate loyalty.*"[60]

By the 1840s new kinds of parties, having a much higher degree of resemblance to contemporary parties than those of the "first party system" had had, organized political participation. The "second party system's" parties were constructed on a mass base, and reached into virtually every neighborhood and ward in the country. The parties came to organize a growing number of voters, selecting candidates for more and more offices as a result both of modifications in suffrage qualifications and of what McCormick has called "the quiet revolution in the electoral environment," which included "the movements toward the popular, at-large election of presidential electors, the choice of congressmen by districts, the popular election of governors, and the multiplication in numbers of locally elected officials."[61] In this context the parties, now nominating candidates by convention rather than by caucus, elaborated an organizational structure, national in reach and highly decentralized, that put party labels on the competition for virtually every office in the land. In the major cities of the East, the sites of large working-class populations, these parties, under the opportunistic provenance of the party leader, converged spatial, ethnic, and political identities.

The political groupings that were created by party activity were based exclusively in the residence community. They had no direct organizational ties to the period's trade unions, and they did not discuss politics in terms of class. As a result, politics in the antebellum city came to be defined in the main, not as a politics of capital and labor, but as a politics of competition between ethnic-territorial communities from which capital was absent.[62]

These developments quite clearly reflected the material realities

associated with the separation of work from home and with the demographic distribution of the population. Capitalist industrialization was experienced directly as conflict over the use of scarce space at the community level. German and Irish immigrants became the tangible symbols (some thought the cause) of the ascendancy of industrial capital. Native-born Protestant artisans who had the most to lose expressed their rebellion against the new order in their neighborhoods by resisting residential incursions. The result was many bloody clashes—between nativists and immigrants, between Protestants and Catholics, and in some cases between blacks and whites. These conflicts heightened the importance of territorial identities and of such institutions as gangs and fire companies that gave expression to them; and these institutions provided the organizational base for party organization. From the immigrants' perspective the integrity of their religion and cultural practices was at stake in their communities. Bitter conflicts over local control of the new public schools reflected these intensely felt concerns.[63]

The new political developments also mirrored the willingness of the old local patrician ruling classes to make way for specialized political leadership in the interest of order. Social peace throughout the antebellum period was extremely precarious. The well-documented experience of Philadelphia was not atypical. In May and July of 1844, Philadelphia was shaken by spasmodic rioting between crowds of Irishmen and native Americans in the manufacturing area of Kensington that brought about a virtual collapse of public order. In 1849, after still another riot—this time racial in content—the city's businessmen and lawyers held a meeting whose chairman, a former mayor, put the case for a reorganization of the city's boundaries, institutions, and political arrangements: "We have a common interest to protect life and property. . . . it has also been made manifest that our property is not secure. . . . property is rendered valueless, comparatively speaking, by popular outbreaks and riots."[64] Though community-based violence was not directed against the ruling classes, it tangibly affected their interests. In the face of these challenges to the social order, the unified Anglo-Protestant elite that had governed the older cities into the age of Jackson was discouraged from making a continuing claim to govern. Its members were ill equipped to manage the new ethnic conflicts. Moreover, they were increasingly absorbed in the economic tasks of a more

complex economy. Business and governmental affairs became too demanding to be worked at part-time. This was particularly the case as cities expanded their boundaries and created new service bureaucracies to cope with the social stresses of the time.[65]

The withdrawal of the traditional governing elite from city politics, in short, was doubly self-interested. The rewards of money lay with private capital, and social cohesion depended on new political relationships they were incapable of creating. One consequence may well have been, as Robert Dahl has stressed,[66] the democratization of local leadership, but the substantive result was a new system of urban politics, city trenches that protected capital.

III

On the eve of the Civil War, all the elements of this system were in place, but just barely. The depression of 1857 decimated urban trade unions. Political machines were still largely neighborhood affairs that lacked coordination. Local services were crude and limited. Many neighborhoods continued to function as integrated worlds of work and home, and some still contained a multiplicity of classes. From the vantage point of 1860, the newly constructed city trenches could not have looked too secure. By the last two decades of the century, however, the uncertainties had been resolved, and as the century turned, the new urban system dominated the political landscape.

Labor unions resumed their path of separate development. Both the short-lived Knights of Labor and the American Federation of Labor (AFL), as their names imply, conceived of workers as "labor" and had virtually no connections of a regular electoral sort with local mainstream or insurgent party organizations. With only rare exceptions, subsequent labor organizations have maintained this tradition.

The residence community became the political forum managed by parties and bureaucracies that were divorced from workplace concerns. These urban working-class neighborhoods were neighborhoods of immigrants who came increasingly from southern and eastern Europe. Like the mercantile cities of the eighteenth century, they were walking neighborhoods; yet unlike the older port cities, these neighborhoods constituted only a part of the ethnic worker's universe. Caroline Golab's sensitive portrait of

Poles in Philadelphia in the late-nineteenth century captures the intense localism and provinciality of these residence spaces:

They walked . . . to the grocery store, to the butcher shop and bakery. They walked to church and to school. They walked to visit friends and relatives (unless they lived in another Polish neighborhood, in which case they took the trolley). Their children were born at home, and when they died in Nicetown, Bridgesburg, Richmond, or Manaynuk, they were not too far from the cemetery. Because all their needs could be satisfied within their immediate environment, they had little reason to venture outside. The beauty of the neighborhood was its self-sufficiency. . . . *The city remained an abstraction, the neighborhood was a reality. It was the neighborhood, not the city, which provided immigrants with their identity, security, and stimulation.*[67]

In these neighborhoods, residents were policed by newly organized police forces, assisted by new welfare agencies, and taught by new public common schools. The prototype of the modern police force was the constabulary established in London in 1829. Before that date the propertied classes had protected their own property by themselves or by hiring watchmen and guards. When public order had been threatened beyond their capacity to maintain social peace, military force had generally been used to quell the "dangerous classes." By contrast, in a policed society, government authorities exercise "potentially violent supervision over the population by bureaucratic means widely diffused throughout civil society in small and discretionary operations that are capable of rapid concentration." It was the job of the police to penetrate the new class-homogeneous neighborhoods of the older cities to maintain order and prevent crime, and in so doing to represent the "continual presence of central political authority throughout daily life."[68] The policeman, often a resident of the policed community, became the instrument of joining local residents to state authority. These relationships, from the start, were often themselves sources of major conflicts between residents and local government, as the police, especially in areas where the policeman came from a different (usually Irish) ethnic group, embodied all undesirable intrusions and traits of "them" or of all who were not "us."

Similar patterns prevailed with respect to welfare and educational services. In the late-eighteenth and early-nineteenth centuries, private individual and associational charity paralleled private police and private schools. As late as the 1830s and 1840s,

it often made little sense to distinguish between private and public benevolent associations. In New York City the Humane Society built a soup house for the poor with public funds; the Society for New York Hospital was funded by legislative grants; the "Society for the Prevention of Pauperism formalized the relationship between public and private bodies by providing that five of its managers be appointed by the common council." The patrician officials who ran city government were often the same people, or at least members of the same families, who directed the city's welfare establishments. By the late 1840s, however, city government came increasingly under the control of professional politicians and had to administer a growing welfare burden. Approximately 57,000 people received public outdoor relief in 1848, compared to about 8,000 four decades earlier. Benevolent societies also expanded their activities, but apart from those of local government. Politics and benevolence had become separate realms of activity; the old ruling class dominated the latter. But in both public and private spheres, paid employees with specialized skills came to take over the delivery of welfare benefits and services to working-class ethnic neighborhoods. The creation of a profession of social work later in the century helped crystallize these patterns, as it also reinforced an emerging set of conflicts between the producers and consumers of welfare services.[69]

Educational issues provided still another new arena for tension between communities and local government. As in the case of the police, the schools were key instruments in visibly linking class and ethnically specific neighborhoods to the larger political and social system. "In almost every city where the population was heterogeneous," David Tyack writes about the late-nineteenth century, "contests erupted in educational politics. Although there were sometimes overtones of class assertion or resentment in such conflicts, the issues were not normally phrased in class terms, but in the cross-cutting cultural categories of race, religion, ethnicity, neighborhood loyalties, and partisan politics."[70]

This language of city affairs was predominantly determined by the increasingly centralized party organizations of the post–Civil War era. Dominant citywide machines came to control the ward organizations, and to impose discipline on neighborhood political actors. In New York City, for example, an era of "rapacious individualism," symbolized graphically by the operations of the Tweed ring, was followed by a period of organization building

under the leadership of John Kelly that culminated in Tammany's triumph over its potential party rivals and in the establishment of a network of district political clubs throughout the city.[71]

The new citywide machines established centralized control on the basis of standardized community organizations. Each of these party clubs—like its pre–Civil War precursors—was enmeshed in the ethnic and territorial culture of the ward or precinct. Ostrogorski well understood the communitarian basis of the machine. He wrote in 1910,

> The small politician has no need to create the political following which he forms around him; he finds it ready to hand in social life, in which neighbourly ties, and above all common tastes and mutual sympathies, give rise to small sets, groups of people who meet regularly to enjoy the pleasures of sociability and friendship. The street corner serves them as a rendezvous as long as they are in the youthful stage. Then, when they grow older and have a few cents to spend, they meet in a drinking-saloon or in a room hired for the purpose with their modest contributions. Several "gangs" unite to found a sort of club, in which they give small parties, balls, or simply smoke, drink, and amuse themselves. This merry crew is a latent political force; when the elections come round it may furnish a compact band of voters. The small politician therefore has but to lay his hand on it.[72]

The centralized machine's political clubs organized this social impulse and made it the cornerstone of an electoral politics through patronage and services. The potency of the community as the locus of political identities lay not merely in the existence of community networks nor in their being promoted by party organizations. Rather, the interaction of the organization and the community base strengthened both, as it gave new impetus to communal ties, and in so doing solidified the prospects of the political party. As a consequence, workers were regularly integrated into the political process on the basis of communally bounded affiliations. The machines, for workers, were "us," yet the machine also limited the content of "us."

Werner Sombart's most acute observations spoke directly to this point. He observed that this kind of party system "makes it extremely easy for the proletariat to belong to the traditional parties. In attaching himself to one of the two parties, even the class-conscious worker need never go against the dictates of his intellect, because these parties do not have to be seen as class organizations and as advocates of a specific class interest." In turn,

this situation "also influences the position they take towards the proletariat." By stressing particularistic rewards and nonclass affiliations, "the traditionally good relationship is maintained intact."[73]

Every election reinforced the split consciousness of the American working class. As a consequence of the mosaic pattern of ethnic settlement and the ward organization of electoral competition, urban political parties, I have noted elsewhere, "to win elections, had to put together electoral majorities composed of blocs of ethnic groups. . . . the opportunity for ethnic communities to enter the political process acted to solidify group consciousness and to perpetuate the division of the city, demographically and politically, into ethnic components."[74] Indeed, the very rules of electoral politics reinforced this system of ethnicity, community, and party. Douglas Rae has stressed how the single-member district system, such as we have in the United States, "strengthens already strong parties by making small party challenges difficult." And he has made the more important point that the system of territorial districts puts a premium on the identities that are to be found where people live rather than where they work.[75]

As most standard treatments of urban politics have stressed, the urban system has been essentially a system of ethnic bargaining and accommodation. Drawing on the political, organizational, and cultural resources of their communities, ethnic groups have been joined in a complex game whose prizes are patronage and city services. I have stressed that the urban system is more than this. By constricting the politics of class to the workplace, the urban system made challenges to the larger social order very difficult indeed. Over a long period of time, the stark division in people's consciousness, language, and action between the politics of work and the politics of community became a tacit mechanism in the selection of alternatives. As Raymond Williams has observed, "in certain social-historical circumstances, there are things which could not be said, and therefore, in any connecting way, not thought."[76] Social control in the United States has depended on just such an imposition of silence. The system of city trenches has produced a working class unique in the West: militant as labor, and virtually nonexistent as a collectivity outside the workplace. Workers have thus tended "to oppose capitalists rather than capitalism."

It is not surprising that there have been attempts to challenge

this urban class system through working-class socialist or laborist parties that would appeal to workers *as workers* both in the community and in the laboring portions of their lives. American urban history is in part the story of such attempts: socialist campaigns in the late 1870s in Chicago; the United Labor party candidacy of Henry George for mayor of New York that utilized trade-union organizations for electoral purposes; socialist strength on the Lower East Side of Manhattan at the turn of the century; and the election of socialist councilmen in many cities, and mayors in a few, most notably in Milwaukee. Taken as a whole, however, these challenges were hardly successful. Indeed, American socialists achieved most when one of two very special conditions obtained: when workplaces and residence communities were tightly bound together as in the Finnish mining communities of northern Michigan; or when the voting public consisted principally of first-generation immigrants from Europe who brought a socialist tradition with them.[77] In almost all other cases, the city trenches held against socialist incursions.

CHAPTER 4

The Making of Northern Manhattan

The "city trenches" constructed just before and after the Civil War were built in the working-class communities of America's large industrial and commercial cities. Rapid and significant urbanization continued after this formative period, well into the twentieth century. Washington Heights–Inwood, encompassing virtually all of Manhattan north of Harlem, was founded and settled as a working-class community after the turn of the century. By examining the making of northern Manhattan, we are able to see how the system of city trenches persisted as the main feature of the urban political landscape and how it determined the rules of city politics.

I

The transformation of northern Manhattan from the last rural enclave on the island at the turn of the century to a densely populated apartment-house area for over 200,000 working-class residents by the Second World War is a story not just of rapid urbanization or of the creation of a "pure" residential community that was spatially separate from where most of its residents worked. It is the tale, too, of how three aspects of the system of city trenches became a part of everyday thought and political life: the separation of community life from work; the isolation of the working class from the dominant classes who resided outside the community; and the segmentation of the society within the territory, dividing workers from each other along ethnic lines.

Washington Heights–Inwood, roughly all of Manhattan Island north of 155th Street, was settled in the seventeenth century by Dutch farmers. The land had traditionally belonged to the

73

Weckquaesgeek Indians, who were compelled to surrender their claims to the territory in 1688 by the new English administration. For more than the next hundred years, the area, as its name implies, took its primary importance from its strategic military location. The rock topography that gave the Heights this significance made it unsuitable for extensive farming. After the Revolutionary War most of the old farm holdings had been converted into country estates for wealthy families living in lower Manhattan. But the farms did not disappear entirely. "Back in the early 1880's one could still meet farmers who . . . 'had not been down to New York for the past twenty-five years.'" In fields still marked by military encampments more than one hundred years after the Revolution, cows and sheep grazed. The area's last grain field was harvested in 1904; fox, mink, and deer were seen in Inwood at the turn of the century.[1]

This landscape must have contained immense beauty and power. Although narrow and compact, the territory has an undulating quality. The terrain rises slowly from the southern section to what is now 181st Street. The eastern and western parts of this plateau feature steep bluffs that terminate in narrow shelves along the Harlem and Hudson rivers. To the north the area is divided into two ridges that run north and south along the edges of the island. Fort George Ridge to the east rises 260 feet above the Harlem River; Fort Washington Ridge, overlooking the Hudson River, rises almost as high to the west. The drop to the valley between the ridges is as much as 175 feet. The northeastern section contains mostly level ground, but there is another major hill to the northwest.[2]

This geography has guided all the territory's settlers. The location of Indian trails was determined principally by the area's topography. The main paths were placed on the floor of the valley between the two ridges, and on the low lands along the rivers. The Dutch and English built on this pattern well into the nineteenth century. Broadway, for example, which follows the Manhattan street grid up to Washington Heights, meanders up the Indian valley path for the rest of its course to the northern tip of the island. The two major east-west thoroughfares, 181st Street and Dyckman Street (the latter providing the rough boundary between Washington Heights and Inwood), follow the level routes between the major topographical features of the area. The Harlem River Expressway and the Henry Hudson Parkway,

built in this century, follow the old Indian paths along the rivers. Land patterns also divided the territory's space into distinctive neighborhoods after the 1920s.

The old rural landscape has not entirely disappeared. Washington Heights–Inwood is ringed by parkland. At many spots it is easy to harbor the illusion that northern Manhattan is rural still, and timeless. But this space has not been divorced from time. Outside of the parks lies a very different kind of landscape. Sometimes pretty, but rarely beautiful, and often dull, drab, dirty. This landscape is almost exclusively the product of the twentieth century, the impress of "a new capitalism upon a new space, installing itself with no overall plan, according to its own internal logic."[3]

The late rural character of northern Manhattan, and the new transport links of New York City's subway system allowed Washington Heights–Inwood to develop exclusively as a residential area. The part-time residential suburb of the wealthy was transformed into the teeming home of Irish, Jewish, and Greek workers and shopkeepers.

As late as the 1880s street grids had been laid out only in the southeastern and northeastern extremes of northern Manhattan. Most of the area's land was still held in large estates comprising from twenty to one hundred acres. Yet some of the largest estates had already been divided into building plots and built on. The naturalist John Audubon's holdings in southern Washington Heights were some of the first to be cut up into plots as the city street system was extended north of 155th Street in the 1870s; by 1910 Audubon Park had completely given way to construction, mostly large apartment houses.[4] Observing this process, the Washington Heights Taxpayers' Association of merchants and property owners predicted in 1880 that "the whole of this section of the city is destined to be transformed in the course of a very few years." Its prescient pamphlet on the future of the area forecast that "a vast business and tide of population is coming," in light of the built-up character of most of the rest of Manhattan, and of the street and transit improvements that had already been made. The area below Washington Heights had already been "improved" by new street pavings and cable-car extensions that had led to the construction of "attractive dwellings" in Morningside Heights and Harlem. What was now required for Washington Heights and Inwood was the extension of rapid-transit railroads

to "attract population to the most beautiful and healthful part of the city" and to "increase the value of property."[5]

A similar theme was the constant refrain of the area's first newspaper, the *West End and Washington Heights Gazette.* A genteel publication, containing many articles on women's clubs, music lessons, glee-club concerts, society events, and local poetry celebrating the picturesque features of northern Manhattan, it eagerly anticipated the construction of housing on a large scale "for the better classes." In 1895 the paper took note of how "building here is steadily progressing; it is astounding to note the number of new stores, flats, and private dwellings projected." But projections they would remain without new transportation to connect residence and work places: "All we cry for is *Rapid Transit;* then New York will become well-acquainted with her long overlooked promising Heights . . . then the Heights thoroughly awake and imbued with new life will look down from its superb eminence with stately consequence." This boosterist call for public works was intended, the paper candidly noted, to bring a "prosperity which will be ours when the distance has been made shorter by real rapid transit."[6] Indeed, as in other rapidly urbanizing areas, there were fortunes to be made: "Rapid development in Washington Heights," a land economist wrote in the 1920s,

has been comparatively recent and it was found possible to trace a tract of about 38 acres through its development from farmland to valuable city property. It now comprises about fourteen city blocks, including the valuable 181st Street and St. Nicholas Avenue corner. In 1850 it was valued at $24,000 and in 1891 was subdivided into 411 lots and sold at auction for $1,490,000. It had been bought and sold several times in the meantime, with one outstanding sale in 1891 for $980,000 wherein practically the whole net increment of forty-one years was taken by those who held the property from 1885 to 1891.[7]

This rapid escalation in land prices, the *Gazette* anticipated, would "preclude the building of anything but high-class residence property" after the extension of rapid transit lines.[8]

The newspaper was mistaken. The first housing built on the Heights after the construction of the Broadway subway to 157th Street in 1904, and then into Inwood by 1906, was not intended for the wealthy. Rather, modified old-law tenements were hastily erected to house second- and third-generation Irish workers and smaller numbers of Jews who sought escape from the crowded and desolate slums farther south. By World War One the land-

scape of this area east of Broadway, from 155th to 178th streets, was largely fixed. The only other development in this prewar period was a much smaller residential area in the northeastern part of Inwood, built adjacent to a variety of new activities that were needed to sustain the new urbanization, including an electric generating station, subway-car-storage and maintenance yards, fuel terminals, and a garbage incinerator. The remainder of northern Manhattan remained mostly vacant, awaiting the construction boom of the 1920s.[9]

The natural geography of Washington Heights–Inwood; the location of the major arterial streets, such as Broadway and Dyckman and 181st streets; the placement of subway routes; and the settlement patterns established by prewar housing—these divided northern Manhattan into four main areas, which in time became distinctive neighborhoods. From north to south these areas were Inwood (and Marble Hill—a small enclave of Manhattan attached to the mainland and not the island proper), West Washington Heights, East Washington Heights (including Highbridge), and South Washington Heights. In order to follow the making and, later, the remaking of northern Manhattan, I have chosen to examine with special care the development of four representative census tracts, one for each neighborhood. Since the boundaries of these tracts have been altered only insignificantly since 1910, they provide an economical way to trace the developing, and changing, community. They are located at the southeastern extreme of South Washington Heights (tract 239), in the heart of East Washington Heights (tract 261), in the Fort Tryon area of West Washington Heights (tract 273), and in what became the residential center of Inwood (tract 295). I shall call these areas by the names of the neighborhoods in which they are embedded (see map, p. 78).[10]

By 1920 East and South Washington Heights had been significantly built up, reaching about 80 percent of their peak population. The other two areas, by contrast, were still largely rural in character, having attained only about 15 percent of their subsequent peak population.[11] Four principal population groups lived in northern Manhattan in 1920: native Protestants, Irish Catholics, Jews, and Greeks. The community had been almost exclusively Protestant at the turn of the century, and it still had a Protestant, mostly middle-class majority or plurality. Yet nowhere did the Protestant proportion now exceed 50–55 percent. The immigrant

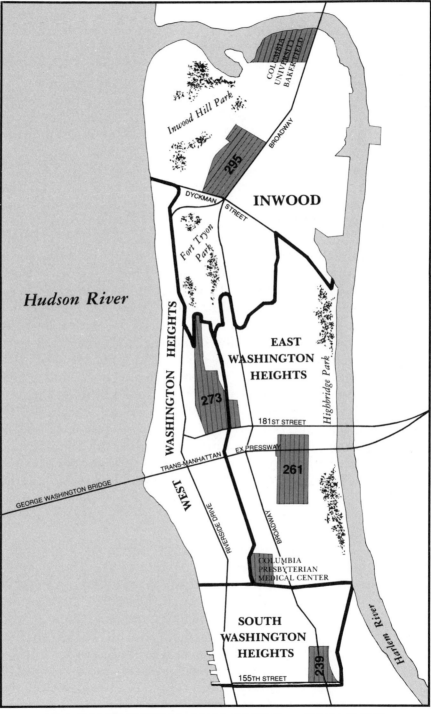

WASHINGTON HEIGHTS—INWOOD

groups were distributed rather evenly across the Heights and Inwood. In our four tracts the Irish constituted no less than 25 percent of the residents, and no more than 29 percent; Jews, no less than 19 percent and no more than 33; and the Greeks, well under 1 percent.[12] For almost all of the Irish and Jewish residents of the community, Washington Heights–Inwood was a second or third place of residence.[13] For them it had become the home of a growing, heterogeneous, and established working class.[14]

The Protestant population continued to fall rapidly in the 1920s and 1930s, and the Irish and Jewish population increased steadily. At the close of this period, the Protestant population north of 155th Street had been reduced to about 10 percent.[15] Jews outnumbered the Irish in Inwood, but only West Washington Heights came to be regarded as "the Jewish Alps."[16] Apart from the Lower East Side, whose Jewish population was now declining, northern Manhattan became the island's main center of Jewish settlement, especially after approximately 20,000 Austrian and German Jewish refugees fleeing nazism settled on the Heights west of Broadway in the 1930s and early 1940s.[17] Western Inwood was also heavily Jewish, but the area as a whole was divided about equally between Jews and the Irish. Since the main Irish parish institutions were located in Inwood, the territory north of Dyckman Street, especially just west and east of Broadway, came to be seen as an Irish area.[18]

Northern Manhattan shared in the massive expansion of Manhattan's housing stock in the 1920s. The First World War had left the building industry depressed. Easy credit and tax write-off policies to stimulate construction produced the desired result. In Manhattan alone, 83,000 new dwelling units were completed between 1921 and 1930; over 60 percent of northern Manhattan's housing stock dates from this period.[19] The main commercial streets, the local public school system, and a majority of the area's religious institutions were developed in the 1920s.[20]

The housing market collapsed in New York in the depression years of the 1930s, but the falloff was less pronounced in Washington Heights–Inwood than elsewhere in Manhattan. New subway construction along the western edge of the Heights, completed in 1932, made possible the urbanization of this hilly and previously relatively inaccessible terrain. On the eve of the Second World War, Washington Heights–Inwood was completed.

II

Washington Heights–Inwood was thus a rather pristine example of the separation of work and home, and of classes from each other. Within northern Manhattan conflicts were waged across an ethnic divide, and Irish and Jewish institutions assumed political roles. The two groups, despite comparable histories, were fiercely separatist, identifying with their own. Their histories, however, disposed them to play the game of politics by the rules established by the system of city trenches.

Consider the Irish. Although the alleged affinity between Irish personality traits and the requirements of political leadership in urban machines should rightly be suspect as the principal explanation of Irish political success in the nineteenth century[21]—the timing of their arrival, their ability to speak English, their Church resources, their command over the same kinds of working-class organizations, like saloons and gangs, that were common to other early working-class cultures, and their participation in collective struggles against the British are among the other compelling factors that would have to be considered in any meaningful explanation—the social and ideological matrix of Ireland strongly shaped the capacity of the immigrants to enter the American urban system already under construction on the terms they did.

An extraordinary religiosity was perhaps the dominant feature of the life in Ireland in the first four decades of the nineteenth century. "In few, if any, of the other European countries was religious observance more widespread or scrupulous, or religious allegiance more decisive and divisive in civil affairs."[22] In these decades a protracted struggle for Catholic parity in religious affairs steadily politicized the Catholic clergy and masses, a politicization that identified Catholic and nationalist interests together against the British regime. Ideologically, the enemy was Protestant and British ascendancy and bigotry. Institutionally,

the main drive of the Catholic Church in Ireland between 1800 and 1845 was the reconstitution of an effective Parish structure after the suppressions and dislocations of the eighteenth century. By 1840, the first stage of this work had been substantially accomplished. A parochial network, with a parish priest and a church for each unit, and a curate for many and parish halls for some, was complete. This provided the basic communal structure for the great majority of Catholics, for the parish and the weekly mass served general social as well as religious

ends. For a large range of matters, they even acted as definers of the group.[23]

The priest in this world occupied a crucial mediating social role. He was at once the protector of the community and the aggressive promoter of worldly interests. He also directed a growing education system, developed after 1800 in defense against Anglican incursions and run by religious orders. By 1845 Ireland had over 100,000 pupils enrolled in more than 4,000 Catholic schools. The priests also commanded complex county political machines within the Irish constitutional system, and they lent support to such extraconstitutional oath-bound and conspiratorial political movements of peasants against landlords as Ribbonism and Whiteboyism.[24]

The Irish did not create the American system of city trenches. But it is obvious that this system lent structural support to the recreation of many elements of political and social life in Ireland, as the Catholic Irish underwent the wrenching transformation from a distinctive category of Irish to a special group of Americans. The nativist reaction bearing a family resemblance to Protestant bigotry and the intensely local forms of political practice found in the newly emerging class-homogeneous neighborhoods of American cities provided a fertile new soil for the growth of the traditions of the parish, the group-centered politician, the separate educational order, and the simultaneous stance of insularity and aggressive assertion. That many of these new class-homogeneous communities became largely Irish is not surprising. Before the Civil War, with blacks still confined to the slave economy of the South, and with the eastern European migrations still to come, the Irish constituted the bulk of the urban proletariat. The importance of the Church in the New World, and the political capacity that the density of settlement afforded further reinforced the tendency to draw together on arrival.[25]

Similar, though not identical, features of the historical background of Russian Jews who came to the United States, mainly between 1881 and 1914, determined the formation of communal Jewish groups in the United States. In Russia, and in the Polish and Lithuanian sections under Russian rule, the status of Jews depended on the protective charter of the authoritarian state. This charter proclaimed an exchange relationship, in which Jews would perform desired functions for the good of the regime and its supporters and would, in turn, accept limitations on the place

of residence and choice of occupation. "The Jewish community became like one of the estates, with its own specific and limited rights and privileges but dependent upon the country's central authority for support and protection." The isolation of the Jewish population, spatially and occupationally, made possible a delicate existence in a world marked by the hostility of the majority of the population, the established church, and local trade and crafts groups.[26]

The Jews of Russia, Poland, and Lithuania lived apart and largely governed themselves. "Given the strong desire to retain religious identity," Kuznets observes,

the effort of the religious leadership of the Jewish community to fortify it against continuous pressure, and the attempt by authorities of the host Christian state to limit contacts between Jews and others, the Jewish community tended to lead an autonomous and distinctive cultural and social life. It was distinctive not only in religion but in language, dress, and the pattern of individual and family behavior.[27]

Furthermore, since the status of Jews depended on a charter granted to the community as a whole, autonomous communal governing units were created within Jewish areas of settlement. This government could tax, run its own courts, and make decisions about expulsion. The boundaries between civil and religious authority were virtually nonexistent.

The regrouping of Jews in New York City allowed them to call on this tradition of collective action, defense, and self-government, even as the community in the New World was sharply divided on ideological and class lines.[28] For both the Jews and the Irish, the heritage of the period of migration was a heritage of "us" and "them" and a series of communal institutional traditions for managing these relationships. Indeed, the leading institutional legacy from the relevant migration periods to northern Manhattan is the church or synagogue: for the Irish, St. Elizabeth's (1871), Church of the Good Shepherd (1912), Church of the Incarnation (1908), and Our Lady Queen of Martyrs (1927), among others; for the Jews, no fewer than twenty-one orthodox, conservative, and reform congregations, virtually all founded between 1910 and 1937.[29]

The similarity of Irish and Jewish backgrounds did not help the two groups build a bridge between them. Similarity reinforced their separateness, even as (perhaps because) the two groups also had much in common in economic and social terms. They shared

comparable incomes and styles of life. Very few were foreign-born. Few were without employment, and most earned more than the median income for the city. Although the Jews were marginally better off than the Irish, both groups had very similar income distributions, and they spent roughly comparable shares of their income for housing. Virtually all lived in sound, modern, and centrally heated, if spare, rental apartments. Census inspectors reported that only a tiny proportion of the housing stock was lacking in major amenities or was in need of major repairs. Vacancy rates were low; rents just above the city median. Scarcely a household lacked a refrigerator or a radio. Northern Manhattan, *within its bounds,* appeared as a classless, egalitarian society.[30]

The absence of class conflict between groups does not mean the absence of conflict. Space itself—housing, shops, and street traffic—is a scarce resource that invites competition among groups disposed to stress their separateness. Conflict about space was especially acute in northern Manhattan between the two world wars because it was such desirable space. Working-class neighborhoods of the kind then available in Washington Heights–Inwood are rare indeed; no other territory on Manhattan Island rivaled it for ease of access to mass transit, parkland, and affordable nonslum housing. Competition for this space was exacerbated in the middle 1930s by the completion of subway and housing construction in the now filled-up area and by the rapid immigration of German and Austrian Jewish refugees. Apartment houses and individual residential streets came to be appropriated by each of the groups. Although the distribution of the population continued to be heterogeneous throughout the area, Inwood came to be identified as the locus of Irish settlement (a disproportionate number of parish churches and parochial schools located there), and West Washington Heights became an area of Jewish symbolic and institutional dominance.[31] The existence of these ethnic fiefdoms affected subsequent population movements, especially as both the Irish and Jewish populations declined in size after 1940.

Relations between the Irish and Jewish residents of northern Manhattan in this period were neither cordial nor peaceful. Conflicts over housing and group symbols were especially prevalent, especially when they were conducted by adolescents and the elderly, for whom, in the absence of work identities, place identities are especially strong and significant. Teenage violence

was common. In the 1930s, Irish gangs frequently attacked the new Jewish arrivals, and there were numerous cases of synagogue desecration. The Christian Front, an offshoot of Father Coughlin's Union for Social Action, was active in northern Manhattan and held well-attended street-corner rallies to protest the immigration of Jewish refugees. Local Irish politicians were generally reluctant to denounce this activity, and some joined in it actively.[32]

Ethnic divisions defined political competition. In the 1920s the Jews and Irish divided largely along party lines in northern Manhattan, the bulk of the Republican and small socialist vote coming from Jewish voters, and the Irish voting Democratic. Political officeholding was almost exclusively an Irish preserve.[33] Unlike the Irish, the Jewish migrants possessed a far more decentralized and voluntaristic religious structure and were much less well located in terms of the date of their arrival and their limited numbers to contest for control of the political parties of the older port cities. An exception was the part of the German-Jewish population that arrived in the 1930s under the leadership of Rabbi Breuer and that brought with it the traditional orthodox set of institutions and practices of an intact congregation. In the prewar period, though, it chose to be aloof from local politics.

As the majority of Jews shifted their allegiance to the Democratic party in the 1930s, ethnic conflict was introduced into intraparty fights. By the end of the decade, "a political shift had taken place, with Jews replacing the former Irish-held monopoly over elective offices."[34] What is significant is not so much that this shift occurred, but that in a period of vital party organizations, political conflict in the community centered almost exclusively on the ethnic possession of the city council, the state assembly, and the congressional seats. Socialist attempts to cast the issues of the depression in class terms met with a very meager response.[35]

III

The organization of social space is never random. People, their homes, and their workplaces are not just placed here or there by accident. Washington Heights–Inwood, as a community, was built up at the end of a long period of expansion of the older port cities of the United States as a place of residence for second- and third-generation ethnic workers that offered access to the burgeoning downtown of New York City. Its patterns of settlement, and the creation of social and political relationships between

ethnic groups, matured under conditions of rapid, confident urbanization and economic expansion, broadly similar to those that had prevailed in the older port cities of the nineteenth century. Since this community was constructed on what was mostly virgin territory, it was not interlaced by remnants of a preindustrial, mercantile environment. It came very close to being the ideal and typical capitalist residence community. Within its boundaries the inherited nineteenth-century system of city trenches was introduced and institutionalized. The two principal groups were incorporated into politics on roughly *equivalent* terms.[36] By maintaining the "society" within the bounds of Washington Heights–Inwood, the larger unequal social structure was obscured, and a politics about the larger social order made irrelevant. In these ways, the ethnic dimensions of community life helped cohere a class society, even in the midst of the Great Depression.

Until the 1950s, blacks were not part of this multiethnic society. To be sure, by 1940 the southeastern extreme (census tract 239) had a clear black majority, as about 2,900 of its 4,000 residents were black; and by 1950 all but fifty of its residents were black.[37] But this small enclave in Washington Heights was treated as an extension of Harlem.

A map portraying the area in 1860 placed the southern boundary of Washington Heights at 135th Street, just north of the semirural, all-white, upper-class community of Harlem.[38] By 1923, after the great migration and real-estate speculation had transformed Harlem into a black tenement area,[39] the conventional boundary had been moved north by ten blocks to 145th Street, where black settlement stopped and Irish settlement started.[40] Yet even as late as the middle 1940s, official reports still placed Hamilton Grange, stretching from 135th to 145th streets, and "Middle Washington Heights," from 145th to 155th streets, in Washington Heights proper.[41] Ordinary usage ignored these traditional boundaries, however. Surveying a sample of "leaders" in 1960, Lee Lendt observed that Washington Heights had shrunk, as its residents had sought to maintain its white ethnic character in the face of the expansion of Harlem:

Most of the white respondents tended to place the southern and eastern boundaries with reference to the northward push of Negroes. Although the respondents were not unanimous concerning the extent of Harlem's growth, they generally defended their boundary line choice by referring to the racial character of the excluded area. It was alleged that Washington Heights begins where Harlem ends. If this is true, the 155th

Street boundary seemed to indicate that this area had been penetrated by Negro residents and was in danger of further penetration. . . . Whatever validity these dividing lines have, they all reflect an exclusionary policy by the white community.[42]

In reciprocal fashion, blacks moving north to what had once been considered Washington Heights thought of themselves as residents of north Harlem, which remained their social base.

The current state assemblyman for this old "border" area recalls the process of boundary change:

They had just begun to allow blacks to live west of Amsterdam Avenue, on 156th Street, and they did it in those days by emptying a building out first, unlike today where they housebreak by moving in one or two families and creating a run. In those days they could afford to go through the building and say "you better move because we're moving blacks in," and they emptied the building out. When my mother went to look at the apartment she had her choice of four or five apartments she could look at, and we moved into the building.[43]

Although he is Catholic, he was excluded from the local parish school, and attended an all-black public school on 164th Street, located in a black enclave, but separated from his home:

There was a constant problem, the fear that you might accidentally cross the line and get killed. I used to have to go home, but I couldn't go down the normal route down Amsterdam Avenue. I had to go down Broadway. Of course, I was then invading white turf. . . . I would leave school at 165th Street, run down 165th Street to Broadway past St. Rose's, make a left turn, and run down Broadway. If I'd been caught by any of the white gangs, I would have been stomped into nothingness. A couple of times I almost got caught, but no one could run as fast as I could.[44]

These attempts by whites to maintain a white Washington Heights were reinforced by the restructuring of political jurisdictions. In the early 1940s the Thirteenth Assembly District, which straddled Harlem and Washington Heights, was divided in two. The western, and white, half of the area from 122nd Street to 161st Street was given by Tammany to Angelo Simonetti, an Italian with an Irish wife, who led the largest political club in the area; the eastern, black section was put in the charge of Raymond Jones, who subsequently became the most influential political figure in Harlem.

PART TWO

The Crisis of the City

CHAPTER 5

The Remaking of Northern
Manhattan

From the period of the First World War to that of the Second, Washington Heights–Inwood became a one-class multiethnic community. The social patterns established in this period and the local game of politics that was played by rules of the system of city trenches appeared durable. Through the depression, when Washington Heights–Inwood continued to grow in housing stock and population, and into the postwar years of economic recovery and prosperity, these arrangements seemed secure. It would have been foolhardy to predict their demise at the time. But perish they did.

In the subsequent quarter century northern Manhattan was remade. The community stopped growing. No new housing of any significance was constructed. The population declined in number. Though the area remained working class, it underwent radical change toward a plural society, divided along racial as well as ethnic lines. The traditional Irish and Jewish inhabitants grew older; their children tended to make their lives elsewhere. Blacks, most of whom came from an expanding Harlem (the site of a massive influx of migrants during the war), and Hispanics, who arrived from Cuba and the Dominican Republic, took their place.

Even a casual visitor after 1960 could not have failed to notice the social character of the community's geography. Inwood and West Washington Heights, covered extensively by parkland, had decently maintained housing at controlled rents and excellent public transportation; they were still the most desirable working-class neighborhoods in Manhattan. South of 181st Street and east of Broadway, however, many buildings clearly had suffered serious neglect, and the shops were smaller, the streets dirtier,

the general ambience more that of a developing slum than a comfortable residential neighborhood. The visitor would have noticed quickly that these physical divisions coincided with ethnic and racial patterns of settlement, and he might have been struck by the very high proportion of children in the southern part of the community and the large numbers of elderly to the north.

To be sure, there were important similarities between the northern Manhattan of the 1920s and 1930s and that of the 1960s.[1] At the end of the period of urban crisis, Washington Heights–Inwood remained a working-class community. In the early 1970s under 10 percent of the population were petits bourgeois, professionals, or managers. At the other end of the spectrum, approximately 15 percent could be classed as underclass, having only marginal incomes and jobs, while roughly three inhabitants in four unambiguously occupied manual or nonmanual working-class positions.[2] Furthermore, the community was still overwhelmingly residential and consumer oriented in character. Only about two adult residents in ten worked in northern Manhattan or in nearby Harlem.[3] Eight in ten worked in Manhattan south of 125th Street or outside of the borough. By contrast, the vast majority shopped for groceries and clothes, attended religious services, went to a doctor, and used the parks in the area.[4]

Nevertheless, the changes overwhelmed the continuities. Race, reinforced by geographic segregation, by differences in age and life-style, and by inequalities of income and housing, made traditional conflicts and old divisions obsolete. Irish and Jewish adversaries found common ground. Likewise, the black and Hispanic newcomers, in spite of very great cultural differences, discovered a convenient unity. Washington Heights–Inwood, like so much of urban America, clustered into two blocs, which may broadly be called "old" and "new," and which were separated by a very great social distance. What had happened?

I

No urban community exists in isolation, even if from within residents find it difficult to discern how changes in the larger society alter the context which their community is embedded. In assessing the ways northern Manhattan changed after 1940, we would be derelict if we did not make these connections. Both the place of northern Manhattan in the larger social order and

the content of its daily life and political conflicts were shaped in the first instance by the loss of traditional economic functions that affected all the large older Eastern and Midwestern cities of this period.

Local governments of the postwar years, which Kenneth Fox has appropriately called "Keynesian-pluralist," took economic expansion and urban development for granted. An essentially optimistic reading of the theories of John Maynard Keynes underpinned their activities. During the Great Depression, President Roosevelt's National Resources Committee articulated a vision of the city as dependent on national policies to guarantee economic growth and security. After the war, attempts to use Keynesian tools to domesticate the business cycle, to provide for acceptable trade-offs between inflation and unemployment, and to manage a steady rate of economic growth made it possible for those who governed and studied cities to take these matters for granted and to restrict their attention to the politics of conflict management and incremental change. City government was optimistically viewed as open, democratic, and responsive, its pluralist character reflecting and guaranteeing these desirable traits. Those left out of the bounty could organize to get what they wanted. The vitality of the local economy that was buttressed by urban renewal to promote local business growth could only benefit the public as a whole and secure the desirable characteristics of the political system.[5]

The turmoil of the 1960s shook these arrangements and assumptions. Most directly, it undermined the social peace necessary for the routine operation of the Keynesian-pluralist city. The challenge to local social control had multiple dimensions, including threats to electoral stability, to existing intergroup coalitions, to the internal organization of local bureaucracies, and to the diffuse authority of government. Perhaps even more powerfully, the turmoil and defiance revealed not only the fragility of the social order and the vulnerability of local property, but also the poverty of the Keynesian assumption of a shared public interest in managed capitalist growth.

Obstacles to insurgency are formidable, Frances Piven observes, so that "extraordinary disturbances in the wider society" are necessary to bring a crisis of social control into being.[6] Such basic changes were in fact occurring in postwar urban America, even if for a time they were not understood. Most fundamentally, they

were the result of the *routine* dynamics of capitalist development that affected local economies and labor markets, the quality of daily life in residence communities, and the organization and policies of government. The crisis of social control was thus caused in the first instance by a crisis of economic function for older cities.

It is important to recognize that the old American cities, not those that reached maturity after the 1920s, were the locales of the urban crisis. Building on the work of Alfred Watkins, the economist David Gordon has contrasted the current economies of eighteen old cities and thirteen new cities, with respect to employment, the incidence of social problems (unemployment, poverty, welfare), and growth rates in municipal budgets. Between 1960 and 1970, he finds, "the civilian labor forces of 15 metropolitan areas grew; 12 of those 15 were New Cities. The civilian labor forces of 15 cities declined; 14 of those were Old Cities." Using an index of social hardship, Richard Nathan has measured the disparity between central-city and suburban problems. "By this standard," Gordon writes, "once again, the Old Cities are suffering the worst. When metropolitan areas are ranked by this measure of central city disadvantage, 13 of the 16 most disadvantaged central cities are Old Cities. Ten of the 13 least disadvantaged central cities are New Cities. The average index of central city disadvantages is 58 per cent higher in the Old Cities than in the New Cities." Gordon's third basis of comparison is that of local government expenditures. In 1972, "10 of the 11 central cities with the highest municipal expenditures per capita are Old Cities. The average in the Old Cities is 42 per cent higher than in the New Cities."[7] Raymond Vernon noted in 1959 that by "almost any objective standard, the major central cities of our nation over the past fifty years or more, have been developing more slowly than the suburban areas that surround them. By many such standards, this *relative* decline has lately begun to appear as an *absolute* decline."[8] He reached this conclusion by examining as a proportion of their metropolitan areas the population, retail-trade employment, wholesale employment, and manufacturing employment in thirteen older cities, all of which had suffered sharp declines between 1900 and 1950. The only countervailing trend, in some of these cities, was the growth of headquarters employment. What do these indicators suggest?

It must be said emphatically at the outset that a crisis of

economic function does not mean an absence of economic functions. Friedland has stressed the crucial functions older cities
continue to play for American capitalism. They remain important
locations for real-estate investment and provide opportunities for
financial institutions to invest in mortgages and municipal debt.
Moreover, the older central city retains its significance for maintaining communication and reproducing social cohesion within
the capitalist class. . . .

To the corporations and the capitalist class whose power is mediated
through them, the city is more than just a profitable location where
inter-organizational relations can best be maintained. The central city
is a strategic political location for the reproduction of a capitalist political
community, for the influence of metropolitan policy-making, and for
access to national political elites.[9]

Virtually all of the headquarters of the hundred largest industrial corporations stayed in America's largest cities. Their central
business districts continued to grow (often with the help of urban-
renewal funds), because corporate offices need to be located in
a place that maximizes access to branch managers, sales executives,
and buyers; because they need a large number of clerical workers
(most of whom are women) to staff their headquarters; and
because they need to be near the "business services which the
corporation cannot internally provide," including printing, ad-
vertising, data processing, and banking.[10] Most new private-sector
urban jobs were created in the 1950s and 1960s by the expansion
of corporate headquarters.[11] Apart from the growth of their
headquarters, firms in the dominant corporate sector expanded
either in the new-technology cities of the South, Southwest, and
West or in the suburbs of the older Eastern and Midwestern
metropolitan areas. As a result, overall, the growth of the old
cities, once at the cutting edge of American industrial development, stopped. Whereas at the turn of the century, cities were
growing very rapidly, the major cities of the 1960s lost population.
Thus from the vantage point of the national corporate economy, these
cities presented an economic paradox: they were important headquarters
cities, but otherwise their traditional economic functions were no longer
needed or performed.[12]

Uneven spatial-economic development, of course, is not new.
It has been an integral feature of modern capitalist development.
From the earliest significant appearance of capitalist industriali-
zation in the United States, there has been a pronounced trend

toward both the deconcentration of production and population and the implosion of managerial and headquarters functions in many areas. As Kenneth Jackson has demonstrated in a corrective essay to the work of Amos Hawley and Leo Schnore, if we define urban deconcentration as a process of population movement "that results in an increase in the proportion of people in a given area who live outside the core city," then we can say that the process was under way in New York, Philadelphia, and Boston by 1820. These population movements have from the beginning coincided with the movement of new kinds of production units to the periphery of existing urban centers, and with the growing concentration of nonresidential-land use in downtown city cores.[13]

The centrifugal growth of metropolitan areas has accelerated since the Second World War, revealing a dual economy divided between behemoth firms of large-capital concentrations employing roughly a third of the work force, and about twelve million small-capital firms employing still another third of American workers; the state at all levels, or state-dependent industries like defense, employs the rest. Aided by the state, the primary sector of large capital (oligopolistic, capital intensive, and highly unionized) has grown relatively richer and the small-capital sector (labor intensive, poorly unionized, usually starved for capital, and limited to local or regional markets) poorer, as those who control the investment of capital have reinvested in products, machinery, workers, and geographic areas that yield the highest returns.[14] As production has been deconcentrated, dispersing it to horizontal factories on large tracts of land outside of central cities, the management of large-scale enterprises has left the factories to concentrate in the vertical skyscrapers of downtown. This division between the conception and execution of work has been a fundamental feature of twentieth-century capitalism. Management in the large-capital sector of the economy "now carries on the production process from its desktops, conducting on paper a parallel process that follows and anticipates everything that happens in production itself."[15] The great army of white-collar workers essential to this process provided one major source of employment in the older cities. Yet even the growth of these jobs could not prevent the declining sector of small capital from carrying the major part of the production and labor-market functions of the economy.

Federal and local policymakers contributed to an acceleration

of these trends. The most important national policies affecting metropolitan development since the New Deal (important in terms of both the size of expenditures and the impact on urban dynamics) have been those of land-use finance—FHA and veterans mortgage programs and urban renewal—and the interstate highway system. With these policies, government did not act as a counterweight to capital, but as its partner. This is logical, given that states everywhere try to make their economies grow and that capitalist states can do so only by reproducing capital. And there can be no doubt that these policies greatly increased the pace of urban deconcentration: "between 1940 and 1950 suburbs grew twice as fast as central cities, . . . between 1950 and 1960 they grew forty times more rapidly, . . . and between 1960 and 1970 virtually all metropolitan growth took place in the suburbs."[16]

But what is rational from one perspective is a disaster from another (is that not a characteristic feature of the remarkably contradictory nature of capitalist development?). Most of the "social problems" of cities in the 1960s were the result of this process of uneven development. As the material base of the cities was undercut, they became the locales of poverty-related problems like crime, drugs, educational difficulties, health pathologies, and housing decay and abandonment. Increasingly, city governments had to cope with crises of finance and social cohesion—not to speak of the quality of life—generated by causes external to the cities where their impact was felt.[17]

All these trends were experienced, like so much else, in exaggerated fashion in New York City. New York began, of course, as a mercantile port city, one of the "hinges" linking commercial and population movements between Europe and a developing hinterland market.[18] By the Civil War, New York was not only the dominant American port, but also a bustling city of small manufacturing enterprises, classically competitive in character. The garment industry, printing, and small-scale machine work, organized in small plants, were prototypical. In such industries there was a premium on craft skills, a high degree of uncertainty, and a broad dependence on a wide array of locally available services. Together, these one-plant firms, with about twenty-five employees each, made New York the largest manufacturing city in the world.[19]

Daniel Bell acutely notes that the character of these firms made them terribly dependent on local commercial banks and factoring

corporations to remain solvent. "Inevitably, the finance agencies achieved a commanding position in the city." After the Second World War these sources of capital shifted their investment strategies. They financed the economic concentration of formerly competitive industries and the introduction of mass-production methods. Many of these investments went to industries that were not locating in the city. Their local investments, by contrast, were increasingly focused on the downtown construction of office towers. New York, Bell wrote in 1960, had entered a new phase, "that of domination by the large corporate headquarters."[20] But the inherited infrastructure of port and competitive industry did not simply disappear. Metaphors of degenerative disease are more appropriate.

The contrast between the growth made possible by investments in large-capital headquarters and the decay of the port and competitive sectors was most stark in the 1960s. Total employment in the city rose by 6 percent in the decade, a net gain of 212,000 jobs. But the composition of employment in the city changed dramatically. The gain of 450,000 new jobs mainly in headquarters employment in the private sector and in government masked the loss of about half that number in manufacturing. Private-sector manufacturing jobs declined from 30 percent of the total in 1960 to 24 percent by 1970; and a declining proportion of workers in manufacturing industries were employed in production activities. Even more dramatic was the shift in private and public employment. While private employment increased by only 2 percent overall, municipal employment increased by 38 percent.[21]

These changes in the economy of the city affected in an especially powerful way black and Hispanic New Yorkers, who by 1970 constituted approximately one-third of the population—and one-half of the economically active population. Virtually two in three were in non-white-collar jobs, and only about one in ten of all managers, professionals, and technical workers was black or Hispanic. The relative decline in precisely those occupational categories in which nonwhite workers labored made the partially countervailing growth of municipal employment especially important; "of the 62,000 jobs added to city government between 1963–71 blacks and Puerto Ricans filled 36,000."[22]

These economic developments were felt acutely in northern Manhattan. As the urban economy that had sustained prewar Washington Heights–Inwood and its working-class population

disappeared, the community began to shrink. The area reached its peak population in 1940. Two decades later the population of South Washington Heights had declined by 27 percent. East Washington Heights suffered a population loss of 31 percent. West Washington Heights lost 3 percent of its population; for Inwood the decline was 13 percent. With the exception of East Washington Heights, the place of settlement for many Cuban and Dominican refugees in the 1960s, this trend continued. The population loss in South Washington Heights was negligible, but dramatic in West Washington Heights and Inwood, whose populations declined by 12 and 15 percent respectively in just one decade, between 1960 and 1970.

Housing construction came to a virtual halt, as investment in residential building was directed more and more to the suburbs. Less than 4 percent of the housing stock in the four census tracts that we have been following was constructed between 1940 and 1960. To be sure, the rate of construction of the 1920s and 1930s could not be sustained, since most of the vacant land was now built-up. But by 1960 a significant proportion of the area's housing was dilapidated or deteriorating. Under 75 percent of the units in South and East Washington Heights were considered sound. Yet no replacement housing was being built, and very little was being done to rehabilitate decaying units.[23]

In 1940 just over one in five of the residents of the four census tracts was either too young or too old to be counted in the active work force. By 1960 this proportion had increased to almost one in three; a decade later it was up to two in five. A declining proportion was self-employed, down in West Washington Heights, for example, from 21 percent of the work force to 6 percent between 1950 and 1970—a decline that was caused mainly by the erosion of the local-retail sector. Of the wage workers, always a majority in northern Manhattan, a growing proportion came to work not in the private sector but for government; one in ten did so in 1950, but one in six by 1970. Just before the Second World War, the working-class residents of Washington Heights–Inwood were moderately well-off, and far removed from poverty. In 1970 a substantial proportion of the area's families were below or just above the poverty level; individuals living outside of families were even worse off. In 1950 the median figure for school years completed was higher in northern Manhattan than for the borough of Manhattan as a whole; in 1970 it was lower in all but

West Washington Heights. By the end of the period, not surprisingly, long-time residents of northern Manhattan rarely spoke
of their community in assertive, confident terms. More often they
resorted to metaphors of decay, associated most frequently with
racial change.

The large-scale economic changes in industrial structures and
job possibilities, in short, were experienced by residents of northern Manhattan not only at work, but away from work as well. In
such residence communities the urban crisis developed, and was
resolved. Washington Heights–Inwood provides a promising locale for illuminating this period of uncertainty. Before the Second
World War, this community replicated the political struggles
played out on the larger plane. It did so again in the 1960s, when
it reproduced on a small scale the conflicts operating at the level
of the city as a whole. Northern Manhattan's population, however,
was large enough (equal to that of many substantial cities) to
reflect the diversity of the American working class and to be a
setting for most of the period's forms of urban discontent.
Moreover, the area was a self-contained political unit. Local
political boundaries coincided with the most common social
definition of the area as all of Manhattan north of 155th Street.
The re-creation at a narrowly local level of the series of economic,
social, and political forces usually found only on a larger scale
makes possible a closer examination of the urban crisis than can
be obtained through a wider focus.

II

"The settlement pattern of a community," James Young wrote
of early Washington, D.C., "is, in a sense, the signature that its social organization inscribes upon a landscape."[24] The changes
that postwar economic developments and demographic trends
imposed on Washington Heights–Inwood transformed the community's space. Above all, it will be recalled, the various neighborhoods had shown, before the Second World War, many more
similarities than differences. No longer; each of the four main
neighborhoods of Inwood and South, East, and West Washington
Heights became more distinctive. The differences between "old"
and "new" northern Manhattan were signed in space.

South Washington Heights comprises the area from 155th to
165th streets. Its population in 1970, according to the census

estimate, was 35,084; approximately half, 17,066, were black.[25] Though geographically compact and relatively small in population, the area was racially and economically mixed. If we divide the region into quadrants, we find that the southeast was overwhelmingly black, its population a microcosm of the internal class differentiation of urban black America in general. The South Washington Heights census tract that we have been following contained enclaves of "middle class respectability"[26] within a rather overcrowded, decaying quasi slum. While a clear majority of black families and over 94 percent of unattached individuals had incomes of under $7,000 per year, 22 percent of the tract's families reported incomes of over $12,000. Much of the southwest quadrant had the same character, and a clear black majority, but the blocks along the Hudson River were populated by a racially heterogenous middle-income population, approximately half of which was white. In the northwest quadrant the population was predominantly white (elderly Jews and Irish), though about one-third of the population was black, whereas only a decade earlier the area had been virtually all-white. The northeast quadrant was much more like the southeast, but there was also a large minority (about 40 percent) of Hispanic residents. The Irish population of the 1940s was completely gone.

By the 1960s South Washington Heights had become an area commonly thought of as principally black. A Puerto Rican cook, who had moved to South Washington Heights in 1952 and who still worked there in a black bar even though he had moved to the suburbs in 1968, described the neighborhood he once knew as a teenager this way:

This was the beautiful thing about this neighborhood. There were a lot of Irish—there were gangs in the streets and there were a lot of Irish guys that would hang out together and be in gangs together. But it wasn't like an ethnic thing. People would meet and say, hey, man, nothing derogatory, everybody could laugh, everybody could joke around. You could talk about the Irish, and the Irish would talk about the Puerto Ricans, and Italians and blacks, and it was beautiful. It was outta-sight growing up over here. People for the most part were not narrow-minded.

And at that time, like comparing it to today, the neighborhood was very much integrated—a lot of Jewish people around, there were your large blocks of Puerto Ricans—like 160th Street would be considered a Puerto Rican block; 159th was a black block; 161st was mixed, Irish mostly and Puerto Rican. We had all the blocks that way, but from my

position there were ethnic lines. Riverside Drive was untouchable and very much white and upper-middle class. Now this bar tells the story. This is northern Harlem.[27]

Of the four neighborhoods South Washington Heights had the fewest long-time residents (over sixteen years), but was not characterized by a large number of new migrants. Long the locus of black settlement in Washington Heights, the area was marked above all, in the postwar years, by the expansion of black residence to all parts of the neighborhood. Indeed, in the 1960s only the existence of the Columbia Presbyterian Medical Center in the northwest quadrant and the pressures of overcrowding in predominantly Hispanic East Washington Heights to the north prevented South Washington Heights from becoming an exclusively black neighborhood.

East Washington Heights had changed even more rapidly than South Washington Heights. To be sure, it did retain small old-timer Jewish and Irish populations. Approximately 17 percent of East Washington Heights's population of 78,611 were Jewish in 1970; Irish residents made up about 12 percent of the population. The great majority of the rest had arrived in the 1960s from postrevolutionary Cuba and the Dominican Republic.[28]

It is exceptionally difficult to count these groups accurately.[29] The 1970 census, which by its own admission undercounted the Hispanic population, found that 43 percent of East Washington Heights's population was Spanish speaking. Approximately three in ten Spanish speakers in East Washington Heights were Cuban. The census divided the rest equally between Puerto Ricans and Dominicans, but this estimate must be approached with a high degree of skepticism. Many Dominicans who are in the United States are illegal aliens and, as a result, have a high incentive to remain unidentified. Because the city has contained a significant Puerto Rican population for some decades, it is relatively easy for native Spanish speakers to pose as Puerto Ricans to gain access to the United States and to remain undetected later. These considerations, as well as my own observations and conversations with numerous local residents, indicate that the Dominican population was at least three times as great as the Puerto Rican. According to this somewhat arbitrary calculation, Hispanic population of East Washington Heights was composed of about 26,500 Dominicans, 14,500 Cubans, and 8,500 Puerto Ricans.[30]

Compared with any of the other neighborhoods, Inwood and

West Washington Heights changed rather little in the postwar years. Parts of Inwood, especially to the west of Broadway, maintained the aspect of an urban backwater. "Some sections," a reporter observed, "look as if they had been lifted intact out of somewhere in Brooklyn from Bay Ridge or Flatbush say in the 1930s. There is a feeling of time stopped."[31] Venturesome children could still find arrowheads in Inwood Hill Park, their parents could still shop on the same streets and in the same stores that their grandparents had frequented, and drink in the same bars. The activities in Inwood's parks—sandbox play supervised by young mothers, softball, casual teasing by adolescents, light necking—not only were the traditional ones, but were conducted in an atmosphere of ease. The area's streets were well kept, alive with use. Inwood in the 1960s had a relatively prosperous, purposeful feel.

West Washington Heights, northern Manhattan's smallest neighborhood, with a population of 19,394, also maintained its traditional character. Some of its streets, like Cabrini Boulevard, were quite stunning as urban environments. Children could be seen after 3 P.M. walking home by themselves from elementary school. And they often took their time, stopping at a candy store or delicatessen that had changed little in four or five decades. At first blush, West Washington Heights, like Inwood, seemed to be home to a form of daily life that had been common to relatively prosperous urban ethnic neighborhoods before the Second World War.

Indeed, the most salient difference between Inwood and West Washington Heights also reproduced the prewar pattern. Although the numbers of Jews and Irish in Inwood represented roughly the same proportion of the population (27 percent and 24 percent of 61,391 residents, respectively), the neighborhood was defined above all by its visible Irish institutions and parish structure. This Irish dominance continued the tradition we noted in Chapter 4. Quite early on, the Irish captured the area's main political and social institutions. Writing about the 1920s and 1930s, Judy Goldstein has noted that Irish control of the local Democratic party organization "provided only Catholics with an opportunity to hold office. The social structure—clubs, police, civic associations—was predominantly Irish. Any kind of permit or license required party intervention; this fact, compounded by anti-Semitism, effectively ostracized Jews from social, communal

and civic activities as well as political jobs. Jews as a minority group
were not seen as a threat since the Irish held the reins of power
so tightly."[32] Indeed, like the Jews of a generation or two earlier,
the Jewish residents of Inwood oriented their communal-insti-
tutional life mainly toward West Washington Heights, where the
Irish population was negligible in the 1960s, where Jews made up
about 60 percent of the population, and where the major synagogue and secular Jewish organizations were located. Thus, as
in the 1930s, "old" Washington Heights–Inwood remained divided between areas of Jewish and Irish dominance.

Yet in spite of these resemblances to the past, "old" northern
Manhattan had altered in important ways. Its age structure had
changed. Once predominantly the home of families with young
children, the population of West Washington Heights and Inwood
was now disproportionately elderly. About one New Yorker in
ten was over sixty-five in 1970. By contrast, in West Washington
Heights the elderly constituted 29 percent of the population; in
Inwood the proportion was only slightly lower at 24 percent. In
West Washington Heights 61 percent of the population was at
least forty-five years old; in Inwood 53 percent.[33] Almost 60
percent of the Jewish and 50 percent of the Irish residents of
northern Manhattan had in the early 1970s lived in the community
for at least sixteen years.[34]

The overall changes in life cycle, schooling, income, employment, and class structure of postwar northern Manhattan were
not distributed evenly over the four neighborhoods. Virtually
identical proportions of the population in each were found in the
working-adult age bracket of sixteen to sixty-five. But the distribution of the population at both ends of the age scale was quite
different in South and East Washington Heights from what it was
in West Washington Heights and Inwood. The young outnumbered the old by a ratio of approximately two to one in the two
tracts in the former neighborhoods; but in the latter two the
relationship was almost exactly reversed. Similar bifurcations
characterized education and income. Only 43 percent of the adult
population over twenty-five in South Washington Heights had
either graduated from high school or studied at postsecondary
institutions; and even fewer, 30 percent, had achieved this level
of schooling in East Washington Heights. The comparable figures
for West Washington Heights and Inwood were 63 percent and
53 percent. These differences in educational background were

consistent with strikingly different patterns of income distribution. Six families in ten in the "new" areas earned under $15,000 a year in 1970, compared with three in ten in the "old" Irish and Jewish neighborhoods. Large majorities of unattached individuals in the "new" black and Hispanic tracts earned less than $4,000; but over half in the "old" areas earned more.[35]

These differences in earnings reflected the jobs different groups held. We have already seen that the vast majority of the population was either employed in occupations or belonged to households that could be identified as the manual working class (46 percent); the nonmanual working class (28 percent), or the underclass (16 percent).[36] Residents of northern Manhattan were not allocated randomly to these positions. More than a third of the blacks and more than two out of ten Dominicans and Cubans were underclass. Manual workers outnumbered nonmanual workers among blacks by a ratio of four to one, by a ratio just under that for Cubans, and by a ratio of better than five to one for Dominicans. By contrast, the underclass Jewish and Irish populations were negligible. As many Irish were nonmanual workers as manual, and among Jews there were nearly twice as many nonmanual workers as there were manual workers. The community's small managerial and professional population was predominantly Jewish; virtually no Hispanics or blacks fell into these class categories.[37]

III

The social distance between groups does not depend simply on spatial segregation. A residence community consists of a multiplicity of networks, as described by John Barnes: "Each person is, as it were, in touch with a number of people, some of whom are directly in touch with each other and some of whom are not. . . . The image I have is of a set of points some of which are joined by lines. The points of the image are people, or sometimes groups, and the lines indicate which people interact with each other."[38] Social fields of this kind provide the "local area" of people's lives.

Such ties need not always have clear spatial boundaries.[39] The networks of the small Greek population of northern Manhattan, for example, both before and after the Second World War, were independent of the area's geography. There was virtually no street in Washington Heights north of 181st Street and Inwood

without some Greek residents. Since they composed no more than 3 percent of the area's population as a whole, the dispersion of Greeks meant that they were not a majority in any single neighborhood. The two Greek Orthodox churches—St. Spyridon, founded in 1931 with 2,000 members, and St. Anagyris, first organized in 1947 and refounded in the late 1960s with just over 225 members—provided the foci for the group's social relations. Through its schools, perpetuation of the Greek language, and the provision of a whole set of activities such as singing, dancing, and talks and slide presentations on Greece, the church provided a relatively complete social world. One consequence was that there was little place for any kind of social life outside the set of activities that it sponsored. The priest, by extension, not only represented religious authority, but was considered the leading man of the communal group. All decisions taken by the parish council and the school board had to be approved by him. The two parish councils were the leading ethnic institutions. The St. Spyridon council, composed of eighteen members elected every year by the parish as a whole, directed the entire panoply of parish activities and competed with no other institution. These activities included the various "societies" made up of people from the same part of Greece; the Philoptochos Society (friends of the poor), a women's charitable organization, the parochial school and its PTA, the Boy Scouts and Girl Scouts, the DOXA soccer club, and the American Hellenic Progressive Association, which assisted immigrants to understand and cope with American society.

This set of institutional and social relations was both smaller and broader than the boundaries of northern Manhattan or any one of its neighborhoods. Greek involvement in non-Greek networks, including political ones, was minimal. "Greekness" defined the working as well as nonworking lives of the members of the collectivity; work relations in Greek restaurants, florists, fur businesses, groceries, and bakeries tended to be between Greeks. But these ties were not limited to Washington Heights–Inwood. Of the ethnic group's ten community leaders that we interviewed (including the priest and the school principal of St. Spyridon, the presidents of the parish councils, the PTA, and DOXA), six lived not in northern Manhattan but in Riverdale, Westchester, or the New Jersey shore.

This divorce of social networks from social space was atypical. For most Washington Heights–Inwood residents, the block and

neighborhood provided the most tangible experiences and ties of daily life. Indeed, for some people, the block and its surrounding turf was so important that it shaped their entire identity. Such was the case for some adolescents who lacked any other context for daily life. Individual and intensely local identities were virtually indistinguishable for the area's numerous teenage graffiti writers. Graffiti was a means of saying "here I am" in a world that seemed not to notice. The names painted on community walls and on the city's subways were joined almost invariably to a street number: not just "Taki," but "Taki-183."[40] In complementary fashion, some elderly, no longer at work and isolated from friends and families who lived in other places, took their cues from the street. There many sat all day long, melding into the landscape.

But this pattern too was not typical. For the great majority of residents, community space was just one element, though often the unifying one and the symbol of others. The networks of northern Manhattan's five main groups (Jews, Irish, blacks, Dominicans, and Cubans) were defined in part by space, in part by extended-family ties, in part by ethnic institutions not necessarily near home, and in part by ties of kinship and friendship in the immediate neighborhood. Friendship patterns overwhelmingly were ethnic-specific; most community residents had relatives in the area. Family and friendship interactions were regular and frequent.[41] The social separation into groups thus did have a spatial dimension—local ethnic networks were in large part circumscribed by well-understood physical boundaries—but it was not space per se that divided them.

Evans-Pritchard observed in *The Nuer* that time and space are socially constituted—that the value of time and spatial distance are determined not by chronology or location but by the social distance between groups in the social structure.[42] In the postwar years the social constitution not just of space but of time in Washington Heights–Inwood changed dramatically. The unitary tempo of historical and social time had been shattered, replaced by a more divergent configuration that divided "old" from "new" Washington Heights–Inwood.

For the Jews and Irish Washington Heights–Inwood became in the interwar years a post-first-generation place of settlement. Their social situation as relatively well-off workers integrated into the political system in equivalent ways made possible the development of a low-intensity political conflict that was not seen to

derive from the larger class structure. In the relatively "complete" world of the residence community, these groups shared a great deal: they had come to the United States at roughly the same structural moment; they were joined to the industrial capitalist order in essentially equal ways; they earned their livings in much the same ways (which is not to say there was no cultural division of labor dividing Jews and Irish more generally); they had achieved respectability through struggles that were not wholly individual, but which represented a collective achievement of ethnic mobility; they shared a life-style that stressed public decorum, discipline, and a lack of overt displays of passion.[43] The logic of their ties to the world and to each other was rather similar. And they shared in their willingness to play by the rules of the urban system of city trenches that had created a wholly separate realm of discourse and action for the community, as if it were isolated from the larger social order of which it was a part.

The black and Hispanic residents of northern Manhattan were different in each of these dimensions. They were, quite literally, newcomers—to the United States for the Dominicans and Cubans, to northern Manhattan for them and the blacks. Clear majorities of the Irish and Jewish residents had lived in the community for more than twenty years. A majority of the blacks, by contrast, had moved to Washington Heights–Inwood between 1962 and 1972; and more than half of the community's Cubans and three-fourths of its Dominicans had been in the area fewer than five years.[44] Both Hispanic groups consisted in the main of political immigrants after the Castro victory in 1959 and the landing of U.S. marines in 1965, respectively. The Dominicans especially maintained close ties to their home villages and, because of their marginal juridical as well as economic status, had only a tenuous hold on U.S. society. For the Dominicans and Cubans northern Manhattan was a port of entry; for blacks, as for the Jews and Irish before them, the area was a place to move to after one or two generations in the north. Yet given the timing of their arrival, which coincided with the uneven economic development of the city and region, the environmental and material conditions of blacks in northern Manhattan were much closer to those of the Hispanic newcomers than to those of the white settlers in West Washington Heights and Inwood.[45]

"Old" northern Manhattan had changed by becoming smaller, increasingly isolated, more conscious of its boundaries. East

Washington Heights was a radically different neighborhood from what it had been before the Second World War, and South Washington Heights had expanded and consolidated as an extension of northern Harlem. From the vantage point of "old" northern Manhattan, these neighborhoods had an ambiguous status. Clearly part of the territory traditionally identified as Washington Heights–Inwood, they were included in the area's boundaries for voting and the delivery of services. Yet the transformation in their ethnic and racial composition excluded them from the "old" social and political networks that had once encompassed northern Manhattan as a whole.

The boundaries between "old" and "new" northern Manhattan were thus based on differences condensed not only in space but also in time. "If divorced from the concept of time," Vilar has written, "the concept of space is ill-suited to old countries in which every stage of production, every social system, has had its towns and fields, its palaces and cottages, each historical totality nesting down as best it can in the kind of heritage of another. . . ."[46] Quite obviously it is not possible to speak of northern Manhattan in exactly these grandiose macrohistorical terms. Yet the impelling logic of this observation is appropriate to our subject. For northern Manhattan, once divided between the Irish and Jews who shared very similar histories in the community, was divided in new ways between groups that did not share essentially similar pasts.

Edelman appropriately draws our attention to the fact that "space itself does not convey meaning as if it were a simple code." Neighborhoods, he notes, objectify meanings, remind inhabitants by their condition whether they are worthy or unworthy, and enclose people who, like automobile drivers on a highway, move "at different speeds, and have no mode of communication and little mutual understanding about how to stay out of each other's way in unforeseen circumstances."[47] The neighborhoods of northern Manhattan contained people who not only scarcely interacted across ethnic and racial lines, but who, because they moved at "different speeds," also came to have very different views about the character of the community.

Such groups do not directly, immediately, or necessarily come into *political* conflict.[48] But in the 1960s they did, in assaults on the system of city trenches, and in defense of it. This theme requires a chapter of its own, which follows.

CHAPTER 6

Assaults on the Trenches

What kind of crisis was the urban crisis of the 1960s and early 1970s? Systematic academic work has conceptualized the "crisis" in many ways: as a crisis of confidence, a crisis of service delivery, and a fiscal crisis (among the more conventional ideas). These approaches all capture partial truths, but they miss the larger point that the most unsettling, and promising, feature of the unruly urban scene was the extent to which the traditional American urban class system was challenged. As such, the urban crisis was a crisis of social control and, more powerfully, a crisis of American class and group relations.

I

The remaking of communities like Washington Heights–Inwood, and of older American cities more generally, according to the dictates of uneven economic development in the postwar years did not automatically call into question the traditional urban system. At least in the first instance, the new currents seemed to fit the inherited logic of city life. Clashes between groups that differed from each other in time as well as space, though new to northern Manhattan, had long been a feature of the traditional urban system. The intensification of conflict within the framework of existing cultural understandings, noisy and unpleasant as it may have been, did not constitute a crisis.

Nor should it come as a surprise that the ways in which residents of older cities interpreted their new situation remained constrained by the political and ideological blinders that the traditional urban system imposed, especially because the changes in the urban world continued to be experienced mainly at the level of

discrete residence communities with their set props, cast, and clearly defined limits. To be sure, alternative interpretations were plausible. The changing economic place of the city might well have produced a fundamentally new city politics, centering on such matters as capital investment and disinvestment and dual labor markets. But such an emphasis, which was wholly lacking in the 1960s, would have required a perception of class relations that simply did not exist. As a result, the most important economic causes of the urban crisis could not be addressed directly, and the urban crisis was in this sense a displaced crisis.

Nor did the experience of uneven development alter the basic situation of urban authorities in a qualitative way.[1] To be sure, the myriad "social problems" experienced in New York and the other large older cities were caused most fundamentally by the spatial trajectory of postwar patterns of capitalist development. As the cities became the repositories of the secondary-sector work force (most of whom were poor and black or Hispanic), poverty-related problems like crime, drugs, educational difficulties, and severe health pathologies intensified, and they had to be dealt with by city government. Yet all, quite obviously, were generated by causes *external* to the cities in which their impact was felt.

Welfare is a case in point. In New York City, with a population of roughly 7.8 million people, just about 1.2 million received some form of public assistance in 1974. This was more than double the number on welfare five years earlier. As late as 1965 only 12 percent of the city's budget was allocated to welfare and related programs. By 1970, a staggering 23 percent went for welfare. In September 1968 fully 60 percent of the persons under eighteen in New York were receiving public assistance. There was no single greater drain on the city's financial resources.[2]

Although the causes of the welfare explosion in the late 1960s were not exclusively economic, it is nevertheless true that the root cause of "the welfare crisis" *was* economic and that the relevant economic factors were not susceptible to control by the city. After studying welfare in New York, David Gordon concluded that "the cause of the welfare crisis is simply the widespread poverty in the city—not chiseling or welfare rights organizations or liberal administrative practices."[3] Indeed, in any given year in the past decade, only from 55 to 60 percent of the eligible recipients were on the welfare rolls.

Neither demographic changes nor poverty rates are caused in

the cities, nor can they be manipulated very much at that level. Urban authorities and citizens could hardly control the characteristics of the national economy, including its rate of growth and the nature of the demand for labor or such characteristics of the industry in which an individual is employed as profit rates, technology, unionization, and the industry's relationship to government; nor could they control individual characteristics like age, sex, ethnicity, and class, which affect employability. Migration patterns, too, depend heavily on "push" factors over which the receiving cities have virtually no control. The increasing concentration and mechanization of southern agriculture and the state of Puerto Rican and other Caribbean economies obviously have had much more to do with the movement of poor people to New York than any causes that could be controlled in the city have had.

This dependent situation of American cities in the postwar years also did not constitute a new situation. On the contrary. At least from the moment of early industrialization, American cities have been the repositories of social problems over which they have lacked control. From the critical antebellum period to the present, urban politics has been a politics of dependency. Cities, more starkly than other arenas of American politics, have been the terrain of social control that has had less to do with substantive problem solving than with channeling and controlling discontent and potential rebellion. Banfield and Wilson's widely accepted distinction between the two principal functions of municipal government—a service function of delivering goods and services and a political function of "managing conflict in matters of political importance"[4]—breaks down, because, historically, both have been inextricably bound in the system of city trenches.

While local business interests have governed many small- and medium-size cities quite openly, this has rarely been the case in the larger cities. Rather, their dependency has for more than a century placed urban authorities in these cities in a situation closely resembling the role that indigenous rulers have performed in classic colonial situations of indirect rule. The "arbiter governments"[5] that they have led had in the near and distant past to manage the consequences of their inability to solve urban problems.

The character of city politics as a politics of social control, in sum, has obtained for a long time. In what sense is it meaningful

to assert, in the face of the many shared elements of urban politics in the 1960s and previous eras, that the turmoil in the Kennedy-Johnson-Nixon years constituted an urban *crisis?*

The new set of groups that emerged on the scene was beyond the reach of the urban political party, the main institution of the system of city trenches. Most black and Hispanic newcomers arrived after the reform movement had weakened the power of the political machine; and even in the late-nineteenth and early-twentieth centuries, when black migrants first came north in large numbers, they were excluded from equal participation in party affairs. The main ties of the new groups to government were direct ones, as clients of service bureaucracies.

The demands of the new groups could not be brokered by local political forces, including city hall, precisely because they were preponderantly in the areas over which urban authorities had no real command. From the point of view of rulers, it was not the unruliness of the demands that constituted a crisis, but the unpredictability that followed from their institutional and substantive inabilities to manage these demands. The result was a major political crisis, a crisis of social control.

Order, predictability, and social control go hand in hand. "The more conduct is institutionalized," Peter Berger and Thomas Luckmann have observed, "the more predictable and thus the more controlled it becomes."[6] The lack of institutional forums for orderly negotiations between the new groups and local governments produced, in the context of the large-scale changes that overtook the older cities after the Second World War, a political crisis of the kind discussed by Pye, Weiner, and Verba in the penultimate SSRC Comparative Politics volume, *Crises and Sequences in Political Development.*[7]

The authors identify five basic kinds of crises that rulers face as a result of "the contradictions and pressures basic to the development syndrome": crises of identity, legitimacy, participation, penetration, and distribution. In spite of the book's linguistic attempts at neutral presentation, it is clear that each is fundamentally a crisis for rulers. Thus, for Pye, "the basic cause of the legitimacy crisis is the fact that the development syndrome always produces a widening of perceptions on the part of ever larger numbers of people and therefore an increase in sensitivities about the possibilities of alternative ways of doing things in all phases of life." A legitimacy crisis occurs when "inappropriately social-

ized" citizens develop "feelings about authority that are not functional for the efforts of the current leaders." Weiner similarly defines a participation crisis as "a conflict that occurs when the governing elite view the demands of behavior of individuals and groups seeking to participate in the political system as illegitimate." Revealingly, Pye concluded with a section called "dynamic leadership and the resolution of legitimacy crises," and Weiner with a section "on the prevention and resolution of participation crises."[8] Verba summarized the book's notion of "crisis":

In almost all cases, what are discussed as crises in the present volume are situations in which the basic institutional patterns of the political system are challenged and routine response is inadequate. We may define *a crisis* as a situation where a "problem" arises in one of the five problem areas (that is, members of the society are discontented with one of the five aspects of the decisional process), and some institutionalized means of handling problems of that sort is required to satisfy the discontent. . . . A crisis is a change that requires some governmental innovation and institutionalization if elites are not to seriously risk a loss of their position.[9]

The dilemmas faced by urban authorities in the 1960s had precisely this character, and, as we shall see, their responses to the crisis took the form of attempts at institutional innovation.

Yet by itself this political crisis would not have directly challenged the century-old pattern of city trenches. Political crises of the kind that required institutional change have been a recurrent feature of the urban system. Rather, it was the multi-*racial* character of urban society that emerged in the postwar years that transformed the struggles of the period into a series of assaults on the trenches.

In numerous ways blacks have been different from white ethnics in America. Since their arrival in the major urban centers of the North and West in large numbers between 1900 and 1930, and again after 1945, blacks have been concentrated principally in employment in the declining sector of small capital. Spatially, they have been confined on the whole to the declining urban cores of a developing dual economy. For blacks working in the secondary labor force, where workplace unionization has been rare, the community-based voluntary association or movement organization has provided the only collective vehicle available for the expression of discontent.

This exclusion from the workplace institutions of the system of city trenches made the historical exclusion of blacks from the local

party system especially significant. As theorists in search of stability in the Third World have understood only too well, the role of political parties "in the institutionalization of the capability to absorb changing political demands and organization is crucial." Similarly, Huntington has stressed the tripartite relationship of political participation, institutionalization, and stability. Where "groups gain entry into politics without becoming identified with the established political procedures," the system's structured patterns of dominance cannot "stand up against the impact of a new social force." The essential issue is the extent to which the system is protected by mechanisms that "restrict and moderate the impact of new groups," either by slowing down their entry into politics or by impelling changes in the attitudes and behavior of the group's most politically active members.[10]

Political machines, the institutional core of the urban class system, performed these functions in older American cities. Shefter appropriately defines the political machine "as a party organization that both distributes patronage to elicit support and is capable of reliably centralizing power within its jurisdiction."[11] The classic American machines, however, which had their heyday in the half century between 1880 and 1930, were more than centralized patronage organizations, since patronage was composed not merely of economic incentives but of coercive and ideological elements. The party's ability to control licensing and the differential delivery of services was the stick that accompanied the organization's carrots. Furthermore, the machine at the mass level defined the realities of politics as being about ethnicity and territoriality rather than about capital and class, and it reproduced and reinforced the segmented-ward principle of political organization.

A crucial feature of machine politics was the segregation of its elite activities from its mass activities. In the community the machine functioned as a *decentralized* institution belonging to the locality. There the mass political party and patron-client ties were fused through a "leader-follower network of clientalistic ties."[12] These same leaders, through the *centralized* apparatus of the citywide organization, were free to make political and economic arrangements, often inimical to their clients' interests, out of the view of their followers. As Scott notes,

Frequently, a three-cornered relationship developed in which the machine politician could be viewed as a broker who, in return for financial assistance from wealthy elites, promoted their policy interests while in

office, while passing along a portion of the gain to a particularistic electorate from whom he "rented" his authority."[13]

The machines, too controlled *both* the "input" and "output" sides of politics; they provided organized, coherent access to government and acted as the key distributors of political rewards. This dual role of the machines, anchored in practices whose origins are to be found in the antebellum period, was especially critical at the turn of the century, because the mass migration of Catholic and Jewish workers from Europe brought into question the traditional hegemony of the Protestant ruling class. Substituting institutional and reward mechanisms of control for traditional deference, it absorbed the political energies of the new entrants into the political system, and as long as it did so successfully, stability and order were relatively assured.[14] By its lack of a class orientation, its emphasis on concrete rewards, and its material support for traditional social ties, the machine form of political organization maintained social order in a setting where the potential for threats to the social order was high.

Even after blacks arrived in the North as citizens with voting rights in the early twentieth century, they were incorporated into the local political system on terms fundamentally different from those that applied to white ethnics. In New York City, for example, blacks were not allowed to join neighborhood political clubs until the middle 1930s; instead, they were linked to the polity by a citywide organization, the United Colored Democracy of Tammany Hall—which sought their votes without yielding control over territorial resources.[15] The exclusion of blacks from the machine on ordinary terms put them outside the central institution of the urban class system and entailed major costs to them. But it also inhibited the development of an understanding that race was divided into the realms of work and residence on the white-ethnic working-class pattern. One consequence is that black social and political interactions tend to be connected more to networks beyond the neighborhood than limited to ties between members of the same residence community. Although black residence communities are organizationally rich, their orientation and focus are more likely to transcend the local community than is the case in white-ethnic areas.[16]

In the 1960s urban blacks were "unmistakably unintegrated"[17] into the traditional urban-class system. Yet they possessed a broad and deep array of institutional resources capable of providing

what Von Eschen, Kirk, and Pinard call "the organizational substructure of disorderly politics." Sociologists who work in the "mass society" tradition have tended to assume that organizational membership "drags people into routine politics, while discouraging participation in direct action movements." This assumption makes sense, however, only if the *content* of the organization's orientations is taken into account. "For an important class of organizations—organizations with goals unincorporated by the larger society or containing members with interests or values that are unincorporated—membership increases rather than inhibits participation."[18]

The position of blacks in the history of capitalist development and in the contemporary economy, and the distinctive character of their residence communities and their ties to the political system, made the urban turmoil of the 1960s a deep-rooted and comprehensive social crisis that challenged the basic assumptions of traditional patterns of class and ethnicity.[19] For blacks, the invocation of any one issue—whether welfare, police, health care, housing, job discrimination, unemployment, or political under-representation—invoked all the others. The combination of being excluded from the system of city trenches and being preponderant in the secondary work force drove blacks to raise issues through different channels (or, in a real sense, nonchannels) from those that white ethnics used. These issues, though raised at the physical level of the community, exploded the community boundaries—they were not just about community control and neighborhood services, but also about wages and jobs and many other aspects of the black condition.

Struggles about the community control of education compose a leading case in point. Education manifestly connects the social structure and political life. Schools link class relations at work and social relations in the residence communities where they are located. For these reasons the global dimensions of the black assault on the traditional American split between work and community relations were most pronounced in the area of education.

To be sure, conflicts about schooling and occupational opportunity are hardly unknown in American urban history. In the United States, capitalist industrialization, urbanization, and the expansion of public education moved ahead together. Boston established free elementary schools in 1818, New York in 1832.

By the time of the Civil War, virtually all large American cities in the North and West had significant educational institutions. In this period, the modern city (with its characteristic separation of work from residence; its segmented class, ethnic, and racial group neighborhoods; and its demarcated downtown joined to the periphery by new transportation technology) was fashioned under the impact of rapid economic growth and European immigration. In this context, where social change was rapid and continuous, education issues intersected the most volatile aspects of the social structure. Many political and economic leaders saw the new schools as insurance against social upheaval. Citizens in the newly industrializing society were to develop the skills appropriate to the new occupational order, to be socialized into a dominant system of values, and to be assimilated into the mainstream of society (or at least to feel allegiant to it). Minority, immigrant, and working people also placed their hopes in education, but for different reasons. They looked to education to alter both individual opportunities and collective group possibilities. Thus, from the nineteenth century onward, school politics for some has meant the preservation of order and the maintenance of the social structure; for others, a lever for altering the social structure or their chances of opportunity within it.

Much traditional educational scholarship has stressed the latter. The expansion of public education has been seen as a result of the extension of citizenship to encompass social as well as procedural possibilities. Schooling in this view is an index of democratization.[20] Revisionist scholarship, by contrast, as in the work of Michael Katz and Joel Spring, has emphasized the need to see education above all in terms of social control.[21] To be sure, workers have often demanded more and better educational institutions, and middle- and upper-class reformers have sought to control educational curricula and administration in order to make schools in their image. But what both dominant historiographical tendencies have missed is the extent to which members of the working class *and* their adversaries have understood, if only imperfectly, the crucial role of education in reproducing the social structure and in shaping individual and group possibilities within it. Schools, it is by now conventional to state, are intimately bound up with the dynamics of capitalist accumulation, with guiding changes in social relations appropriate and necessary for the changing economic order, and with legitimating inequalities.

Mostly tacit, but sometimes explicit, understandings of education in these terms have been basic sources of educational struggles over time. What is crucial, though, is that while the dominant have been more likely to perceive education in terms of capitalist reproduction, most urban Americans have understood school politics in terms of ethnic and territorial conflict. As David Tyack notes in his treatment of nineteenth-century school patterns, "Although there were sometimes overtones of class assertion or resentment in such conflicts, the issues were not normally phrased in class terms, but in the cross-cutting cultural categories of race, religion, ethnicity, neighborhood loyalties, and partisan politics."[22] For them the issue has been, not whether schools reproduce capitalism and its class structure, but whether the schools function to provide the children of a specific ethnic group and residence community with the chance to be mobile within the larger class structure. School struggles within this traditional understanding have been most acute in periods of sharp alteration in the objective dynamics of economic development, and when, as a consequence, there are sharp discontinuities in people's perceptions of opportunity. The 1960s proved to be such a period in both respects.

In traditional fashion, the public schools became a focus, and a barometer, of the period's urban struggles. Available popular and scholarly interpretations, it should be remembered, generally accepted, at least until the late 1960s, the conventional wisdom that linked education and opportunity. Schooling, available by right of citizenship to all, was understood as a potential equalizer by some and as a mechanism for individual gain by others.

In all these ways the school struggles of the 1960s were much like those that had preceded them. Even the term "community control" invoked, in its imprecision, some of the most powerful and warmly persuasive symbols of the traditional system of city trenches. At one level, "community control" connoted the long-familiar intersection of residence space and ethnic capacity; as a slogan and platform it thus reflected a community rather than a workplace orientation. But such a limited reading of black demands for community control of schools would be terribly inaccurate. At a second level, and in the context of the more general nationalist analysis, the character of schooling as an issue potentially connecting work *and* community made a focus on education by black activists a challenge to the political separation of the two. Blacks did not demand community control of the schools only to

change patterns of governance in order to secure this or that distributive good, but as an aspect of the larger struggle to redistribute life chances between blacks and whites. In this limited but tangible fashion pre-1969 school struggles did constitute an assault on the distributive, issue-specific, and residence-community-based ethnic features of the traditional urban class system.

Black-white relations can be compared to the situation of English workers during the first industrial revolution. Much as collective protests in English working-class residence communities invoked their status *as workers*, not just their status as residents of this or that community, so the collective protest activities of urban blacks invoked their status *as blacks*, not just their status as residents of Harlem or Brownsville. Like the terms "capitalist" and "worker," the terms "white" and "black" had a general application.

Black nationalism, as theory and as ideology, recognized the special total character of the black experience. The nationalist program in the North took its force from the particularity of the conditions of black city life, as the analysis and the rhetoric of internal colonialism addressed the links between blacks and the service bureaucracy where they lived. In this way, to be sure, the movements that were organized within the nationalist embrace took as their concerns the very issues that had been at the center of traditional urban political practices for more than a century. But by placing these concerns under the rubric or "internal colonialism," they signaled the break with tradition, for they understood these issues as aspects of a larger situation, not as isolated matters to be taken up on their own terms at the community level. It was this special *racial* dimension of the urban crisis that made the events of the 1960s so unsettling for so many.

In the winter of 1964, *Commentary* magazine featured a round-table discussion of race relations. Norman Podhoretz, its editor, posed the following question to James Baldwin: "Is it conceivable to you that the Negroes will within the next five or ten or twenty years take their rightful place as one of the competing groups in the American pluralistic pattern? Or is something more radical—or perhaps less radical—more likely to happen the way things are going now?"[23] Baldwin's answer was rather uninteresting, but the question itself was significant. Would blacks—indeed, *could* blacks—be incorporated into the traditional system?

The next five years pressed the issue and raised the specter of the more radical solution. The intermittent riots in the ghettos

of the North, Midwest, and West in the middle and late 1960s were the most visible indications that the ethnic-territorial formula was unable to manage racial conflict and to secure its expression within the limits of "the American pluralistic pattern." Yet the rebellions themselves, and the most common decodings of their meaning, contained enough ambiguous elements to make Podhoretz's question as germane in 1969 as it had been in 1964.

The racial disorders, like the black condition more generally, were an amalgam of partly contradictory tendencies. One observer perceptively used the analogy of the wildcat strike. The violence, David Boesel wrote, represented a revolt of the "ghetto rank and file against an established black leadership which . . . has failed to deliver the goods, and a form of direct action intended to communicate grievances and apply pressure on the white 'managers' of the ghetto."[24] Wildcat strikes are militant by definition, and their existence threatens more regular patterns of conflict management. But they do not call essential features of industrial relations into question, at least not directly. Rather, they are demands for "more" and pleas for more inclusive participation in ongoing workplace relations. The wildcat-strike aspect of the ghetto riots was in its own terms ambiguous: on the one hand, it accepted the traditional boundaries of the community-work dichotomy by striking at targets in residence communities and by articulating in an inchoate way a demand for justice in traditional terms. This political thrust closely resembled the form of English and Continental urban unrest that Eric Hobsbawm calls populist legitimism, in which the populace uses proscribed forms of political action to demand just treatment according to the manifest logic of prevailing arrangements. Whether in the Paris of 1588 or the Naples of 1799,

the ruler . . . represents justice. Though it is patent that the local lords, officials, clergymen and other exploiters suck the blood of the poor, this is probably because the monarch does not know what is being done in his name. . . . The populace therefore riots for justice under the banner of King or Tsar.[25]

Indeed, it became a commonplace for interpreters of the rebellions of the 1960s to note how often blacks said they were taking to the streets to command the attention of the regime that was assumed to be on their side but inattentive.

On the other hand, the wildcat-strike dimension of the rebel-

lions attacked the segmented tradition of the system of city
trenches. It did so, not only by rejecting a traditional leadership
and by communicating grievances, but by embracing in action
and language the essentially nationalist, holistic interpretation of
internal colonialism. Blacks might not be able to have a nation in
the United States, but they could seek to seize their own territory
and replace white authority with indigenous control.

Indeed, the rebellions are explicable in this view only as part
of a larger movement for ghetto control, articulated in the
language of Black Power and of colonialism, of the most conse-
quential agencies of social control located in the residence community—the school system, the welfare bureaucracies, and the
police. These activities were joined by the common thread of
community control, understood as decolonization. Echoing the
demands heard in the 1960s in the ghettos, Blauner wrote the
following:

The various 'Black Power' programs that were aimed at gaining control
of individual ghettoes—buying up property and businesses, running the
schools through community boards, taking over anti-poverty programs
and other social agencies, diminishing the arbitrary power of the police—
can serve to revitalize the institutions of the ghetto and build up an
economic, professional, and political power base. These programs seem
limited; we do not know at present if they are enough in themselves to
end colonized status. But they are certainly a necessary first step.[26]

These demands were limited in a different sense: they did not
address the basic questions concerning large capital and the city,
and they did not directly address those of employment. From the
point of view of urban authorities, the movement for community
control was unsettling nevertheless. It challenged decades-old
trends of political institutionalization. Neither the party nor the
bureaucracy could manage or control the black insurgency; indeed
both were targets of the period's militancy. Blacks discovered that
the party positions they could now secure were far less rewarding
than the same positions had been for their white-ethnic predecessors. And the service bureaucracies, of course, were directly
assaulted by demands for community control.

But these aspects of the black insurgency were less threatening
than some of its other features. The holistic world view of black
nationalism produced demands that in two respects were radically
different from the usual articulation of urban issues. First, it did
not respect traditional boundaries between issues. School, welfare,

police, and housing issues were treated together, as aspects of a total condition.[27] As a result, authorities had to manage conflict that was much more intense and less susceptible to piecemeal solutions than they had been accustomed to. Second, these policy areas were the objects of demands for a radical redistribution of resources and opportunities. At issue was not simply a set of divisible benefits of patronage and services; rather, such questions, which had been at the core of modern urban politics since the antebellum period, were joined to questions of governance, and together they were connected to a larger analysis of black-white relations that demanded a fundamental transformation of the social structure. These demands could not be resolved at the urban level within the assumptions of the prevailing political economy.

I I

At precisely the moment when blacks mounted this assault on the trenches, its institutional elements were in a vulnerable condition. Over a period of some four decades, the locus of urban political power had shifted from the party organizations to largely autonomous, but not apolitical, service bureaucracies. This shift weakened the social position of authorities, for unlike the machines, bureaucratic control mechanisms deal only with the output side of politics. They took over the machines' functions of distributing services and benefits, without assuming the organization of participation in politics. As a result, bureaucratic, as opposed to party, control left authorities potentially more vulnerable to challenges from below.

This shift in the urban political scene had its roots in the challenge to the prerogatives of party organization that had been mounted from within the Republican party at the national level in the 1870s. From its founding through Reconstruction, it had built powerful state and local organizations by utilizing patronage resources. By the mid-1870s it had been transformed "from a political movement into a political party that advantaged the professional politicians within it." Many of the groups that had been drawn to the party for moral and policy reasons were distressed both by the diminished importance of issues and by their own loss of influence. Many of the party's professionals fought to develop channels of policy influence outside of the

traditional party structure, in such nonpartisan groups as the National Civil Service Reform League, and, as the title of this organization implies, they took up the cause of civil-service reform based on merit, not on partisanship.[28]

The middle-class professionals who led the Mugwump movement were part of a new class that was growing in size and capacity. Their political aspirations were reinforced by the logical imperatives of their position in the social structure. Professionals are people who produce and deliver special services. They typically seek "to constitute and control a market for their expertise"; and they act collectively to assert a "special social status" in the interest of achieving upward social mobility.[29] The contextual conditions of attempts by professionals to translate their special knowledge and skills into social and economic rewards changed in important ways in the late-nineteenth century. The model of the profession had initially emerged during the antebellum period, when it had been shaped by the matrix of competitive capitalism. After the Civil War, but especially toward the turn of the century, the development of large-scale corporate capitalism altered the dominant professional pattern from that of lone practitioners competing in a market to that of salaried specialists in large organizations.[30]

This shift had various consequences. Organized professions were unified under the leadership of groups of reformers. A common language between people sharing the same profession was forged; common standards of training and licensing were developed. The internally generated professional consensus, which fashioned a "community of fate" for all its members, had to be ratified and sanctioned by the state in two ways: first, the professions of law, medicine, social work, and education, among others, had to be granted their autonomy and the capacity to regulate themselves. Second, government itself expanded its service bureaucracies, especially at the local level. Welfare agencies and public-school bureaucracies grew in size; they were joined by city-planning bureaus, public-library and museum establishments, and public-health clinics. Claims by the new organized professions to control the market for their skills and for special social and economic status rested on an ideology of classlessness, efficiency, and expertise.

After the election of 1896 the new professionals were joined by politicians and businessmen who found use for the ideology of

merit and efficiency; and, in turn, the professionals were prepared to support the broader political goals of their allies in the Progressive movement. The unbalanced, regionally based system of single-party dominance ushered in by the realignments of 1896, Shefter notes, created groups of permanent losers. Minority parties could not credibly expect to become governing parties. As a consequence, he argues, "the political actors who found it impossible to advance their interests *within* the party system were joined together by the Progressives in an attack *upon* the party system."[31] Such politicians were aided by many businessmen. The standard equation of reform and business versus machines and workers is much too simple. Not all businessmen broke with local machines; indeed, they often thrived personally and tangibly from machine largesse, and they benefitted, as a class, from the existence of the machine, since the pattern of class formation embodied in machine relations helped reproduce the social order. Yet there is no doubt that many businessmen at the local and national levels were the key supporters of the Progressive movement. Research on the question of why they rejected the machine form is terribly inadequate; only a speculative answer is now possible. In a period of rising labor unrest, capitalists sought to deny workers as many of their autonomous or semiautonomous institutional resources as possible. They wished to extend the social-control capacities of local governments and their service bureaucracies. They shared an interest in promoting the ideology of the neutral state, embodied in the ideology of the nonpartisan professional. They wished to create rationalized, predictable links between business and government. They were repelled by the "foreignness" of the immigrants and their political language, style, and practices, and they wished to protect the Republic from perceived alien threats to republicanism and free enterprise. And, as Clifton Yearley suggests in a little-known but superb monograph, they may have tired of the cost of supporting a system of double taxation: funds for government, and funds for party coffers.[32] The professionals who backed progressivism did not necessarily share these views or these interests. Yet there was an ideological convergence between the professionals and their allies that was structured around the goals of rationalization, efficiency, education, and merit. At the local level, one result was a series of coalitions of reformers who preached these values and an antiparty gospel.

Another outcome was the development, from the turn of the century to well after the Second World War, of the reform-machine dialectic that is the stuff of basic-textbook treatments of city politics. Electoral competition has been organized less as a competition between parties than as a choice between party and nonpartisan governments. In his study of New York City, Lowi notes that reform victories at the polls tended to be short-lived, since reform coalitions that were spurred by their animosity to local Democrats lacked the persistent organizational structure to fight successfully for reelection (the La Guardia mayoralty was the major exception, but he built a party base in the American Labor Party; John Lindsay was reelected in 1969 only because his opposition was divided). In New York, he observes, reform governments have been the major sources of organizational innovation. Reform has not advanced a program of policies opposed to those of the machine.[33] Rather it has taken the evils of the party system as its central target, to be modified by changes in the form and structure of local government:

Since the overriding tenets have been the elimination of corruption and the introduction of efficiency, the most important goal for political action has been the merit-alterations in personnel. . . . This has been the goal of reform: No integrated program, no concept of the public interest to which all Departments and agencies would be devoted, but an instrumental view in which responsible programs and the public interest would emerge from elites of skill.[34]

Although reformers did not often control city hall for long, their institutional innovations did last. Thus, Lowi concludes,

largely due to the efforts of the reform movement, there is independent, non-party access to the mayoralty. Perhaps of greater importance, the reform principle of insulating the bureaucracies from the parties has become so strongly operative that it has created a separate political force in the community. The departmental bureaucracies are not neutral, they are only independent.[35]

Measured by the degree of centralization and professionalization of municipal civil services, reform has clearly triumphed even in cities like Chicago, where political organizations have thrived in the past three decades. During the Great Depression national housing, public works, and welfare programs on an unprecedented scale provided local governments with the means to balance budgets, keep services going, reward friends, and punish

enemies. In order to receive, administer, and distribute this federal largesse, municipal governments of both the reform and machine types were compelled to reorganize and modernize their bureaucratic structures. The growth in local government employment, accompanied by the growth of local bureaucratic power, dates principally from this period. As the private sector of small capital has declined in the postwar period, and as social problems have been exacerbated by federal programs favoring the "natural" motion of capital, local bureaucracies have been expanded in an attempt to cope with and to manage the problems of social order. In these ways, the reform impetus has come to be largely detached from the electoral game of machine versus reform in which it originated. It has made little difference to the triumph of reform whether machine or reform governments have been in charge, though it has made a significant difference in the area of fiscal management, where machine governments have usually done the more effective job in keeping a lid on spending.

The question of whether a given city in the postwar era was to be governed by machine or reform regimes after the depression hinged largely on the type of regime that was in office during the depression. Where, as in Chicago, machine politicians controlled city hall, and thus had access to the federal bounty of the New Deal, they tended to reinforce their leader-follower ties. But where, as in New York, the machine was out of power, there existed no alternative sources of money, jobs, and services to be distributed (except perhaps those contributed by organized crime), and thus the machine's mass links tended to wither.[36] The survival of machines in the depression depended, in short, on developing instrumental relationships with the national Democratic coalition. As Scott notes, machines flourish best in expanding economies that can afford their expensive habits. In a period of profound scarcity, machines not fattened by programs funded in Washington lacked sufficient rewards to compete with the reform-managed social-welfare programs. In this period the balance of exchange between the patron-bosses of the machines and their client-followers shifted perceptibly, as the machines in reform-governed cities like New York were less and less able to secure means of subsistence, manage economic distress, and provide influential brokerage services.[37]

At the level of the community, as a consequence, the institutional mediation of the party organization that had acted as a buffer in

the relationship between the citizen and the state was virtually eliminated. In 1935 Roy Peel published the best available study of the political clubs of New York City that had initially been created by Tammany Hall in the years following the election of 1886, when the organization had been challenged by the city's labor organizations. The work focused on the late 1920s, by which time, it is clear in retrospect, the heyday of the Tammany club had passed and the party was shaken by factionalism. Nevertheless, Peel portrays a world of vigorous party organizations that were *the* major political presence in their neighborhoods. Although most active at election time, these community organizations held meetings on a regular basis throughout the year. They were, in Raymond Jones's words, "the welfare bureaus and social service agencies of those days";[38] perhaps most important, they were major community centers of social activity. Peel writes of community sings, programs celebrating ethnic accomplishments, special entertainments with hired dancers and actors, big-band dances, amateur theatricals, theater parties, picnics, and presentations of new films. In overheated prose, he described the "crowd" at a typical club:

The assembly district leaders of the major parties and the organizers of the minor parties are the chief actors. . . . Next to them come superior party officers; officers of the government; councillors, marshals, club officers, captains, workers, members, aspiring members; interested citizens with definite aims in mind; candidates and prospective candidates and used-up party hacks; curious citizens impelled by habits of gregariousness; men wanting to meet other men; hungry people wanting food; shivering citizens attracted by the warmth of the club's quarters; lonely citizens anxious for recognition; reckless or desperate or bored men wanting to gamble; unemployed looking for jobs; misdemeanants and criminals craving pardons, protection, and legal aid; orators burning to make speeches; women craving work in the kitchen; and citizens of all ranks thirsting for knowledge.[39]

In the period 1927 to 1933, Peel counted 1,177 individual clubs within the city's boundaries, of which 703 were Democratic. A replication of the Peel study in the early 1970s found that the number of clubs had declined to 268, of which only 154 were affiliated with the Democratic party. Individual clubs tended to be smaller, moreover. Most, though by no means all, the active clubs in the early 1970s were survivors from an earlier age. Much of the activity of these clubs was involved with maintaining the

organization—publishing a newsletter, keeping the club open on one or two nights a week, soliciting advertisements for an annual journal. Less than a third of the city's clubs held the traditional picnics, card and theater parties, or athletic outings. Annual dinners and dances were held outside the club premises; fully a third of the clubs did not engage even in these events. More than half did not provide any kind of welfare, employment, or housing service; only a small majority stated that they provided "contact with government." The clubs also failed by and large to place their members in top city jobs. "Of the clubs responding to the question, 'How many members of this club held government appointments to positions of Deputy Commissioner or above on the state or city level?', 66 percent answered 'none.' An additional 25 percent had less than five such members, and only 2 percent had more than ten."[40]

By this standard, the principal Democratic party club in northern Manhattan in the late 1960s and 1970s, the Washington Heights Progressive Democrats, was one of the city's most vigorous and successful neighborhood party organizations. In the early 1970s its two most important members were a city councilman (David Friedland) and the minority leader of the state senate (Joseph Zaretzki). The club had nearly five hundred members. The organization had access to some high-level patronage. One member was a state liquor commissioner, a job requiring only two mornings of work each week and paying a salary of $31,000. A second position on the commission was secured for an insurgent candidate who had announced he would run against Zaretzki in the 1970 primary, but had then withdrawn. The club opened every Monday and Thursday evening. Zaretzki and Friedland personally met constituents with problems and tried to help, with information, phone calls to appropriate administrators, and legal tax advice. "This is a strong club," its president stated, "one of the best in the city." The liquor commissioner added, "Yes, this is a strong club. Fifty years of existence backs this up."[41]

With all this, however, the club in fact was a rather weak and precarious institution. In the 1960s its membership declined from over twelve hundred to over five hundred, the majority of whom were over sixty and had been members for a long time. A small number of people in their twenties and thirties had joined the club, mainly in search of political careers. But there were virtually no middle-aged members at all. The club was run autocratically

by its leadership; the most important decisions were made by Zaretzki, an elderly man in frail health who had served in the state senate since 1946 and who had become the Democratic party leader in 1958. The club was essentially an extension of his influence and personality. This personalism was a strength of the organization for a time, and it helped sustain the club for much of the postwar period; but as his health and energy declined, so did his organization.

It will be recalled that Shefter defined the political machine in terms of its centralized capacities. No local club can flourish if the larger party structure of which it is a part does not. In the context of the diminished state of Tammany Hall, the Washington Heights Progressive Democrats had little patronage to distribute to its members. Because its leaders understood that "patronage is essential to keeping a club going," they lamented the fact that "there is very little patronage available. There is practically nothing in the City Council. In the Senate and Assembly there is a little, some few minor committee positions with respect to the legislative function. Some judicial positions are available, but our members do not have the qualifications."[42]

Perhaps most significantly, the club had over time been content to withdraw to a smaller and smaller territorial area, in the hope of maintaining the organization with the support of its traditional Jewish and, in lesser numbers, Irish constituents. Until 1950 the club had been the official Tammany organization for all of the Fifteenth Assembly District, which then included the whole of Washington Heights–Inwood. That year the Fifteenth was divided in two; and subsequently each of the new districts was subdivided again, more than once. By 1970 the club's territory had shrunk to one-fifth of its size two decades earlier. Its leadership welcomed this contraction to a more secure base in a manner reminiscent of the redefinition of the southern boundary of Washington Heights before the Second World War in order to maintain the area's traditional white-ethnic character.[43]

The contraction of the party organization to "old" Washington Heights was accompanied by the expansion in the number of direct ties between community residents and city service bureaucracies. These connections varied by race, ethnicity, and neighborhood. In 1972 approximately one in three residents received subsistence help from government. But the distribution of such assistance was hardly random. Of those receiving cash assistance

from the state, 76 percent of the Irish, Jewish, and Greek residents were retired recipients of Social Security. Only 11 percent of the inhabitants of "old" Washington Heights–Inwood were on the welfare rolls, or had been in the past year. The contrast with "new" northern Manhattan is striking. Fewer than 2 percent of the Hispanic service recipients were on Social Security, and only 22 percent of the blacks. But 61 percent of both the blacks and the Hispanics getting some form of government aid were receiving, or had recently received, welfare benefits.[44] In this way they were enmeshed directly in relationships of major consequence with service bureaucrats. Links to the public schools showed a very similar pattern. Roughly nine in ten Irish and Jews had no children in state schools, compared to about seven in ten blacks and Hispanics who did.[45] In part, of course, this divergence was the result of the area's age distribution, but only in part. A majority of the children of elementary school age in West Washington Heights attended parochial or private schools; in Inwood this proportion approached two-thirds. Although one in four Hispanic children of this age did go to Catholic schools, and about one in ten black children enrolled in private schools and one in twenty attended parochial schools, the overwhelming majority were schooled in public institutions.[46]

By the 1960s the erosion of party links, even in areas like Washington Heights that had relatively strong party institutions, was significantly facilitating the urban crisis. The direct ties between citizens and bureaucrats became basic causes and targets of urban discontents. The very triumph of reform threatened its political, business, and professional supporters.

Almost all citizens come into contact at some point in their lives with school systems and health-care organizations; millions of city dwellers are on welfare; all are conscious of the police either as a source of protection or harassment, and some are processed through the police-courts-prison complex. Lower-level employees in these agencies—teachers, social workers, nurses, clerks, policemen, lower-court judges—most directly represent government to the governed.[47] These contacts are fraught with tension. Low-level bureaucrats are in extremely sensitive positions, but, unlike local machine politicians, they lack the affective ties that bind party bosses to followers. They constantly interact with the public and have a great deal of power over the lives of captive clients. The bureaucrats, moreover, are hardly ever responsible to those

nonvoluntary clienteles, but are, rather, accountable to their bureaucratic supervisors.

The bureaucrats have difficult jobs. They must typically operate in an environment that makes it impossible for them to satisfy their professional goals. Too often the resources available to them are inadequate, in part because of the dependency of cities. There are too many children in the classroom; the court caseload is impossibly heavy; not enough policemen are available in high-crime areas. Bureaucrats work in a situation in which their authority is challenged regularly and in which there is a higher than average possibility of physical and psychic threat.

To deal with these work-related circumstances, they act in ways that heighten urban conflict. Policemen may come to see and treat all young blacks as potential criminals. Lower-court judges process cases so quickly as to transform judicial decision making into administrative routinization. Social workers often penalize clients who rebel against the agency's routines. Health-clinic doctors and nurses, under the pressure of their workload, may act as if their patients were not human. As a result of this kind of activity, the gap between bureaucrat and client inevitably grows, as does discontent with a remote, unresponsive, irresponsible urban government. This process of interaction, in short, takes on a dynamic of its own that is profoundly alienating.

III

In this institutional context, city struggles came to revolve, first, around two territorially based political blocs—white ethnics versus blacks and Hispanics—and, second, around the ways these blocs were tied to the party and bureaucratic institutions of local government. The urban crisis in motion was a three-cornered game between the "old" and "new" political blocs and the government.

Even where blacks composed a numerical minority of the "new" bloc, they usually took the leadership role. Such was the case in northern Manhattan. Blacks composed only about half of the population of South Washington Heights, less than 20 percent of the residents of East Washington Heights, and negligible proportions of the population in West Washington Heights and Inwood. For every black resident of northern Manhattan there were at least two, and possibly as many as three, Dominicans,

Cubans, and Puerto Ricans. Yet, for a variety of reasons, it was impossible for the Hispanic population to have any but a subordinate role in the political bloc of "new" Washington Heights–Inwood.

Citizenship, or rather the lack of citizenship, was the most important barrier. We have already noted how difficult it is to make accurate estimates of the noncitizen population. But there can be no doubt that the large majority of Dominican and Cuban residents of northern Manhattan in the 1960s and early 1970s were not citizens. Of the Block Survey respondents only 35 percent of the Cubans and 18 percent of the Dominicans were citizens; and the very nature of the survey enterprise makes it likely that these are inflated figures.[48]

It should come as no surprise, therefore, that most Hispanics had very little information about local politics and only a very tenuous connection to organized local political activity. A minority of the Cubans and Dominicans read an English newspaper. Two community newspapers were published in northern Manhattan; virtually no Dominicans or Cubans knew of their existence (and of the few who reported that they did, only half had read one). A majority of the Cubans and more than three in four Dominicans could not identify the positions of Congresswoman Bella Abzug or Senator Jacob Javits. Well over 80 percent of both groups reported that they understood New York City issues "not too well" or "not at all." Fewer than one in seven Dominicans and one in three Cubans reported belonging to any social or political organization. Not until late 1973 was there an attempt to create a Hispanic political organization, La Alianza, that cut across the Cuban, Dominican, Puerto Rican distinctions.[49]

In spite of all these impediments to a leadership role, Hispanic residents of northern Manhattan were available for mobilization as subordinate members of the black-led political bloc. Large majorities of the Cuban and Dominican respondents endorsed ethnic political action, and as high a percentage of Dominicans as of blacks thought such activity should be militant.[50] The Hispanic political role was especially considerable in the policy area of education, where parents of school children were accorded the right to participate in school-board elections irrespective of their larger citizenship status. They visited their children's schools and contacted school-board members in numbers roughly proportional to their share of the population.[51]

The "old" northern Manhattan political bloc, composed of Jewish, Irish, and Greek members, was directed by leaders who were disproportionately Jewish. The low visibility, lack of a territorial base, and small numbers of the area's Greeks made it impossible for them to take a leading role. The Irish and Jews shared similar histories, economic positions, and synagogue- and church-based institutional resources. But local Jews possessed a number of advantages that propelled them to the bloc's leadership. As in many other working-class communities, local political elites in northern Manhattan were disproportionately lawyers and other professionals, shopkeepers, and tradesmen. We have already seen that half of the area's professionals and more than half of its petits bourgeois were Jewish. The majority of the party activists and Community Board members came from these groups. The Jewish role in its bloc's leadership may be gleaned from the fact that of the forty-seven members of the Community Board, twenty-five were Jews and only seven were Irish.[52]

The two political blocs shared a very deep distrust of the fairness of local government. Only one-fourth of the Block Survey respondents thought they could "trust the government in New York City to do what is right" almost always or most of the time. More than half said that local government "is pretty much run for the benefit of a few big interests." About six in ten expected to get a runaround at city agencies or to be treated "like a number." Large majorities of all groups thought that city government discriminated on an ethnic basis and that, moreover, their own ethnic group was the one most discriminated against. Although blacks were more disaffected than any other communal group, the differences between groups on these measures are much less important than the widespread *ressentiment* they all shared.

This common disaffection reflected at least in part the way in which national and regional economic developments were transmitted as local social problems to members of the community. Although there was some variation across neighborhoods and ethnic and racial groups, the Public Survey found that residents in all parts of northern Manhattan complained of the same major problems: crime, dirty streets, a dilapidated environment, decaying housing, and drug addiction. But the meaning of these social problems was quite different for each of the main actors in the three-cornered urban "game" of the 1960s.

The white-ethnic bloc judged the new situation of northern Manhattan against the memory of an older community. The newcomers were very visible to residents of "old" Washington Heights–Inwood, both as the source of the community's social problems and as the recipients of political favoritism. The white-ethnic bloc defined its interest in the game of the urban crisis as the defense of the status quo.

The disaffection of white workers was at least in part independent of the resentment generated by the influx of the newcomers. White ethnics, like blacks, were affected by the basic changes in the economy of the city, which produced disinvestment in housing and industry. The common elements of black and white discontent—commonalities based on class—could have found expression in at least a partial alliance with the newcomers. But this coalition never developed, not only because the new groups were beyond the reach of the weakened system of trenches, but because the trenches became the defense apparatus of the old groups. The defensiveness of the whites imbued the party remnants of the old system with more efficacy than they in fact possessed. They became symbols of the protection of scarce residence space, public employment, and municipal services.

For the black-led bloc, white ethnics were visible at every turn as the politicians who controlled the party structure and the Community Board, and as the street-level bureaucrats in the police department, welfare bureaus, and schools.[53] The predominantly black social movements politicized these relationships. "It is no accident that some people strike, others riot or loot the granaries, or burn the machines," Frances Piven writes, "for just as the patterning of daily life ordinarily assures mass quiescence, so do these same patterns come to shape defiance when it erupts."[54] Since welfare, housing, police, and educational services are distributed in residence communities by local governments, they act as organizing incentives for ethnic and racial groups to behave as interest groups, much as the ward organization of party politics historically has acted to solidify group consciousness and perpetuate the division of the city, demographically and politically, into ethnic components. This was especially the case for urban blacks, whose collective situation came to be defined in large measure by their relationship to the schooling, housing, welfare, and police bureaucracies. The differential pattern of party and bureaucratic institutions thus overlapped with and reinforced the racial divi-

sions of the city. In this setting, race proved to be the most important solvent acting on the traditional urban class system. For if the division between the worlds of work and residence has been the most basic element of the American pattern of class, the racial dimensions of the urban crisis undermined its presuppositions, at least for a time and at least indirectly.

Faced with this situation, local authorities had to manage their inability to solve the substantive concerns of blacks and their social movements. Within the limits of this incapacity, they had to contain and defuse the urban crisis. And so they did.

CHAPTER 7

Innovation and Reform, 1969–1974

A central feature of the response to the assault on the system of city trenches by those who governed was the fashioning of a new genre of institutions. These programs, initiated by local mayors, included little city halls, offices of neighborhood government, decentralized school boards, and neighborhood service councils. Complementing existing federal programs like Model Cities and Community Action,[1] they altered the political landscapes of Boston, New York, Los Angeles, and numerous other large cities where party organizations had been attenuated severely. The main principle of these innovations was decentralization, whose family resemblance to community control was high.

Theodor Geiger observed in the 1920s that "counterrevolution is part of revolution. Not that it is a revolution. Rather, counter-revolution belongs to it, results from it in the form of a refluent movement. It is literally a *re-action*."[2] Building on this insight, Arno Mayer has insisted that all crisis situations have a double-edged nature and impulse. All situations of revolt are moments of counterrevolt; and the internal relation between the two is quite important: "As if by reflex," he has written, "the counter-revolution borrows its central ideas, objectives, styles and methods from the revolution."[3] Such a mimetic response, I argue, occurred in American cities in the late 1960s and early 1970s. The objective of the new urban public policies was not only to overcome the threatening gap between citizenry (especially black citizens) and government, but to reinvolve them in the terms of the traditional trench system. Moreover, in instances like schooling, in which a

---

The education sections of this chapter were written in collaboration with Henry C. Wells.

virulent issue produced a social and political crisis, authorities sought to fragment the issue into manageable community-sized components.

In New York City most of the new programs initiated by the Lindsay administration were implemented citywide. But when city officials had some discretion over where to locate the new organizations, as in the case of the mayor's 1970 plans for neighborhood government, Washington Heights–Inwood was invariably selected as a test site. Because of its multiracial character, its proximity to Harlem, and the history of political conflict in the 1960s between "old" and "new" residents and neighborhoods, northern Manhattan became an important location for the mimetic public policies of the late 1960s and early 1970s. By 1970 northern Manhattan had an appointed Community Planning Board, the rudiments of a new multifunctional community-level government (the Neighborhood Action Program), and an elected school board.

I

In June 1970 Mayor Lindsay proposed a "Plan for Neighborhood Government." The program's stated goals were the improvement of the delivery of services "by making city agencies more responsive and accountable at the neighborhood level," and the reduction of "the distance that citizens feel exists between themselves and city government" by creating the "basis for a single coordinated governmental presence in each neighborhood, recognized and supported by the community, the municipal government, and all elected officials." The plan called for the establishment of sixty-two "neighborhood government" units that would utilize the prevailing boundaries of the city's advisory community planning boards.[4] As an initial step, six pilot programs were announced, including what came to be called the Neighborhood Action Program in northern Manhattan.

It is important to avoid the functionalist trap of imputing a causal motivation for neighborhood government from its consequences. Since the new program was designed to absorb the "functions, powers and duties" carried out by an existing array of agencies and boards—including urban-action task forces, neighborhood city halls, and community planning boards—we would do well to examine these organizational roots of neighborhood government.

Running as the Republican-Liberal candidate in 1965, Congressman John V. Lindsay lacked even the inadequate organizational support that the atrophied Democratic party organization was capable of providing for its candidates. To compensate, his campaign manager organized storefront headquarters in the city's neighborhoods to assume the functions of traditional machines. After the election, these storefronts, in spite of Democratic opposition in the city council, developed into neighborhood city halls, which served as grievance centers that dispensed information, services to individuals, and, on occasion, jobs. The results of the creation of these new institutional brokers, Lindsay has claimed,

were almost immediately encouraging.... For example, more than 2,300 problems were brought to the city's attention through one neighborhood city hall located in a city-owned health center in Queens. The complaints ran the gamut from housing to street and sewer conditions, from abandoned cars to welfare problems and requests for traffic lights—all the services a city tries to provide for its people. The hall was staffed by three professionals supplemented by volunteers who ... both as residents and "ombudsmen" ... could channel complaints and problems directly into the machinery of the city administrations.

The results were impressive. The number of cases handled jumped from 2,200 in 1967 to more than 8,000 in the first nine months of 1968. *More important, however, was the fact that local residents realized their neighborhood city hall was an effective mechanism for getting grievances resolved.*[5]

The second organizational predecessor to neighborhood government was the program of urban-action task forces formed in a conscious effort to cool the ghettos and prevent riots. Barry Gottehrer, a journalist appointed as assistant to the mayor when Lindsay took office, has described the establishment of the riot-prevention system in some detail. In July 1966, shortly after Lindsay had taken office, a series of racial clashes between whites and blacks in the East New York section of Brooklyn ("We hardly knew where East New York was; we read about the trouble in the newspapers."[6]) nearly had produced a major race riot. The mayor and his staff were determined not to go into the summer of 1967

as ill-prepared as we were in 1966. It was time to concentrate on neighborhoods, the poorest neighborhoods, before troubles blew up in our faces eight or ten months later. We were under pressure to alleviate the long term injustices of inadequate housing, health care facilities, sanitation collection, job opportunities. For these needs we required a

massive infusion of state and federal funding, as well as planning; but with or without those funds, we needed to head off the confrontations in the streets that now seemed inevitable.[7]

Together with fellow aides Sid Davidoff and Jay Kriegel, Gottehrer prepared a proposal for the creation of a Summer Task Force operation that could act to keep the peace in the absence of large-scale structural changes. As Lindsay later put it,

What we saw in early 1966 was that within the ghetto, discontent and alienation were at the breaking point. We saw that a basic commitment to ending that alienation through greater contact was essential. And we knew that words alone would not do the job. . . . Thus, throughout the fall of 1966 and into the spring of 1967 we made plans for a structured, formal link between the neighborhoods and the city.[8]

The first task of this new structure was that of intelligence gathering: "We were interested in creating a network for getting information from the street right up to the mayor, and for getting information from different departments to do so."[9] The aim was to tap street-level activists, including gang members, and to enmesh them in a series of relationships with the administration—in effect an exchange of information for discrete summer programs of employment and entertainment. Each community would have a representative of the mayor, at the level of a city commissioner or deputy commissioner, to meet weekly with local leaders and street-level bureaucratic administrators working in the community. "We now had the makings of a new kind of structure. We had access to the complaints and real problems of citizens in poor neighborhoods, and they had a direct route to City Hall if the civil servants in their neighborhood had given up trying to respond to them."[10] In April 1968 the Urban Action Task Force was put on a year-round, permanent basis in order to "open channels of communication . . . act as a vehicle for coordinating city services . . . and ensure that the agencies of city government are responsive on a direct basis to neighborhood problems."[11]

The structure of the task force had a number of significant organizational features. One was its domination by the mayor's office. At the city level, a task force, whose chairman and vice-chairman were appointed by the mayor and whose membership consisted of the heads of eighteen city agencies and departments, the borough presidents, and the chairman of the Board of Education, the Council Against Poverty, and the Housing Au-

thority, supervised the work of the local task forces. The mayor's executive order establishing the program spelled out "examples of groups that should be invited" to join its structure, including "poverty corporations, local community action agencies, religious organizations, district planning boards, community and civic organizations, block associations, and educational groups led by parents." With their participation, the document noted, it will be possible to remedy the "serious communications gap between government and the residents of the disadvantaged neighborhoods in the City."[12]

Lindsay has maintained that while the task-force network might appear to have been nothing "but a peacemaking operation . . . in fact the task force did more than that by coordinating services, transmitting grievances, and providing a popular means of participation."[13] While such services and activities were in fact provided, this formulation misses the point that their principal purpose was not the solution of substantive problems, but the maintenance of social order. The Kerner Commission, on which Mayor Lindsay served, recognized that these actions were the key means to this end. By constructing "input" mechanisms that functioned much like those of traditional machines, the task forces, it found, had made "a major contribution to the prevention of civil disorders." It thus recommended that the New York model be widely adopted and noted that success depends on gaining "the confidence of a wide spectrum of ghetto residents. This will enable [political authorities] to identify potentially explosive conditions, and working with the police, to take action to defuse the situation."[14]

In northern Manhattan, as in the other areas in which task forces functioned, the program took the form of an umbrella organization, bringing together representatives of the service bureaucracy, of the mayor's office and of voluntary groups. The chairman of the local Task Force, Emmanuel Savas, a Greek who worked for the mayor as deputy city administrator, issued invitations in May 1969 to the inaugural meeting. "I have tried," he wrote, "to identify and invite representatives of all major business, civic, educational, fraternal, institutional, neighborhood, parent, political, religious, social and tenant groups in the area, as well as each of the elected public officials."[15] By bringing together the existing institutional structure of the community, the Task Force aimed to quickly fashion an "input" mechanism that officially

sanctioned these organizations as access points to government and that, in turn, created an authoritative presence in the area that had to be dealt with directly by the area's leaders.

Working closely with the existing Neighborhood City Hall (the Task Force shared space and some staff with the NCH), the Task Force quickly identified the range of the problems with which it could deal, the actors who might be involved, and the scope of conflict. The minutes of the first meeting reported that "this whole idea was reported by Dr. Savas as an experiment at the fourth level of government: down from federal, state, city, to the neighborhood. It is not likely by itself to solve the big problems of poverty, education, or housing, but, besides achieving its three-fold purpose, it can promote the exchange of information and experiences among neighborhood groups, so that local 'people power'—through mutual assistance—can tackle and solve these problems which government cannot."[16]

Though the schools had become the central issue of local mayoral politics, and, indeed, the focal point of the major urban struggles of the period, the issue of education was explicitly excluded from consideration. Formally, schools were not within the province of the mayor; hence they could not be dealt with by his task forces. Shielding the task forces from educational issues that deeply divided "old" and "new" northern Manhattan made it possible to engage both the white-ethnic and black blocs in the new organization.

With the Neighborhood City Hall the Task Force conducted its main activities. At its monthly meetings anger could be vented. Such expressions typically occurred at different levels. Those who attended frequently expressed their hopes and fears for radical urban changes. Blacks often used the language of nationalism and internal colonialism; whites demanded neighborhood stabilization. Exchanges were often heated, especially when they were directed at service bureaucrats. But given the limitations of the Task Force, these conversations had no more than symbolic value. They did allow irate group leaders to talk directly to local officials, but the definition of what the task forces could do, and the separation of each task force from all the others, limited the practical work of the organization to repairs of public facilities and to the distribution of low-cost but highly visible goods, especially in the summertime. Many meetings of the Task Force had an almost surreal character. Much of the time would be taken up with generalized gripes; the remainder of a meeting would

deal with a very narrow and specific agenda, including such items as the placement of litter baskets, the inspection of trees blocking traffic lights, the removal of abandoned cars, block cleanup campaigns, the installation of bright lighting, park permits for ice and roller skating, the repair of broken fences, potholes, fire hydrants, and sidewalks, and the restructuring of bus routes. These matters were obviously important to the quality of life in the area, but they were relatively noncontroversial and connected not at all to the more generalized angry concerns about the police and courts, the schools, landlord-tenant relations, and public housing.

The Task Force collected gripes from individual citizens. Most were about housing: poor conditions, code violations, illegal rent increases under the terms of the city's rent control statutes, peremptory evictions, and the like. The Task Force and NCH staff were very efficient in collecting these complaints and in transmitting them to the relevant bureaucracies, but their work typically stopped there. Very little follow-up occurred. A former employee explained why he resigned partly in these terms: "The UATF-NCH program has been successful in processing complaints; however the resolution of a complaint tends to be *ad hoc,* temporal, often incomplete, and often placed outside its hands by insurmountable bureaucracy in the regular city service agencies and programs."[17] In performing this grievance-collection and transmission function, the UATF did make a tangible difference to some community residents. Yet it is important to note that the grievances were collected almost exclusively on an individual basis and that the act of listening to angry people was, to judge by the staff's allocation of efforts, more important than the substantive resolution of their requests.

The UATF also conducted a very long list of summer activities, including bus trips, the distribution of free tickets to New York Yankee baseball games, visits to the New York Jets football training camp, a Jazzmobile, a program of movies in the street, the registration for senior-citizen half-fare bus tickets, and the management of a small temporary swimming pool. Explicitly aimed at keeping angry people busy to prevent disorders, such programs were very different in their carnival character from alternatives that were not provided: legal services, preventive medicine campaigns, information about welfare, tenant, and Social Security rights, and tenant and block organizing.

The third organizational precursor of neighborhood govern-

ment was the network of community boards. Unlike the Neighborhood City Hall–Task Force structure which had its roots in the electoral and riot-prevention aspirations of the Lindsay administration, the community boards were existing institutions that were adapted by the Lindsay administration in the late 1960s as part of its strategy of decentralization.

In July 1947 the Citizens Union, a reform organization, proposed "subdividing the boroughs into recognized districts as a basis for more orderly planning and decentralization of municipal services and community development." The proposal, it argued, promised to make government more efficient, save money by avoiding duplication (agency construction programs could be consolidated, as in a fire house and police station that shared premises), and make citizens identify more closely with their neighborhoods in order to "bring back the sense of 'home town' that New Yorkers used to have." The timing of this proposal was motivated in part by the death of Fiorello La Guardia and by the return of city hall to Tammany Hall. Community planning boards not only could contribute to longstanding Progressive goals of efficient government, they could also provide local centers of good government as competing legitimate entities to neighborhood party organizations.[18]

Robert Wagner, Jr., the aspiring son of Senator Wagner, picked up this proposal and made it his own. First as head of the City Planning Commission and then as the borough president of Manhattan, the community-board program allowed him to build a reform constituency outside of regular Democratic party channels, even as he was allying with the insurgent efforts of Carmine De Sapio within the Tammany organization. The twelve "planning councils" that Wagner created in Manhattan were designed to serve as "logical units for the planning of schools, housing, hospitals, libraries, playgrounds, local street systems and other public facilities, as well as for consideration of land use and zoning patterns."[19] Councils were to be composed of from fifteen to twenty volunteer members nominated by civic groups to be appointed by the borough president. Their powers were advisory. No funding was provided for their operation.

This organizational model was replicated on a citywide basis after Wagner's election as mayor in 1953, and, following a change of name adopted in 1952 in Manhattan, the councils were now called community planning boards. In spite of their rather grandiose responsibilities, the character of the membership of the

boards, and their lack of staff and funds, made them very peripheral organizations throughout the 1950s and 1960s. The northern Manhattan Board was "a fairly quiet, relatively unpublicized group whose meetings were little more than gripe sessions and a place for community leaders to get together, a group that made few decisions and took little action." Much time, according to the minutes, was devoted to small-construction items, such as traffic lights, or to the discussion and usual approval of the city's capital budget and the making of occasional suggestions for minor changes in it. In no meaningful sense did planning proposals originate with the Board; rather, most of the time "it reacted to other agencies' proposals and plans rather than taking the initiative." As a result, one observer noted, the Board functioned "as an agent of legitimation" to city agencies, since their activities gained the imprimatur of a local representative body. And on the few occasions when the Board responded negatively to an agency proposal, its advice was usually ignored, since the Board lacked a formal veto.[20]

The community planning boards were granted legal standing in the new City Charter of 1961. In 1969 the Lindsay administration sought successfully to amend the charter to expand the role of the boards at precisely the same moment that it activated the task-force structure on a citywide basis. Local Law 39, passed in July 1969, changed the name of the boards to "community boards," set the membership size at fifty (to make room for new minority representation), and increased the range of topics that fell within the jurisdiction of the boards. Among these tasks were mandates to "consider the needs of the district for which it serves and develop plans for the district's welfare and orderly development"; "advise, either on its own initiative or when requested, any public officer, agency, or legislative body with respect to any matter relating to the welfare of the district"; "hold public or private hearings or investigations with respect to any such matter"; "cooperate and consult with the local administrators of city department and agencies"; "assist city departments and agencies in making contacts with and transmitting information to the people of its district"; and "use all practical means to keep the public informed on matters relating to the welfare or development of its district."[21] This impressive set of paper responsibilities, however, remained mostly symbolic. The "community boards" remained unfunded and without veto power.

The Board was at this time an institutional extension of the

leadership of "old" northern Manhattan. Of its forty-one members, thirty-one were white. Most were professionals (several teachers, social workers, and nurses, an architect, at least eight lawyers, a clergyman, and an anthropologist) or managers or executives. Most, as we have seen, had party ties. Members were drawn disproportionately from the northern and western parts of the community. When an M.A. student at Columbia asked them to describe their motivations for taking on the nonpaying position, they gave a high priority to wanting "to conserve and protect the community character."[22]

II

Following the mayor's proposal for the creation of units of neighborhood government in June 1970, Emmanuel Savas prepared a "Pilot Program for Neighborhood Government in Washington Heights–Inwood" that proposed that his neighborhood be one of the program's experimental locales. He argued that northern Manhattan was an ideal test site. It was, he noted, an area that was "still relatively stable, but in serious danger of decay," with "enough positive attributes to offer good chances for success." The new program, under the heading of the Neighborhood Action Program (NAP), would supersede the Task Force–Neighborhood City Hall organizations and develop ties with the existing Community Board. In addition, and this was the key new component, NAP would have at its discretion approximately $500,000 a year in capital funds that could be spent by the neighborhood government on projects requiring little or no continuing maintenance by the city. The advantages of merging the old operations into the new NAP, Savas argued, included the development of a single coherent focus for citizen demands, increased possibilities for mayoral control of the performance of service bureaucracies, and the enhanced chance "to improve community cohesion and build consensus in a neighborhood which is socially, ethnically, racially and economically mixed." The participation of local groups, including those that were angry and insurgent, would be facilitated, he presciently suggested, by the availability of new city funds; in the words of his proposal, "NAP money serves as incentive for citizen participation in all aspects of the project."[23]

When this proposal was conveyed to the Community Board,

"the first question we asked was 'What is the administration trying to pull?' " They were convinced, first, that Lindsay was attempting to institutionalize a new electoral machine that bypassed the existing party organization and, second, that he wished to impose a competing nonboard leadership on the community. The mayor's provisional selection of his former campaign organizer in Washington Heights to direct the new NAP reinforced these fears. The Board reacted by passing a resolution which proposed that a steering committee of seven Board and four mayoral representatives should fill the position of executive director, and that this committee, to be chaired by a Board member, should have complete authority to create the structure for the NAP. "We said that if these conditions were not acceptable, then the Community Board of Washington Heights was not interested in the establishment of a Neighborhood Action Program in the area."[24]

The city responded by withdrawing its original candidate for executive director and by offering the post to Jordan Linfield, the chairman of the Community Board. In the winter of 1971 Linfield presided over a series of negotiating sessions held between six representatives of the Community Board and three designated by the mayor in order to determine who would control the NAP funds and to set up an operating structure for the new unit of neighborhood government. These sessions, three of which I attended, began with the negotiators' taking apparently contradictory positions. The Board members argued that they were the legitimate representatives of the Washington Heights–Inwood community, since they formed a microcosm of the organized population. Accordingly, the Board should be "the sole legislative body" for NAP, and the Board should control a majority (seven of eleven) seats on an NAP governing committee. The city negotiators countered that a Board role was legally impossible. NAP funds were the mayor's responsibility, and he could not yield them to another unit of government under the appointive control of the borough president. Furthermore, they argued, and here they were joined by Linfield, Board control would negate the central objectives of the program: "We need to gain the confidence of other new groups," Linfield asserted in late January. "A sole reliance on the Board will cut out whole groups. The Board has left a vacuum which we will fill." He indicated that he planned to involve black and Hispanic groups especially in the new organization by establishing "wide and broad functional committees"

and a functional coordinating committee to make recommendations for spending NAP funds.[25]

The central issue with which the negotiators dealt, in short, was how simultaneously to obtain the cooperation of the new groups and to retain the support of the leadership of "old" Washington Heights (of which Linfield was a part). The solution was rather ingenious. A neighborhood government with two branches, an executive and a legislative, would be created. Under these arrangements, the Board would in fact have the final say over NAP expenditures, but its role in the process would come only at the very end. An executive unit would operate in the storefront that had been occupied by the Neighborhood City Hall–Task Force operation. There it would take over their grievance functions and serve as the community's officially sanctioned access point to government. The executive staff would organize the process of assessing community requests for expenditures of NAP money by referring them to a series of functional committees which the director would appoint, and which would include at least one member appointed by the Community Board "as official liaison and member." The chairs of the new committees would be the NAP's executive committee which would decide between various committee recommendations and then take a consolidated budget request to the Community Board. The Board could then approve or reject the budget proposals or return them to the NAP with recommended modifications.[26]

By spring 1971 the new NAP was functioning. It was, by any account, a low-budget operation. Its unprepossessing office symbolized the small resources with which it had to work. The long, narrow enclosure of its storefront was badly in need of a paint job and substantial renovation. The reception area was furnished with very old desks, filing cabinets, and a few uncomfortable hard-backed chairs. Thin metal partitions made "private" offices out of the middle section of the store. The back consisted of a bathroom, a rarely functioning Xerox machine, and a small "conference" table. Physical comforts throughout were at a minimum. Phones were constantly ringing, and a general air of busy chaos typically prevailed. The staff occupying these spaces consisted of three full-time paid employees, the director and two assistants, as well as a volunteer receptionist, a part-time secretary, and an indeterminate number of high-school and Urban Youth Corps workers who were assigned to the office.

In spite of its minimal expense budget and overburdened staff, the NAP succeeded at a crucial moment of the urban crisis, when a noisy, more radical politics predominated, in serving significant numbers of the local community and, more important, in engaging the energies of most of the traditional and the new community activists.

At the street level the NAP functioned much as its predecessor, the Task Force–Neighborhood City Hall structure, had. Each week it processed about 200 to 250 individual grievances. In January 1972 Linfield reported, "We have provided assistance in resolving the complaints and problems of more than 10,000 area residents. This involved us in informing people of their tenants' rights, helping them to fill out the proper forms for housing problems, and acting as liaison between tenants and landlords and city agencies. We have also dealt with problems of traffic, sanitation, public safety, and health; and helping people find and contact that agency best suited to help them." The NAP also continued the attempt to emphasize entertainment activities in the summer. It made buses available for trips by community groups. It distributed widely a calendar of "free happenings" that promised "the most exciting summer, theatrically speaking, our community has ever had." It made available almost 4,500 free tickets to Broadway and Off-Broadway plays. And it coordinated the distribution of 3,000 free lunches each day in July and August.[27]

In these ways the NAP, like its predecessors, sought to acquire a constituency by playing the role for the new migrants that the machine in the past had played for the old immigrants. Its success, measured in the minimal terms of recognition by local residents, was mixed. It did not achieve the recognition that such party organizations as the Progressive Democrats still had. Approximately half of the white-ethnic respondents to the Block Survey could identify State Senator Joseph Zaretzki's position, and almost one in ten blacks and Hispanics could do the same. One-third of the respondents said they took their grievances and service problems to political party organizations or to political leaders first. By contrast, only 2 percent had heard of Jordan Linfield, and only about 6 percent identified NAP as their "broker organization" of first choice. But in its first year, the NAP did establish relatively strong ties with blacks. Located just a few blocks from the southern boundary of Washington Heights–Inwood, it drew

much of its clientele from this predominantly black area. Significantly, the Public Survey discovered that about one in four residents of northern Manhattan answered the question "Does this part of the city have an office of neighborhood government?" affirmatively, but that one in two residents of South Washington Heights answered yes. Overall, blacks were best informed about the existence of NAP (40 percent), followed by Jews (36 percent) and Hispanics (21 percent). The Irish, who lived farthest away in Inwood, were least likely to know of NAP (9 percent).[28]

The main effort of the NAP, in any event, was not the construction of a mass constituency, but a reorientation of the activities of the most important local leaders. The NAP used the $500,000 of available capital funds (a small sum for a community of 200,000) to induce local individuals and groups to participate in the program. By the middle of the first year of operations, the NAP had established an elaborate executive that included, in addition to the paid and voluntary staff, fifteen functional committees (parks, safety, health, narcotics, housing, arts, social services, and so forth), having a total of over 250 members, almost all of whom had organizational affiliations. These committees met regularly, at least once a month, to hold hearings and to consider budget proposals from groups in the area and from service bureaucracy representatives. Those that the committees approved were passed on to the executive committee for final budget preparation.

In early November of 1971 the Community Board met to consider NAP's first proposed budget. Linfield opened his presentation by explaining that "there is very little one can do" with just over $500,000 of capital funds. "We have looked for areas where we can make a visible impact on the community with small amounts of money. . . . We have looked for stopgap possibilities and for things no one else is doing."[29] The main proposals included park rehabilitation and extensive tree planting on community streets ($80,000); new street lighting and electronic and radio equipment for the police and citizen groups ($95,000); new equipment for the sanitation department and new litter baskets ($75,000); athletic equipment for the local high school and other youth programs ($95,000); wall murals and the installation of four pieces of sculpture ($35,000); and a communications program that included community bulletin boards and the establishment of a community TV studio ($30,000). All of these proposals were

approved by large Board majorities (in the face of a lack of alternatives and the availability of funds that would be lost if not spent, rejection was seen by most who participated in the discussion as out of the question). Such unease as was expressed concerned the issues of whether NAP funds really added to community resources or whether they were being spent on programs that ordinarily would have been charged to the city budget; and whether the tree-planting and parks-rehabilitation programs would be shared equitably by all of northern Manhattan's neighborhoods (the Board's blacks were skeptical, since most of the community's parks were in the northern parts of the district). One white radical community activist argued that in the face of the area's pressing needs, the emphasis on tree planting, sculpture, bulletin boards, and police and sanitation hardware was "asinine." Yet, as he conceded, within the terms of the NAP program the more basic questions of employment, welfare, and housing construction could not be addressed.[30]

One year after the establishment of NAP, serious planning began in the mayor's office to set up another experiment in decentralization that aimed to reverse the loss of power by city hall to the city's bureaucracies by creating coordinating bodies at the community level that could impose mayoral priorities on local bureaucrats. An Office of Neighborhood Government (ONG) was established with a central office downtown to supervise the development of the administrative decentralization of city agencies. Its catchwords were the fashionable policy jargon of interagency cooperation and coordination, "partial internal devolution" of authority to the local level, and "coterminality" of district boundaries, which, in English, meant that the different services of police, garbage collection, and welfare would use the same district boundaries, and that within those districts officials would have limited authority to coordinate their activities and take some action on their own initiative. There can be little doubt that the Lindsay administration saw these "output" mechanisms as a complement to the "input" capacities of NAP. Together they would provide the possibility for neighborhood government units that could join both sets of traditional machine functions together at the community level under the tutelage of city hall.

The ONG experiment was initiated, like NAP, by the establishment of district field offices of neighborhood government in selected planning districts in the city. District managers, recruited

from among men with considerable experience in program development and implementation, along with experience in local government or community service, were to head these field offices. They would hold monthly "cabinet" meetings, which all the local line agency chiefs would attend and at which they would initiate and develop the coordination and cooperation that the program proposed. The managers would not have any line authority over cabinet members, but the central office of ONG would have made agreements with all the city agencies involved that the job specifications of the local agency chiefs would be rewritten to give those in the experimental districts greater authority and independence in the running of their operations. The field offices of ONG would be purely administrative catalysts and would have no special funding beyond their own operating expenses, i.e., office space and equipment and staff salaries.[31]

Northern Manhattan was chosen to be one of the first five experimental districts. NAP would be subsumed under ONG and the district services cabinet would pass over to it. In the fall of 1971, Don Middleton, who had until then been the director of innovations at the city's Addiction Services Agency, was appointed district manager. News of his appointment reached local political and Community Board members through the pages of the *New York Times*.

Under these circumstances the Board and NAP mobilized to resist the new ONG. They feared that their own previous relations with the city administration would be impaired considerably. Their contacts with local bureaucrats would be cut off. Community groups might be tempted to reorient their efforts away from the NAP-Board nexus to ONG. The consequence would be a much weakened political structure for "old" northern Manhattan and a declining ability to incorporate the black political bloc on traditional ethnic-distributive terms. As it turned out, the conflict between the Board and NAP and ONG weakened all three protagonists.

During the early months of 1972, ONG downtown sought in vain to placate local leaders. Finally, in March, an agreement was made between the Community Board, NAP, and Middleton's office, which provisionally laid down the basis for coexistence. The Community Board and NAP were to be Middleton's channels of contact with local community groups. NAP was to retain control of programs and proposals, which they would present to the

Board in the usual way. ONG's role was restricted to administrative coordination and to the achievement of the goals laid down in the mayoral plan for "administrative decentralization."

Although in similar, though less highly charged, situations of community hostility other district managers had sought to change their approach in an attempt to gain at least a measure of local acquiescence, Middleton adhered to orthodoxy and found his hands officially tied. Moreover, another agreement gave Linfield the right, as director of the Washington Heights NAP, to sit in on Middleton's cabinet meetings, attended by the former members of Linfield's cabinet. Since the two men were by this time often not on speaking terms, the situation remained very difficult.

To add to the hostility and uncertainty surrounding the early months of Middleton's tenure, communications between the local ONG and NAP and the Community Board were poor indeed. The attempts Middleton made to approach the Board in order to suggest possible new programs were met with taunts that he was a "Johnny-come-lately." Middleton subsequently contacted community groups on his own, and he was attacked by both NAP and the Board for breaking their joint agreement.

NAP continued to identify itself as the Office of Neighborhood Government in Washington Heights; ONG in turn took to adopting Community Board and NAP programs and proposals and calling them its own, much to the chagrin of its opponents. To further complicate matters, Middleton and his staff continued to work out of ONG's downtown office, since they could find no suitable office space in the district. It was not until September of 1972 that they would finally find a place—ironically, next door to NAP.

One of the major dilemmas confronting ONG's field operations—and one serving to change the directions taken by their district managers once they got out into the field—was that it seemed impossible to generate interagency coordination unless they had meaningful programs that would afford opportunities for developing patterns of working together. The district managers therefore had to find out what the people of their districts wanted done. This required that contacts be made with community groups and organizations. Moreover, having no line authority over local agency operations, they had to show their cabinet members that there was a demand in the district for the programs they proposed. They were thus forced to enlist the support of

constituencies in their districts. They also had to deal with citizens' grievances, aiding them in their need to contact the appropriate arm of the city administration. Meanwhile, devolution of authority to the local level had not been forthcoming within the city agencies, and coterminality was proving too complex and controversial an issue in the bureaucracies for the field offices to be able to deal with it. ONG field offices rapidly came to take on the appearance of variations on the NAP scheme. In Washington Heights, for example, Middleton fought with NAP to win over similar constituencies, but with comparatively little success.

By January 1973 Middleton had come to regard his position as untenable, and he contemplated resignation. He pledged to quit if he was not granted complete authority over NAP. NAP resisted and mobilized its neighborhood political contacts in response to this threat to its partial autonomy. After a series of meetings between Middleton, Linfield, and John Mudd (director of the mayor's Office of Neighborhood Government), ONG and NAP declared a peace of sorts with one another. This "burying of the hatchet," as it came to be called in Washington Heights, implicitly recognized that both ONG and NAP ultimately had much to lose in the course of a long, drawn-out conflict. Indeed, some members of both local staffs came increasingly to feel that the animosity between the two offices was politically motivated and mutually destructive.

Soon after this peacemaking initiative had been successfully concluded, Middleton began to introduce some proposals before NAP and its committees. The most notable example was a precinct-on-wheels scheme, which would have involved the outlay of some $25,000 for a van equipped with desks and a telephone, to be manned by a desk sergeant and a patrolman from the local police precinct. During each week of operation the van would be moved to different locations throughout the district, in order to show a stronger police presence in the community and thus perhaps to allay local fears of crime. The scheme was presented jointly by Middleton and Captain Santaniello of the Thirty-fourth Precinct, with Middleton consciously playing down his own role in the development of the program. The NAP Public Safety Committee, meanwhile, handled the proposal diplomatically, even though there was considerable opposition to the idea. It was, however, indicative of the very tentative nature of the peace between the organizations that Middleton's scheme still aroused animosity.

Relations between the warring parties generally followed a

similar pattern. Each side approached the other warily and with diffidence, while openly trying to give the impression of its willingness to cooperate. Thus Middleton would inform one inquirer of his attempts to help the board stop plans to close a local hospital. Similarly, in an October 1973 press release, the Community Board chairman stressed, "It is nonsense for anyone to suggest that Linfield, Cooper, and Middleton have personally frustrated the administrative decentralization program," and he argued that, together, the Board, NAP, and ONG "have important complementary and supportive roles to play in developing effective local government for Washington Heights, Inwood, and Marble Hill."

These possibilities remained untested. When Mayor Lindsay announced that he would not run for reelection, the electoral possibilities of his neighborhood government units went unrealized. The period of urban rioting and massive threats to the social order, moreover, had passed. Mayor Abraham Beame, a traditional party Democrat, assumed office early in 1974. He moved quickly to dismantle the Lindsay programs of neighborhood government, reinvigorate local party organizations with the patronage available to him, create an Office of Neighborhood Services to replace ONG and coordinate neighborhood patronage, and promote charter-revision proposals in order to enhance the powers of community boards and mandate the rationalization of service-delivery boundaries. The instruments of decentralization were absorbed into the traditional idiom and practices of local politics. A slightly altered system of city trenches was in place.

III

Northern Manhattan's Community School Board met in public session in May 1973, in order to vote on the appointment of a new district school superintendent. The meeting ended prematurely after a scuffle broke out among Board members and the audience. When the Board's chair called for the vote, the two dissenting members began to shout into the microphone, "You're wrong, you're wrong." Members grappled for the mike, many in the audience rushed to the front to join in the melee, a table was overturned, and at least one person was cut by flying glass. Three of the seven board members present crossed the street to the police precinct to press criminal charges.[32]

Almost two years later, in March 1975, the appointment of a

white principal in a predominantly black elementary school was the Board's main agenda item. The post, vacant for three years (an interim principal had been filling in), had become a visible symbol of the differences between the local parents association and the Board. After voting approval, the meeting broke up in violence. The meeting itself was marked by "the shouting of obscenities, chanting, singing, and the chasing of one school board member." Although police were stationed in the auditorium during the meeting (a new practice), the session ended after the vote when a group of parents rushed the speaker's table, one Board member was pursued out the door, and another had to be escorted out by the police and school security officers.[33]

These two meetings were exceptional only in the level of interruption. School Board meetings regularly occasioned outbursts of passionate anger, interruption, and physical jostling. In no other arena of local politics were discontents so frequently and openly voiced; and in no other facet of public life were people's expectations for better lives so palpably felt. These discontents and expectations crystallized in demands for "community control." The disenchantment with bureaucratic centralization that this slogan and program emphasized was, for blacks, linked directly to the inability (or unwillingness) of the Central Board of Education to deliver on its civil-rights promises. These matters came to a head in 1966 when a new school, IS (Intermediate School) 201, opened in Harlem.

Shortly after a period of school boycotts and counterdemonstrations in the heyday of the civil-rights movement in 1963 and early 1964, State Commissioner of Education James Allen issued a report that took the Board of Education to task for its failure to achieve racial integration and that proposed to facilitate integration through a reorganization of the schools. The existing system of six years of elementary school, three of junior high school, and three of high school would be replaced by a system of four years of each. Little attempt would be made to integrate the four primary grades, which would be "in the neighborhood and as close as possible to the homes of the children." The new middle, or intermediate, schools would achieve much more integration, since their feeder lines would transcend neighborhoods. New high schools, combining vocational and academic streams, would be built in predominantly white neighborhoods, to insure their integrated character.[34] In 1965 the Board of Education

announced it would accept the Allen plan; it began the abolition of junior high schools in September of 1966. This new policy appeared to be the major tangible gain of nearly a decade of civil-rights activity in New York.

When it accepted the Allen plan, the Board of Education announced that IS 201 would be one of the city's first intermediate schools. Local Harlem activists pressed for guarantees that the school would be racially integrated; school officials refused to make precise commitments but did assert that the school's "proximity to the Triborough Bridge would make the school accessible to white students from Queens and the Bronx, who would be attracted to 201 by its superior educational program and outstanding facilities."[35] One result of these discussions, and of the climate of distrust they caused, was the formation of an ad hoc parent council, composed principally of black antipoverty workers from MEND (Massive Economic Neighborhood Development) in East Harlem in order to press the Board to keep its commitments.

The Board did not. In early 1966 the district superintendent announced that the school's population would be divided equally between black and Puerto Rican students and that there would be virtually no white enrollment whatsoever. The ad hoc parent council, in response, petitioned the Board to keep 201 closed "until such time as our community is satisfied that the education to be offered by the school meets the critical needs of our children." But that spring the ad hoc parent council changed its demand from integration to the transfer of authority from central school headquarters to local parents of school children. They proposed that 201 become an experimental school governed by a "School-Community Committee" with powers to hire and fire administrative staff, the principal included.[36]

In the very short run these demands failed, because IS 201 opened only one week behind schedule as a segregated school led by a white principal to whom the parents objected. Nevertheless, the IS 201 dispute had a profound impact on New York City school politics. It shifted the axis of school disputes from integration to community control. It mobilized new participants for school struggles—parents, union officials, and the mayor. The turmoil which followed is well known. The mayor appointed McGeorge Bundy to head an Advisory Panel on School Decentralization in New York City, which reported in favor of substantial decentralization of the school system in November of 1967. In

the interim, under the sponsorship of the Ford Foundation, experimental school districts with community boards of limited powers were established in the Lower East Side of Manhattan, in East Harlem, and in the Ocean Hill–Brownsville area of Brooklyn. An attempt by the Ocean Hill–Brownsville board to extend its powers by recommending the removal of thirteen teachers, five assistant principals, and one principal, and the bitter resistance of the United Federation of Teachers (UFT) to community control in general, and to the actions of this local board in particular, produced a citywide politicization of the schools, a remarkable level of interracial and ethnic animosity, a series of school strikes in the fall of 1968 that kept the schools shut for over two months, and, perhaps most important, threats to the social peace and the governability of the city that appeared at the time to unhinge decades-old arrangements of social control.[37]

The turmoil of school politics in the late 1960s in the city as a whole had important effects in northern Manhattan. In 1968 approximately half of District Six's elementary schools had school populations that were more than 60 percent white. All of these schools recorded reading scores above the national average. All were clustered in two sections of the district—northwest Washington Heights and Inwood. The remaining schools had populations with black and/or Hispanic majorities and with reading scores just at or below the national average.

During the 1968 strikes Leonard Strauss, president of the parents association of PS 187, a predominantly white school in West Washington Heights, organized a steering committee of representatives of all the parents associations in the district (which, at the time, extended south of Washington Heights–Inwood into northern Harlem). The initial purpose was to insure that parents of local school children, acting through their parents associations, would have a substantial say in the design of local school-board elections, should a decentralization law be passed. A central premise of the steering committee was that the parents of children actually enrolled in the schools compose the electorate and the membership of the school board. The committee, to this end, proposed that at least three-fourths of the board be composed of school parents and that employees of the Board of Education be ineligible to serve.[38]

The steering committee of 1968 was predominantly white, although some blacks and two Hispanics did participate. Many

black school activists, however, remained aloof. Five parents associations, all from Harlem schools, refused invitations to join the committee. Strauss's parents association played the leading organizational role. Although at this time the group was united on the position of parent control, it was internally divided as a result of the fall strikes. Strauss and most other white members had supported the striking UFT, while most nonwhite members had supported the efforts of District Superintendent Haas to keep the schools open.

The most significant impact of the strikes on the local schools, however, was the acceleration of white withdrawal. Of the fourteen schools in the district, seven had white majorities in 1968. Only three years later all had majorities that were either black or Hispanic, while only two had as many as four in ten whites among their pupils. After 1971 the white public-school population continued to decline far more rapidly than the school-age population; only the white population of PS 187 stabilized at approximately 40 percent. These demographic changes led many white school activists, including Strauss, to abandon the principle of parent control. They were then prepared to join with the UFT and the Catholic Church, which became involved intermittently in school elections, in order to secure control over the school board in the face of racial change.

To the demand for the community control of education, the most significant policy response in New York was the School Decentralization Act. After a period of prolonged negotiations, ably chronicled elsewhere,[39] the state legislature restructured New York City's school system in May 1969. The new act created an interim Board of Education empowered to divide the city into thirty to thirty-three school districts, to be governed in part by community school boards elected by proportional representation.

Although the resources that the act offered to residence communities were insufficient to realize the aspirations of the advocates of community control, they were sufficient to engage large numbers of school activists in a new, organized, predictable political arena at the district level. From the vantage point of the neighborhoods, the local boards were not insignificant. They were given the authority to hire teachers outside the city Board of Examiners' lists for schools in the bottom 45 percent of city performance, judged by comparative reading scores. They could hire nonprofessional staff and exert virtually complete control

over the selection of supervisory personnel. They would administer specially targeted federal funds. And they would hold regular open meetings that could provide local groups with the means to amass visible symbolic and solidary incentives to build and mobilize constituencies. In a universe of declining resources, the new school boards seemed to be worth fighting for. Nevertheless, the community boards were given only limited powers. Virtually all the budgeting authority remained with the central headquarters, as did the responsibility for school construction and maintenance. Personnel issues, crucially important to the UFT, including wage scales, work rules, work loads, promotions, and most hiring and firing, remained the subjects of negotiation between the central administration and the union. Moreover, the new Board of Education was directed to appoint a chancellor of the school system with the authority to suspend or remove a community board or any of its members who failed to comply with Board rules, regulations, or directives.

IV

The School Decentralization Act of 1969 made the entire voting citizenry the school-board electorate, in contrast to the earlier situation in which neighborhood school-board officials had been appointed rather than elected.[40] In northern Manhattan between 1970 and 1975 there were no fewer than four school-board elections. These contests pitted "old" and "new" Washington Heights–Inwood against each other. Elections were not fought about issues, but about which political bloc would control a school-board majority. The outcome of each election was the same: a majority for the white-ethnic bloc, this in spite of their composing a minority of both the school- and the voting-age populations. The reasons are not hard to find, however, because old northern Manhattan commanded a disproportionate share of economic, political, and organizational resources.

The first election after decentralization was scheduled for March 1970, only five weeks after district boundaries had been established (eventually the date was pushed back to May in order to allow more time for campaigning, but undoubtedly the date change added a new element of uncertainty in an already indeterminate situation). A complex system of proportional representation,[41] which few appeared to understand and which authorities

failed to explain with even a minimal degree of clarity, combined with an unfamiliar election date worked against widespread participation. Moreover, the inexperience of parents associations with electoral politics, their lack of ties to a nonschool electorate, the short time allowed for campaigning, and the unwillingness of locally elected officials to take sides in school issues gave a significant advantage to candidates with established union and church ties, and with access to resources generated beyond the district. Much as in primary campaigns with low turnouts, candidates with organizational links had a clear advantage. Furthermore, some of the most outspoken advocates of community control proposed a boycott of the elections.[42]

Throughout the city the May election returned local boards dominated by candidates supported by the Catholic Church and the UFT. The average voter turnout was 15 percent. Although the school system's population was over 60 percent black and Hispanic, only 15 percent of those elected were black and only 10 percent Hispanic (proportions close to, but under, their respective 21 percent and 12 percent of the city's population as a whole).[43]

The results in northern Manhattan generally followed the citywide pattern. Just over 12,000 voters went to the polls, about 13 percent of the eligible electorate. Voting was in large measure disciplined by slate. Following a directive of the New York Archdiocese, the parish councils of all the Catholic churches in the district endorsed a slate of three (Cashin, Ayala, and Halloran). The Church was particularly interested in the new boards because it anticipated that they would distribute federal ESEA Title I funds for schools serving disadvantaged populations. In fact, the Central Board retained authority over these funds, but the expectation that local boards would have a controlling voice led the Church to mount an intensive citywide effort to assure representation of its interests. Apparently misunderstanding the complicated electoral rules, the Church endorsed only three candidates, though up to nine could have been supported without fear of diluting the group's impact. Richard Cashin, an accountant, who had been a Republican candidate for the state assembly in 1966 and was active in the affairs of Good Shepherd parish, led all the candidates by a considerable margin. But even more impressive than his vote total was the internal vote discipline that the Church slate achieved. All were elected, as was John Fenwick, a young Irish lawyer who was an active member of the parish council of

St. Elizabeth.[44] The Catholic slate's campaign was almost entirely waged through Church channels—phone calls made through Church organizations, announcements from the pulpit, and literature sent home with children attending the area's parish schools. Cashin appeared at only two of the public candidate forums held at each of the public schools; he stopped going because of the hostility directed at him as the representative of the Church and its schools.[45]

Four of the other elected candidates (Strauss, Rabbi Abraham Pinter, of a large orthodox congregation, Franklin Nieves, an aide to the area's Democratic congressman, and Joseph Bailey, a black politician with support from a local Democratic club) were endorsed by the UFT. The last successful candidate, David Goodman, like Strauss and Pinter, was backed by a variety of local synagogues and secular organizations. Of those elected, only Strauss had also run with the support of a local parents association. No candidate running wholly as an independent, attempting to mobilize friends and neighbors without organizational support, was elected. Reflecting the more developed organizational life of northern Manhattan, 65 percent of the vote came from the area north of 181st Street.

With the election of the first Board, northern Manhattan school politics turned inward. School struggles became struggles over the limited pie available in the district, and about the relationship between Board members and parents-association activists. At first, the uncertain character of Board politics—there were no inherited roles and cues to guide members' behavior—and the independent role of the Church-supported members (who quickly discovered that the stakes they were elected to fight for did not exist) combined to produce Board politics with much heat, but little direction.

The nine-person Board constituted a group with shifting coalitions. The most cohesive voting unit proved to be the three members from the Jewish West Washington Heights neighborhood of Fort Tryon, two of whom had been elected with UFT support. In the aftermath of the school strikes of 1968, they saw the defense of the merit civil-service system, which had served Jewish teachers well, as their most pressing task. A corollary interest they shared was an attempt to maintain their neighborhood's public schools, especially PS 187, as attractive magnets to discourage the dispersion of the local Jewish community to the

suburbs. The UFT group, with which the Fort Tryon group interlocked, divided often on ethnic and racial grounds. Bailey and Nieves frequently voted against Strauss, Goodman, and Pinter on issues of appointments and contracts for services. The Church slate quickly lost its initial rationale for existence, since the Church as a corporate body lost interest in school affairs when it became apparent that the Board had no authority over Title I funds. The level of commitment of the individuals endorsed by the Church (as well as the commitment of Fenwick) declined accordingly. But at critical moments, such as the vote to select a district superintendent, the Church group joined with coreligionist Hispanic parents to support a man opposed by the Fort Tryon group.

Throughout the period 1970–1972 Board meetings were heated affairs. Expressions of anger often had little to do with the formal agenda. The Board existed; it was a public authority; and it provided a forum. Meetings rambled from topic to topic; shouting and interruptions were common. Ethnic slurs became part of the routine discourse. Black and Hispanic school organizers, active in parents associations, poverty corporations, and tenant groups, frequently led ad hoc demonstrations in the middle of public sessions. Long, rambling speeches were common. In July 1970 a Mrs. Lopez demanded "equal representation for all minorities" and a larger role in the local poverty corporation. At other meetings, parents from the local high school (which fell outside the Board's authority) used Board meetings to denounce the UFT's opposition to their plan to establish a parent-complaint table in the school, and to complain about the local UFT representative. Board members often came under personal attack for their alleged racism, Uncle Tomism, and absenteeism. In the fall of 1971 parents from a school half black and half white disrupted a meeting in order to demand approval of their association's plans to appoint two school principals, one white and one black. When the Board refused to accept their proposal on the grounds of questionable feasibility and legality, parents from the school would not allow any other items to be discussed, and the meeting collapsed. In an attempt to keep control over meetings, the Board adopted ever more complicated rules to channel public expression. Participants wishing to discuss specific agenda items had to sign up to do so before any discussion of that item had begun; many quickly learned to sign up for the discussion of every agenda item even before the meetings began.[46] The Board's adherence to strict

parliamentary procedures became more rigid as time went on. Proceedings took on an increasingly tendentious character. Unsatisfactory as the meetings were, however, the important fact is that they were held and that people and groups with grievances came to them, not elsewhere. Public attendance, while not always high, was usually over a hundred, and for important meetings, like the one to choose the district superintendent, was over four hundred.

In this period of the first elected Board, there were three main foci of activity: the complaints and protests about overcrowding; the competition for very limited funds to be allocated locally; and the selection of supervisory personnel.

The Board and the public shared the view that the schools were overcrowded (it was hard not to). At the Board's second public meeting, in July 1970, Joseph Bailey opened the agenda item on the capital budget for 1971–1972 by stating, "We are here tonight to listen to parents and interested public tell us what their views are on conditions within specific schools. The district is terribly overcrowded, and as long as it is overcrowded and the children are being shortchanged we are going to be pushing hard for the new PS 172." He added, however, that outside of a maintenance budget, only $65,000 of capital monies were available. Representatives of almost every district school then stood up to tell the Board of the deplorable conditions in their schools. "Unhealthy, dingy, sham, fraud, disgrace" were recurring terms. The discussion did not stay at this expressive level alone, but quickly took on competitive tones: black parents saw their schools as being shortchanged; the minutes record that "the Spanish speaking contingent arose saying their race had been disgraced; they were walking out," and as they did so they voiced complaints over the absence of a bilingual school. Parents from near-majority white schools also voiced complaints about conditions, and some said that whites were losing out as more and more funds were going to minorities. In short, the collective problem of overcrowding came to be defined as a problem of the inequitable allocation of resources *within* the district, a perspective that received some credence when it became clear that PS 187 was the only under-utilized school in the area.[47]

The one notable success the Board had in this area came in the winter of 1971. For a number of years local educators had attempted without success to secure a replacement school for PS

186, a dilapidated, unsafe, depressing facility in South Washington Heights that served a majority black population. The new school had been placed in the city's capital budget year in and year out, but had always been eliminated at some stage of the budget process. To prevent a recurrence of this, the parents associations of the entire district sponsored a boycott of their schools in 1971. After the boycott had begun, the Board belatedly endorsed the tactic, and the district's schools were closed for several days. As a result, the replacement school was put in the final capital budget, and it has since been constructed. It is striking that this singular success in Board-community cooperation was possible when the chief adversaries were *outside* the district.

The second major cluster of issues before the Board concerned the allocation of relatively small amounts of money. Although the district employed approximately fifteen hundred people and had an annual budget of over $23 million, the Board controlled the expenditure of only about $580,000 in discretionary program funds each year (about $40 per pupil). Competition for these monies was fierce, nevertheless, since from the perspective of any single school they seemed quite large, and, in any event, they potentially provided the only available opportunity for undertaking innovations in school programming. Special reading and guidance programs, theater and arts presentations, and extra staffing were understandably coveted by each parents association. Initially the Board decided to use $205,000 of state urban aid funds to assist schools not eligible for federal Title I money. The schools that could have benefitted most all served the more affluent neighborhoods in the north of the district. At meeting after meeting, parents from the southern half of the community insisted that the money be reallocated to the schools with the greatest demonstrated need (measured by reading scores). Finally, after much acrimony, $50,000 was reallocated to schools eligible for Title I.[48] The outcome nevertheless left a residue of considerable suspicion and bitterness toward the Board, which was unable to make its case stick for some measure of equity across the district in the distribution of discretionary funds. Most important, one observer has noted, the dispute revealed "the preoccupation of both the Board and the public with the relatively small stakes when substantive issues arise. This reflects the impotence of the Board and of the district, at least in the short term, in dealing with large budgetary items, which are controlled

almost entirely by the Central Board of Education."[49] Indeed, much of the acrimony surrounding local board decisions was the result of the assumption by many school activists that the Board had more budgetary discretion than it actually did.

The third major area of Board activity and controversy concerned the appointment of school and district supervisors. In this period, by contrast to what was to come, the selection of school principals proved a relatively pacific task. The job was delegated to each school's parents association, which had its choice ratified by the Board, usually by unanimous vote. The appointment of a district superintendent, however, proved a much thornier issue; one, in fact, that made an already ineffectual Board incapable of exercising even the limited powers it had.

The appointment of a district superintendent was the most important decision local school boards across the city had to take. The Board was composed of unsalaried, part-time, lay members who set and ratified policy and appointments. The District Office was staffed by full-time, salaried individuals who carried out policy, made recommendations, and found personnel for appointments. The District Office, and its superintendent, was the most valuable resource provided by the Decentralization Act of 1969. Moreover, as Michael Krasner has stressed in his comparative study of two community school boards, the superintendent was usually a focus of intergroup competition, especially because the ways in which he used his resources affected the ability of different parent groups to contest successfully for school-board office.[50]

In June 1971 the Board divided five to four in favor of reappointing Erwin Haas community superintendent. During his period as acting superintendent, Haas and the Fort Tryon group had become adversaries. Haas, it will be recalled, had attempted to keep the district's schools open during the 1968 strikes; henceforth he was identified as sympathetic to the aspirations of black and Hispanic parents. Puerto Rican, Cuban, and Dominican activists—internally divided though they were—were unanimous in praise of Haas, on the grounds that he had been sympathetic and responsive to their constituents. More concretely, they cited his support for bilingual education. Indeed, the local school system had become the major source of public employment for Hispanic leaders, social workers, and nonprofessional teacher aides.[51]

For Strauss and his closest Board allies, this behavior appeared

scandalous, since it violated the canons of the civil-service merit system. Strauss claims he opposed Haas because Haas was a poor administrator who gave in to "illicit political pressures" and who appointed incompetents as a result of a policy of "catering to" Hispanic pressure groups.[52] His preferred candidate was Paul Treatman, a Brooklyn school principal, a UFT supporter, and a civil-service enthusiast.

The divisions that had characterized the period of school strikes in 1968 were re-created on a small scale during the period when the Board was reviewing candidates for the position. At the meeting immediately preceding Haas's election, a local group of parents led a demonstration on his behalf. The minutes record that when the second item on the agenda, funding of programs for the fall, was introduced,

Mrs. Bajador at this time stated that the Board was "getting rid of Dr. Haas." She stated that there was no community representation on the panel. Miss Morris stated the Screening Panel in the district, operating under Professor Strauss, was operating in a very underhanded way. She stated there were people up for superintendent of whom the community knew nothing about. Their credentials were Prof. Strauss' personal choices. She added that the screening panel was supposed to be made up of Parents Association and Community groups, and there were no community groups represented. . . . At this point signs being carried by members of the audience went up. Some read "Haas is the Community's Choice"; "Hamilton Grange supports Dr. Haas"; "Haas Stays"; "Permanent Status for Haas Now."[53]

When Haas was elected (with the support of the Church representatives and half of the UFT slate), the decision was greeted with jubilation by the people in the audience, who erupted in a demonstration and carried Haas around the auditorium on their shoulders.

From this point until the next Board elections, the Board not only remained sharply divided, but underwent a decline in the commitment of individual members. By forcing latent cleavages into the open, the Haas appointment destroyed the relative calm that had prevailed on the Board. Not surprisingly, Board membership came to seem increasingly unalluring. The Fort Tryon faction, after its defeat, all but withdrew from Board affairs. Pinter rarely attended meetings, and Goodman shortly resigned. Of the Church members, Fenwick and then Halloran (who moved out of the area) also resigned. By early 1972 four of the nine

members of northern Manhattan's Board had left, and other members participated in its affairs only sporadically. The Board was now faced with the need to fill vacancies. Yet no rules existed to guide its deliberations. The 1969 act had made no provisions for such a situation, and in district after district those with minority representation sought to fill the vacancies in ways that would alter the character of their Board.

In Washington Heights–Inwood, after Halloran resigned in 1971, the audience at public meetings insisted for months to follow that no business could be conducted unless the vacancy was filled. By this time, meetings were routinely surrendered to the floor—motions were made by speakers from the audience, the agenda was usually discarded, and Board members were reduced to playing passive roles. Finally, after a six-month period of agitation and acrimony, the Board solicited resumes from interested candidates. Ten applied, including two leaders of predominantly black parents associations. Their applications were rejected (thus further exacerbating the district's racial and territorial divisions) in favor of a white applicant without visible public support who was later found legally ineligible to serve because he resided outside the district.

No sooner had the immediate problem of filling one vacancy been solved than Goodman, Fenwick, and Bailey resigned. In February 1972 a group of parents association leaders joined with Dr. Thomas Matthews of NEGRO to take control of the Board meeting and then nominate and seat a "People's Community School Board" to dramatize the issue of representativeness. As a protest action, the people's board had considerable success; its meetings were much better attended than those of the elected Board had been in the past. Complaints against the Board, in fact, had become so vociferous that it ceased holding public meetings.

The main activity of the people's board was the filing of a complaint with the Board of Education against the local Board's failure to fill its seats. Although the hearing officer rejected most of the charges, he did urge the Board to fill the vacancies as quickly as possible. Since only the Board had the legal authority to appoint new members during its term, plans to hold an advisory election were made. This election proved to be the turning point in the history of district school politics, because it created a clear majority, independent of the Church, for the Strauss faction.

The Board announced in early September of 1972 that the advisory election would be held on October 24. Three organized groups mounted slates and campaigns: the UFT, the president's council of the parents association of District Six, and El Concilio, a coalition of Hispanic groups. All four places were won by the UFT slate.

The UFT selected candidates with close and dependable organizational ties. Two of the members of their slate (chosen by a vote of the union's chapter chairmen from each district school), Mary Saunders, a black, and Ernst Lilienstein, were school teachers in other districts, and union members. Ramon Pedraza, a Cuban immigrant, was the president of a large local of the International Ladies Garment Workers Union (ILGWU) in New Jersey. His union connections, his lack of any alternate neighborhood constituency, and his ethnic background made him an appealing choice for the UFT. Their slate's final candidate was Gideon Chern, an electrical engineer who directed his own consulting firm and who had been recruited by Leonard Strauss, a close personal friend.

The UFT campaign relied mostly on advertisements in the *Daily News,* editorials and stories in the union paper, word of mouth, and one-on-one direct mailing. The UFT did no canvassing or street soliciting. Union statements characterized their main opponents as a "take-over group," which had tried in 1968 to keep the district's schools open. In addition, the UFT slate had two main community-based resources. Local synagogues and Jewish organizations ran their own slate, which with the exception of a West Washington Heights resident (Ezra Fleishman) was identical to the UFT slate. Moreover, the UFT commanded the resources of many local administrators and employees at the district office. The Church played no role in this election, a withdrawal that left the UFT as the dominant organization, directing its appeals to the white Inwood residents, and that left the parents slate without the resources of the Hispanic parishes.

The parents-association slate consisted of two black candidates (Ramona Morris and Eric Illidge, both employees of the local poverty corporation), and two Hispanic candidates (Rudi Garcia, a reporter for the *Daily News,* and Helen Torres, president of her parents association). This time, as opposed to 1970, when only the Church and the UFT had mounted effective campaigns, the parents slate did challenge the UFT with a strong effort. Under

the direction of Ellen Lurie, a long-time white activist in the community-control movement, the president's council set up a campaign committee, and each candidate was asked to find a manager. Canvassing and pull lists were compiled and used. Candidates held press conferences covered by community media. An aggressive street campaign was mounted, making extensive use of leaflets. And, most important, local politicians with considerable black and Hispanic constituencies did not stay aloof. Rather, most political leaders with any visibility endorsed the parents slate, and the leaders of the Tioga Club, a Democratic organization in the southern half of Washington Heights, provided considerable resources, including good advice and facilities.

The third slate was exclusively Hispanic, organized principally by Ben Garcia, who had been employed since 1970 as assistant coordinator for the state urban-aid program in the district office. When Rudi Garcia of the parents slate turned down the backing of El Concilio, the group joined in the UFT selection of Pedraza. Although El Concilio's campaign was the weakest of the three slates, its limited success in mobilizing votes in the home school areas of its candidates allowed it to play a spoiler role in the election. Pedraza's vote total led all others, and if the Consilio votes had been added to the parents slate, it would have elected at least two of its members, and possibly all four.

Very few people voted; just under five thousand turned out, about 6 percent of the electorate. In spite of the UFT's appeal to the memory of 1968, on the whole the campaign was not organized around issues. Rather, the kind of friends-and-neighbors political style characteristic of the one-party South and of poverty elections predominated.[54] In an electoral contest for an office whose powers were not clear, and which was relatively obscure, an intense localism triumphed. Leaders could mobilize their existing followers, and those who mobilized best won. Especially notable once again was the uneven distribution of the vote. Although voters north of 181st Street furnished 40 percent of the public school children in the district, they provided 55 percent of the votes.

Neighborhood voting cohesion, among those who voted, was very high. The schools were the polling places. Every school returned a clear majority of its votes for one of the three slates, and in only three of the eleven cases did the winning slate garner less than 60 percent of the votes cast. Even more impressive, especially given the existence of Hispanic candidates on each

slate, was the result that in eight of the eleven schools, each of the four nominees on the locally dominant slate was named individually on more than 50 percent of the ballots. Voting cohesion by slate was low only in schools located in heterogeneous neighborhoods serving an integrated student body.

Residents of West Washington Heights (tract 273) voted at PS 187. This predominantly Jewish neighborhood had the highest and most disciplined turnout. Although PS 187 had by far the lowest number of pupils of any school, and although the neighborhood had the lowest percentage of its population in elementary school of the four tracts, 70 percent more voters turned out than at any single school. Here neighborhood solidarity was truly extraordinary. Fully 73 percent of the voters named all four of the UFT candidates, while 90 percent named three of the four. The union slate by itself accounted for 88 percent of all votes cast at the school, a figure that would have been even higher had the synagogues endorsed all the union candidates. Inwood residents of census tract 295 voted at PS 98. In 1970, and again in 1973, when the Catholic Church supported candidates explicitly opposed to the UFT, Church candidates in this area won by wide margins. Without Church participation, however, this neighborhood returned a majority of 68 percent for the UFT. The parents slate, by contrast, did extremely well in census tract 239, where over 95 percent of the population was black. There, at PS 28, the parents received 81 percent of the votes cast. Finally, in overwhelmingly Hispanic tract 261 the Concilio slate carried PS 115 with 57 percent of the vote.

After the 1972 election the District Board had a stable majority, since Strauss and Pinter were joined by four new supporters. Now that the Board was controlled by one group of northern Manhattan's population, it was free to act as it wished. This change was most noticeable in the conduct of public meetings. During the weeks immediately following the seating of the new members, when few matters of controversy were on the agenda, and, later, when the sharp conflicts between the public and the Board developed, the majority came to meetings with well-thought-out, clear positions on the issues at hand. As had not been the case in the period before the 1972 election, the Board was no longer reluctant and defensive. Questions for consideration were now clearly initiated by the Board. Agenda items in the winter of 1972–73 were announced, discussed, explained, and acted on.

With Strauss in the chair, supported by a steady majority, the Board could now focus on the routine items it had under its jurisdiction. In this period, too, the Board moved decisively, in advance of the 1973 elections, to consolidate its authority in three ways:

First, the Board established a rigid formula for the distribution of state and federal funds among the schools of the district, thus depoliticizing one of the most important sources of conflict that had confronted the pre-1972 Board.

Second, the council of presidents of the parents associations was formally dissolved and removed from its offices in district headquarters. Its successor was a committee of presidents, limited in membership to current leaders of parents associations, and greatly restricted in its role. In this way, the Board eliminated a major political resource of black and Hispanic organizers. The presidents council had in the past obtained much of its strength from the participation of previous association officers, and from the use of outside consultants, such as Ellen Lurie.

Third, and most important, the Board moved to take close control over the staff and leadership of the District Office. A new community coordinator (a public-relations post), a new drug-program coordinator, and a new coordinator of bilingual programs were appointed. Several weeks after the election, Superintendent Haas resigned. For some time the Fort Tryon members of the Board had been dealing directly with school principals and district staff, ignoring Haas. Now that the Board had a majority hostile to Haas, his position was untenable. Just as the appointment of Haas had been the most important single act of the original Board, so his resignation and the appointment of a successor were the most critical events during the period that preceded the 1973 elections. The dispatch with which the Board acted, and the relative ease with which it handled criticisms of its procedures, highlighted the significant difference a clear majority made.

The impending election of an entirely new Board created an awkward situation. Board members repeatedly stated that it would be improper to saddle an incoming Board with a superintendent not of their choosing. They stated publicly that the appointment would be an interim one, good only until the following September, when the new elected Board could make its selection. The first choice of the parents associations was the superintendent of

schools of Bridgeport, Connecticut, but he withdrew his name from consideration, not wishing to accept a temporary post. The Board instead offered a contract to Paul Treatman, Strauss's candidate in 1971. In spite of its public position, the Board hired Treatman for a full three-year term, a move that produced renewed bitterness between the Board and many parents groups. But whereas in the past the angry adversaries of the school authorities had placed their hopes for redress in the protest tactics of demonstration and boycott, in 1973 they mobilized instead to fight an electoral campaign whose outcome ratified the existing balance of political power between the two political blocs of the community.

With two successful elections behind them, the UFT–Fort Tryon group felt itself firmly in control as the regularly scheduled 1973 elections approached. Its electoral tactics were designed to keep it in firm control of the Board, rather than to broaden the base of the political majority. With the exception of Nieves, who had become a political adversary of the Fort Tryon–UFT group, all those on the Board who had previously been endorsed by the union were renominated. To take Nieves's place, Rabbi Pinter recruited another Fort Tryon resident, Hadassah Hersh, who taught in the public schools in another district. The UFT thus entered the election with a ticket of seven nominees (for nine places), five of whom were teachers and union members, and five of whom were residents of the Fort Tryon area.

The managers of the parents associations, by contrast, sought to widen their base by uniting all the dissident forces in the community. The overriding need, in their view, was to secure the cooperation of the Concilio leaders and to present a single slate that could mobilize supporters in all parts of northern Manhattan, except for Fort Tryon. Ellen Lurie and her associates encountered many problems in putting such a slate together. Slate-making discussions were heated affairs between black and Hispanic competitors. Many black leaders who had dominated the 1972 parents' campaign felt very strongly that the long residence of blacks in the community, their leadership in local protest movements, and their history of oppression in the larger society entitled them to the dominant role in electing candidates and in determining the policies of the coalition. The Dominican, Cuban, and Puerto Rican representatives were at least equally adamant. In spite of their poor showing in October, they argued that they

held the balance of power in the district. In the end, the coalition slated three blacks, four Hispanics, one Irishman, and one Jew. Two of the black candidates, Morris and Illidge, had run in 1972; the third, Gwen Crenshaw, directed a day-care center and was married to a member of a local reform Democratic political club. Two Puerto Ricans were slated: Nieves, the incumbent who had been elected with UFT support in 1970, and Juana Lopez, director of the Puerto Rican Guidance Center and a member of the local Community Planning Board who had been an outspoken opponent of the School Board at many of its public meetings. The remaining Hispanic candidates were David Caro, a Cuban who had run on the Concilio slate in 1972, and Victor Espinoza, a Dominican engineer. The white candidates were Tom Marino, an Irish Catholic from Inwood who had led two parents associations effectively, and Jack Mannheim, a refugee from Nazi Germany, who had been outspoken in his criticism of Strauss.

The coalition slate, in sum, represented a subtle balance of the dissident groups in the district. Blacks won more places on the ticket than their numbers in the population warranted, yet not as many as their superior organizational strength would have permitted. Otherwise than in 1972, the parents this time had white candidates, but the largest number was Hispanic, reflecting the majority status of Hispanics in the public schools.

The results were close. The UFT won five of the nine seats, with 53 percent of the vote on the first ballot being cast for members of its slate; the parents' coalition captured the other four seats. As in 1972, a plural-society pattern of electoral appeals and voting prevailed; the difference was the greater breadth of the parents' slate and a renewed role for the Church, which endorsed the coalition, whose candidates composed a Catholic majority. As in 1972, there was little discussion of specific issues and little attempt at debate between candidates. As in 1972, campaign efforts paralleled and supplemented, rather than supplanted, existing social and organizational networks. Among the organizationally rich white groups, independent campaign organizations were superfluous; among blacks, they reinforced existing protest and party organizations; and among Hispanics, they were virtually useless, having little upon which to build.

After the 1973 election, the Board, though elected by a narrower margin, was controlled unambiguously by the "old" bloc, which moved assertively to govern in its own interest and to use the

rhetoric of community and local control to legitimate its activities in conflicts with the central school administration. Two issues dominated the Board's agenda between the latter half of 1973 and early 1975: the addition of grades seven and eight to PS 187 and an attempt to purchase the Academy of the Sacred Heart in Inwood for conversion to a public elementary school. In both cases, the Board majority acted against strong local opposition to preserve the racial mix and academic standing of the district's one remaining school with a large white population.

PS 187 was the least-overcrowded, best-integrated, and academically most successful school in Washington Heights–Inwood. Instead of opening up its underutilized space to other children outside of the school's regular feeder pattern, the Board voted, with the customary five-to-four division, to allow sixth-grade children to continue through the eighth grade rather than attend a mainly Hispanic junior high school. The School Board meeting of 21 March 1974 captured the strong feelings on both sides of this question. At issue for the parents of 187 was the maintenance of a very good public school. The president of the parents association of 187, the minutes record,

invited the community to visit 187 to see what education of children really is. This past week they had the privilege of being host to various members of the media. They had television reporters, newspaper reporters, all kinds of reporters visiting the school. They walked into this school and were amazed at the integration, at the economic integration, at the decorum, at the learning and at the pleased faces of the children and the teachers. It was a good school. It was the kind of school they remembered going to. This is the kind of school the parents of 187 wish for every child in the district. If they don't have this in their school, they should get what the parents of 187 have.[55]

From the perspective of parents with children at other schools, 187 was being given special privileges in order to keep its children isolated from theirs.

Mrs. Omura stated that PS 28 is overcrowded to 140 per cent capacity and asked why PS 187 did not come to the community and tell them of their space and give overcrowded schools the option of sending their children to PS 187. She stated it was pure racism. . . . Mrs. Crenshaw stated she would address the speaker and said the reason why 187 comes under attack is because of this attitude to other people in the district. They want the same things for their children. If they have to fight to get it they will. They don't have a personal lawyer as they do in 187.

They don't have the chairman of the board and another member to go downtown. They are working mothers and don't have maids or baby-sitters.[56]

The decision to expand 187 to eight grades had more than one irony. Although, in effect, the District Board had implemented the old Allen plan, and although racial integration was thus maintained for a longer period, the Central Board of Education disallowed the expansion. As a result, the District Board majority was brought into conflict with downtown, when it sought to institute the four-four system at 187. It thus asserted that what was at stake, in Strauss's terms, "basically was a problem of decentralization and the question of who runs the various districts, the Community School Board or the Central Board."[57] By contrast, the black and Hispanic School Board members, who had long advocated community control, fought the PS 187 expansion on the grounds that it illegally violated Central Board directives.

In October 1973 Board members were summoned to Central Board headquarters, but they did not attend. Four months later the school chancellor threatened to cut off funds from the district unless it complied by March 15. The order was defied; some two hundred pickets surrounded the school on the fifteenth in support of its extended organization. The District School Board voted again to resist the Central Board at a stormy public meeting in late March. On the last day of school in June, representatives of the chancellor arrived at the school in order to remove the records of sixth- and seventh-grade students. A parents' picket line prevented their entry. In July the chancellor offered to negotiate in order to avoid further confrontations in September. Three days before school began in September, an agreement was reached that allowed seventh and eighth graders to stay in the school, but the grades would administratively be considered part of a nearby junior high school, and would be under its principal's administrative direction.

Throughout this period, PS 187 was the only underutilized school in the district. At virtually every monthly School Board meeting, parents associations from the other schools demanded that their children have access to 187's empty places. These demands grew more insistent during the period of visible confrontation between the District Board and the chancellor. In September 1973 the Board voted to consider the purchase of Sacred Heart, which was closing for want of pupils and funds, for

use as an intermediate school. Opposition developed quickly. Predominantly Irish residents of the eastern part of Inwood, where the school was located, formed Residents Involved in Neighborhood Growth (RING) to fight the plan. Though the schools their children attended were slightly overcrowded, they feared that the conversion of Sacred Heart would create empty places in Inwood schools, with the consequence that black and Hispanic children would be bused in. At the Board meeting of November 15, their spokesman stated that RING's members

wanted to control their neighborhood. The public school system is inaccessible to the average person when the neighborhood loses control. They are afraid of a massive influx of people from outside who will disrupt the calm of this neighborhood. The fears are real. The area around Junior High School 52 has deteriorated. We do not want another area to go down like this, businesswise and communitywise.[58]

Parents from the southern part of the district, black and Hispanic, also argued against the acquisition of the school. They contended that their schools were the most overcrowded, yet the Board was prepared to spend money in a chiefly white area in the north. Gwen Crenshaw, a black Board member, spoke for this position. Parents, she argued, should have the option to have their children travel to underutilized schools

or to keep them close to home. But there can be no option if you have no junior high schools and intermediate schools in the lower end of the district. Certainly parents have the right to have schools in the lower end of the district if they so choose. This does not mean that their children do not belong anywhere. In addition, why must their children always travel? If the schools are located in a certain part of the district then there is a possibility that somebody else in the other end can travel to a point that is convenient to all the schools in the district. Their children always do the traveling.[59]

Only the Fort Tryon representatives supported the acquisition, which allowed for some relief of overcrowding without adding children to PS 187. The Board approved the purchase by a vote of five to four, the UFT–Fort Tryon group voting affirmatively.

Because this question involved not only education but also land use, RING was able to take up its opposition in another forum, the Community Planning Board. Here Inwood was better represented; the Fort Tryon area alone could not control policy. Indeed, at the February 1974 meeting to review the School

Board's decision, only the two Fort Tryon members voted to buy Sacred Heart; the other seventeen present voted against. Later in the year the school was sold to the Seventh Day Adventist Church.

The 1973 election for Board membership had carried a two-year term. In 1975 the parents-community slate endorsed fourteen candidates for the nine seats, a number that reflected their difficulty in agreeing on a ticket acceptable to all coalition members, and the hope that a larger number of contestants would make possible a more intensive friends-and-neighbors campaign. The parents-teachers coalition, endorsed by the UFT and the parents association of PS 187, continued the tradition of nominating union members who come predominantly from the Fort Tryon section of Washington Heights. The campaign was marked by even lower public participation at candidates' forums than had been the case in the past, and voting turnout in northern Manhattan, as in the city as a whole, declined. As in 1973, the vote was closely divided between the slates, and the five-to-four Board split held. Strauss and Pinter, the candidates most closely associated with the Fort Tryon area, again garnered the highest vote totals. As in 1972 and 1973, the campaign and the results followed the familiar pattern of territorial, ethnic, and personal loyalties, and the outcome produced a Board that sharply over-represented one segment of the community. As a result, school politics after 1975 continued along the lines of divisions that dated back to the earliest community-control disputes.

V

The resistance by blacks to their urban condition in the 1960s was reminiscent of aspects of plebeian culture in eighteenth-century England, "in its experiential ground, . . . in its picaresque flouting of the provident bourgeois virtues, in its ready resource to disorder, and in its ironic attitudes towards the Law."[60] Like the eighteenth-century English crowd, too, the black social movements of the 1960s did not see or fight their battles as ones of "class." The fissures of society were not comprehended in terms of the antinomy of capital and labor. In neither case was this understanding of class culturally or intellectually possible. In England it was impossible because the modern usage of class had not yet been developed. In the United States the very pattern of

city trenches that was under siege by the black urban revolt had provided an inheritance that made it very difficult to incorporate class into everyday thought and action outside of the workplace. Yet in both cases the targets of revolt were, ultimately, structured patterns of class relations that affected the dominated groups adversely. The plebeian crowd of the eighteenth century found itself arrayed against the gentry. The urban crowd of the 1960s experienced and was disadvantaged by the uneven investment patterns of capital. In both cases E. P. Thompson's phrase "class struggle without class"[61] seems apt. The source of power of the assault on the trenches was this "class struggle," and its demise was caused principally by the vulnerability of social movements "without class."

At issue was the attempt to take the radical impulse away from the politics of race by the creation of mechanisms of participation at the community level that had the capability to limit conflicts to a community orientation, to separate issues from each other, and to stress a politics of distribution—in short, to reduce race to ethnicity in the traditional community-bounded sense. The new institutions of decentralized schools, neighborhood government, local planning, and the like were developed to perform the functions for blacks and their political blocs that party machines had performed for white ethnics.

The starting point for an assessment of this process is the two-edged meaning of the term "black community." On the one hand, as we have noted at length, conflicts between blacks living in a specific residential community and local government or other groups were understood almost automatically as being not just about their interests in this or that place. Yet the territorial dimensions of demands for community control, the focus of the black bloc on the linkages between government and the residence community, the inability of the period's ideology of black nationalism to address fundamental questions of political economy on a macroanalytic scale directly, and, above all, the resilience of the political culture of the traditional urban system and its close resemblance to the ethos of black protest made it very hard for blacks to get a confirming response to the global features of their insurgency from the larger society, and tended to dissolve the nationalist thrust under the impact of the mimetic policy responses of local government. The racial challenge was transformed into an ethnic politics of a traditional kind even as the activities of city

governments allowed militant nationalist black leaders to claim substantial victories.

"We are all decentralists now," Irving Kristol conceded in 1968. The broad appeal of decentralizing reforms should hardly have been surprising. For the authorities, decentralization held out the possibility of renewed contacts between citizens and the state that could be used to integrate the polity. Decentralization in these terms represented intervention on behalf of the traditional urban system. To the people, and especially to blacks, urban decentralization appeared to promise not only more efficient government, but government that they would be able to control. "What some social scientists only dimly sensed quickly became a reality: that for the indigenous leaders of the poor, particularly the militant blacks, the movement for 'participation' became a drive for 'power,' "[62] a thrust that implied that others would be displaced from their position of power.

These antagonistic bases of support for programs of decentralization found expression in academic treatments of the subject. Milton Kotler argued too simply that the history of American cities is a history of the imperial domination of neighborhoods by "downtown" interests. As cities expanded by incorporating surrounding autonomous communities, new centralized loci of power eroded traditional municipal liberties. In his view, American cities became "foundering empires," no longer in control of the neighborhoods they annexed. This crisis of social control should be resolved by radical decentralization. Territorial liberties would "be vested in the neighborhoods, which will federate in a common city government." In this vision the neighborhood is seen as "the source of revolutionary power, and local liberty as its modest cause."[63]

A sharply contrasting academic view, that of Alan Altshuler, captured the potentially conservative possibilities of decentralizing reforms. "The central issues," he wrote, "are social peace and political legitimacy. . . . The critical issue is what it will take to persuade blacks that the system is fair."[64] To this end he endorsed "plausible" versions of community control. In a personal postscript to his monograph on the subject he explained why:

I address myself to fellow whites who believe this nation's highest priority must be to achieve a peace of reconciliation. The question for us is more than one of peace: it is one of legitimacy. It is first: how can we sustain the interest of blacks in peaceful compromise—in sharing

laws, institutions, even a common nationality with the white majority? And it is second: how can we pursue this aim effectively within the American political system?[65]

Needed, he proposed, were "sources of liaison with the smoldering ghettos" that could replace "violent disorder with non-violent political protest activity" and "establish a form of government that is widely perceived as legitimate in the ghettos."[66]

Of all the demands blacks were making in the 1960s, including massive income redistribution, better jobs, and access to positions of economic and political power, Altshuler suggested that "participatory reform . . . for all the obstacles to it, is probably the most feasible," since most whites "really have no stake in who governs the ghettos."[67] In his view, decentralizing concessions by city elites would be *substitutes* for other substantive changes, rather than means to redistributive ends. In making this proposal, which, we have seen, echoed much of the thinking of the Lindsay administration in New York, Altshuler perceived that carefully implemented decentralization could shatter the global challenge that race presented to the urban system and restore the territorial boundaries of regular urban conflict:

Perhaps its most important positive potential, from the standpoint of citywide elected officials, would be to divert much of the force of community dissatisfaction from them to neighborhood leaders. There would still be pressure on the citywide leaders to find resources for the decentralized functions, but they would be far less vulnerable than currently to blame for day-to-day operations. . . . It would provide an arena in which blacks might engage their energies and experience power. . . . It would provide a focus for black political organization. . . . But most important, it would give blacks a tangible stake in the American political system. By giving them systems they considered their own, it would—hopefully—enhance the legitimacy of the whole system in their eyes.[68]

In northern Manhattan the Neighborhood Action Program and the District School Board were new set institutions that refocused neighborhood politics in traditional directions. They did so by appearing to be responsive to the period's demands for community control. But their activity, at a moment of social and political crisis, not only absorbed the energies of insurgents, it also transformed their protests and rendered them harmless. These institutions did so by reconnecting the disaffected to political life

and in this way making them part of the regular, legitimate, and
predictable political process. And they did so by fragmenting
issues into community-sized components, thus separating community from community, and one set of concerns, such as
education, from each of the other policy areas. Once activists
joined in this new version of the old game of city trenches, they
lost their ability to challenge the urban system and, in time, their
capacity to lead popular constituencies. The uncertainties of the
"moment of madness" yielded to the cautious politics of austerity
and cutbacks.

Of course, the tale of institutional innovation in the late 1960s
and of the relationship between community control and decentralization is hardly the entire story of the resolution of the urban
crisis. Police forces were substantially strengthened by adding
officers and equipment. Riot commissions helped quiet the racial
turmoil.[69] Spending by service bureaucracies was increased dramatically in order to create new jobs and appease angry claimants.
Municipal budgets and payrolls skyrocketed. The New York City
payroll expanded from 240,000 to 380,000 jobs in the 1960s, most
of the increase coming at the end of the decade. Its budget had
increased at an annual rate of 6 percent in the 1950s, at just over
8 percent in the early 1960s, but at 15 percent after 1965. In one
decade, the city budget quadrupled. "The pattern of crazily rising
municipal budgets," Frances Piven noted, "is the direct result of
the diverse and pyramiding claims on city services, claims triggered
by political instability."[70] The rapid increase in city employment
and spending represented a desperate attempt to adapt the
payoffs that bureaucratized regimes could provide in order to
win allegiance to the existing institutional order and to restore
social peace.

Yet by itself such a strategy for order could not work. Not only
did the process have fiscal limits, but even in its heyday bureaucratic expansion further politicized client-bureaucrat relations
and actually heightened conflicts about policing, schooling, and
welfare. For, paradoxically, increased spending did not create a
positive-sum relationship between the black and white-ethnic
urban blocs, but tended to promote more elaborate and tension-
ridden zero-sum competition. Moreover, available resources were
never enough to alter the black condition in any basic way, and
the pumping of resources into traditional institutions highlighted
and called into question their very legitimacy as "colonial" agencies.

Piven and Cloward have argued in their treatment of welfare that social spending has been used in a politically countercyclical way: expenditures are increased in times of crisis and turmoil, as in the 1930s and 1960s, and then decreased as order is restored to allow the welfare system to revert to its traditional function of channeling people into low-wage dirty work.[71] Their argument, in my view, is persuasive in accounting at least in large measure for the expansion of social-welfare expenditures and, in an extension of the analysis proposed by Piven,[72] for municipal spending in the 1960s as well. Furthermore, they persuasively demonstrate that when the crisis passes, the concessions that were accorded to the poor are mostly withdrawn; if anything, the pattern of city spending in the 1970s after the publication of their work supports this view. But the part of the argument that is unpersuasive to me is that spending per se can absorb discontent. Rather, as Piven and Cloward's more recent work demonstrates, the impact of spending can be assessed only together with changes in the institutional ways that insurgents are linked to the political system, and in the terms of political participation which are then made possible.[73] Such organizational changes, and their impact on group perceptions and political capabilities, were at the very core of the resolution of the urban crisis.

The stories of neighborhood government and school decentralization in Washington Heights–Inwood suggest how such a process worked. The energies of virtually all local activists were caught up in the new arenas of highly localized and issue-specific conflict. Cut off from struggles in the other communities of New York City, northern Manhattan's politics of decentralization and education became a politics of the distribution of limited resources and of symbolic posturing that utilized a language of racial and ethnic competition. While the new organizations absorbed much heat, they contributed to the cooling of potentially redistributive issues from a citywide perspective. The activities of these new institutions permitted the incorporation of the community's new political bloc without disturbing the dominance of white ethnics in northern Manhattan and, more generally, of the traditional city-trench system.

The emergence of the Community Board as the legislative branch of the NAP structure made possible a reciprocal process in which the NAP executive was given the imprimatur of the Board and, by extension, of "old" northern Manhattan; in turn,

the Board's status as the "legitimate" representative body of the community was enhanced, since its authority prevailed over the functional committee apparatus of the NAP. The program that was meant above all to link insurgent blacks to the local political system (and that to a large degree succeeded in this aim) thus also strengthened the organizational capacities not only of older, more traditional groups but of the linguistic, institutional, and ideological features of the traditional urban system within which they comfortably operated. The Board's basic operating norms were geared to reproduce the appearance of incorporating groups equally into the polity, the autarchy of community politics, and the notion that since issues at the community level were distributive, a high degree of consensus and a relative ease of conflict resolution were possible. The Board almost always succeeded in avoiding open conflict at its public meetings. Much of the real debate took place prior to important votes, either in committee meetings or, more often, in telephone conversations between members. Participants spoke regularly about a telephone "hot line" network as the means by which they determined outcomes in advance. Conflict between community groups in "old" Washington Heights–Inwood was resolved outside the formal context of the Board itself.[74] Membership on the Board was limited self-consciously to those willing to play by these rules. Many new community organizations were excluded in part for this reason (their behavior on the Board was unpredictable, since there was no precedent on which to base predictions about how they would act), and in part because of a long-standing practice of replacing departing members with new representatives of their organizations. In this way the older party-dominated leadership of northern Manhattan was re-created even as its base and capacity contracted. These patterns of behavior and membership were complemented by a Board ideology of "one community," which enhanced its ability to claim to speak for all of Washington Heights–Inwood.

The NAP fulfilled its purposes above all by building a coherent functional committee structure which succeeded in reorienting the activities of the active leadership of local community organizations, and in separating issues from each other. Each issue area was considered in its own terms apart from every other. As a result, community organizations, especially black groups, that had a multi-issue focus were compelled to treat each issue separately.

However holistic their orientation, they were precluded from joining their various concerns together in a coherent fashion.

The leaders who served on the NAP committees directed a good deal of their time to making the NAP process work. The housing committee, for example, included the chairman or leading activists of the major tenants and housing associations in all parts of northern Manhattan—among them the Riverside-Edgecombe Neighborhood Association (RENA), the leading militant black organization in South Washington Heights; the Marble Hill Community Council; the Inwood Tenants Association; and the Washington Heights Tenants Association. Their organizations, each of which made presentations to the committee, had to expend numerous hours in voluntary effort in order to draw up proposals, put them in writing, and testify orally on their behalf. For volunteer organizations, time and effort are precious commodities, and they were now deflected from organizing to achieve goals through the NAP process. The work of each committee was largely invisible to each of the others. Committee members were forced to become issue specialists, and they also operated in a situation where they were uncertain about the relative importance of their work within the larger budget process. As a result, they tended not only to be more optimistic, at least in the short run, than was warranted about the possibility of funding their favored projects, but also advocated the importance of their concerns above those of any other. Although all the committees contained new, angry, and therefore "unreliable" members, their chairs were either old-time party or Community Board leaders from "old" Washington Heights–Inwood or blacks who had developed close ties with the white-ethnic bloc in years of service on the Community Board. Militant activists thus became part of the NAP apparatus without entering its leadership. The executive committee was dominated by a core membership of the present and the past three chairs of the Community Board. The participation of "new" northern Manhattan was thus secured, but under the tutelage of the "old" political bloc.

A separate but parallel process was played out in the explosive politics of education. To defuse educational struggles, local authorities have in this century relied on two main strategies. First, they have sought to isolate educational conflicts from other frictions in the political life of the city; industrial conflicts, housing disputes, and class animosities have been treated as if they were

irrelevant to the individualistic educational mission of the schools. The principal device in this respect has been the separation of school boards and board member recruitment from other aspects of municipal government. Second, substantial efforts have been made to neutralize conflict within the educational arena itself. Here the principal device—even as early as the 1860s—has been that of proliferating organizational complexity, which diffuses personal and role responsibilities for the state of the school.[75] Taken together, these two strategic thrusts created a closed system of educational governance, scarcely rivaled in complexity and breadth.

The closed-system organization of the schools, which isolates and neutralizes educational conflicts, carries the seeds of its own failure as a strategy of social cohesion when educational issues, for whatever reason, become the subject of intense concern to large numbers of people. The concurrence of economic decline and racial change in the 1960s produced such an occasion. Under these pressures, the existing organization of the schools was identified as the major barrier to change, and was itself a major source of school struggles. Over the years the politics of education had institutionalized a recurrent set of black and Hispanic losers, and institutionalized losing creates a disposition to act collectively. Moreover, the political isolation of the schools could only mean that autonomous school authorities would eventually lack the means to enforce order within the educational arena on their own. At the same time, the construction of massive city school bureaucracies necessitated wide areas of policy stagnation and the creation of a highly interested corps of personnel who were not so much opposed to innovation as they were institutionally unable to accommodate change. In short, in the 1960s the dominant strategies of managing education produced a frustration of initiatives that in time undermined the interests both of those concerned with managing conflict and of those hoping for better individual and collective life chances.

Reactions to pressures to change or reform New York City's schools in the early 1960s essentially took the form of attempts to maintain existing arrangements intact. Exhortations to overcome parochial divisions for the good of the children were common. Special blue-ribbon commissions multiplied. New proposals emerged regularly from governmental and private agencies.[76] By the middle 1960s, the noises got louder and the

noisemakers refused to go home. Promises of reform, especially after IS 201, were no longer believed. The unwillingness of all the major actors to give much credence to educational leaders between 1966 and 1969 indicates that the defenses erected around the public schools had finally collapsed, breached from within by the union organizing of the UFT, and from without by the demands of the civil-rights and black-power movements. Both movements explicitly and successfully linked educational issues to much wider questions of resource distribution and social justice. Both turned aside offers of due process with selective, and effective, uses of civil disobedience. At the time, both were perceived to threaten to turn school fights into a much more general social conflict, whose terms and outcome it was not possible to discern.

The collapse of the conflict-management potential of the old system of school governance was especially threatening in more direct and tangible ways to the city's political and economic leadership. School disputes threatened to destroy the career ambitions of Mayor Lindsay, and did severely weaken his capacity to govern. Long-standing and relatively stable electoral coalitions between white-ethnic workers and black voters no longer seemed certain to endure. Through the Urban Coalition and in other forums, businessmen took notice that New York's schools no longer seemed able to bolster the social order, to police the offspring of the deprived population of the city, or to teach a sufficient variety of marketable skills to insure that the needs of the local and regional labor markets would be fulfilled. Public schooling, in short, which traditionally has been an integral element of the state's functions of reproducing capitalist accumulation and managing social order, now threatened to accomplish neither and actually to become a major source of the disorganization of American capitalism. Or so it seemed at the time.

The ripple effects of school politics thus moved significantly beyond the traditional limits of school disputes. Not surprisingly, an attempt to find an organizational format for New York's schools that could satisfy the major claimants and adversaries, reassert predictable and coherent channels of school politics, and contain conflict within traditional boundaries became a matter of some urgency. School decentralization was the product of this search.[77]

The new rules of school politics delicately balanced incentives sufficient to secure the participation of school activists with protections sufficient to insure the continuing allegiance of school-system bureaucrats and teachers. At issue no longer was the *framework* of school politics, the subject of so much turmoil in the middle 1960s; all the contestants were once again enmeshed in a shared political game with two parts: electoral contests to elect the nine-member community boards and distributive contests to secure the limited new public goods that the boards had the capacity to deliver. Both of these contests would be marked by much passion; indeed it is by no means clear that pre-1969 school politics involved more anger or mobilized more energy by participants than did post-1969 school politics. But as the framework of school politics changed, so did the meaning of school struggles, since they were now conducted within a *shared forum* that defined the terms of conflict and provided mechanisms to manage and resolve conflicts. The new act predisposed this outcome. It displaced school politics from the city to the district level, at which communities tended to be class homogeneous, from which capital and relations of production were absent, and which functioned socially and politically in ways that segmented society understandings made comprehensible. And it created electoral and distributive contests *within,* not *between,* these community units; this caused school politics to turn inward—into contests between people sharing roughly equivalent places in the social structure, rather than into ones between different classes.

Unlike Mayor Lindsay's programs for neighborhood government, which were dispensed with when he left office, the decentralized school boards continue to function. They constitute one of the very few remnants of the cluster of mimetic public policies that were developed in the period 1969–1973. Created as responses to a "moment of madness" when so much that had been taken for granted seemed indeterminate, most of the new urban institutions were set aside after they had deflected the black movement from its radical, holistic, and redistributive possibilities. As survivors, the school boards have become relatively inconsequential institutions, which have "outlived their original purposes but refuse to die."[78]

Faced with their failure to capture local boards and with the assimilation of the board structure into the traditional idiom and practice of local government, the activists whose anger and activity

had been absorbed by school decentralization went away.[79] Left without credible challengers, the UFT captured the vast majority of seats in the 1977 elections. With the passing of the urban crisis of the 1960s and early 1970s, the time had come, its president suggested in the aftermath of his union's triumph, "to rethink the whole question of decentralization and whether it makes any sense in terms of economy, efficiency and education."[80] To this call there were no passionate rejoinders. The boards' constituency had been reduced to their members and appointees—contractors, janitors, supervisors, and some teachers.

School politics had moved on to a new agenda, one that made the issues of community control and decentralization seem beside the point. A future chancellor of the school system accurately predicted this change in 1973. "The entire thrust of decentralization," Frank Macchiarola wrote, "has been based on a desire to change the ways in which the City of New York *spends* its money," but "clearly the role for the future of the City involves it in *reducing* its governmental activities."[81] That this point of view quickly came to be the conventional wisdom of the middle and late 1970s reflected in large part the triumph of the mimetic policy formula: for community control, decentralization; for protest, elections; for redistribution, modest but sufficiently tantalizing distribution. The noise of schooling now signified nothing.

This analysis leaves many questions unanswered. Why did local activists join in the activities of the mimetic organizations? How did their participation change their relationship with their constituencies? Can we assess the gains that their participation achieved? Did the process of resolution of this urban crisis differ from that of past social and political crises?

The decision by local activists to participate in the new organizations had been made well before the organizations were created. The substance and rhetoric of the demands for local control, whatever their potential for ultimately challenging capitalist patterns of economic development and privilege, were compatible in large measure with traditional city politics. If in the middle 1960s urban movements had one foot in the traditional trenches and one foot out, the imbalance of this stance made them terribly vulnerable to mimetic policy responses that pushed both feet back in the trenches. As soon as school decentralization and neighborhood government were initiated, the leaders of community-control movements were compelled to participate

because, to all appearances, key elements of their demands had
been granted. There is a broad parallel here to the experience of
socialists in late-nineteenth-century Europe who, having railed
against voting restrictions based on class, had to embrace electoral
strategies once they were offered. And just as electoral participation "imprints a particular structure upon the organization of
workers as a class"—it creates parties and unions that are distinct
organizationally, it leads to a delegation of responsibility from the
masses to their representatives, and it produces a disavowal of
"extra-constitutional" tactics, among other effects[82]—so the incorporation of the leadership into the new organizations altered the
relationship between movement leaders and followers, and transformed movement tactics and possibilities.

Once enmeshed in the new institutions, leaders were forced to
fight for the rewards and resources these organizations could
distribute, and to fight for them on the terms these organizations
made possible. From a neighborhood perspective the new resources in capital funds, programs, and jobs were sufficiently
tangible to engage large numbers of people. Quite simply, it was
unthinkable for a leadership devoted to community control to
eschew struggles for these goods. But to struggle for them was to
accept the organizational demands the new institutions imposed:
demands of time and of substance. NAP and local school politics
required a great deal of attention and effort, which competed
with the time needed to maintain the organizations of independent
movements. But more important were the demands of substance.
Issue areas now were dealt with only one at a time, in separate
forums. Participants tacitly accepted the dubious notion that the
resources offered could make a major substantive difference.
They defined politics at the community level solely in terms of
the distribution of new kinds of patronage; and conflict, solely in
terms of ethnic and racial struggles within the community. The
boundaries of conflict were those of the geographical community.
Struggles were turned inward, now taking place between groups
who happened to inhabit the same territory. The gains activists
had made in opening up new channels of political participation
and influence (the reforms of 1969 and 1970 would never have
been made without the movements of the 1960s) proved in fact
to be *substitutes,* as Altshuler had predicted they would be, for
structural economic changes and for a basic redistribution of
wealth and power among classes and races.

Caught up in the new participatory system, movement leaders were doubly frustrated in their efforts to produce change. They frequently lost their electoral and substantive battles within the new organizations. And even where they succeeded, their successes were too limited to have much of an impact on the lives of their constituents. Enmeshed in the new institutions, and compromised by them, local activists were driven simultaneously away from a politics of protest and away from their followers.

To a very large degree, then, this story of mimetic responses shares some of the general features of movement protest and response that Piven and Cloward note in their treatments of the unemployed- and industrial-worker movements of the 1930s and of the civil- and welfare-rights movements of the 1960s. Concessions, they observe, are not offered readily, but only under compulsion. Authorities respond to movement pressures not only by dealing with immediate grievances in limited substantive ways, but also "by making efforts to channel the energies and angers of the protestors into more legitimate and less disruptive forms of political behavior, in part by offering incentives to movement leaders." Furthermore, responses often appear "to meet the moral demands of the movement, and thus rob it of support without actually yielding much by way of tangible gains." And apparently conciliatory responses free authorities to use repressive tools legitimately to quell protest.[83]

This process, Piven and Cloward argue, although debilitating for social movements, produces what they call a residue of reform—the right to organize unions, to vote, and to benefit from new social policies. But in the case of the mimetic policies that helped resolve the urban crisis, such a residue is hard to find. The NAP structure was entirely cast aside once it had achieved its purposes, and the school-board system remains in existence without any substantive purpose or strong supporters. The gap between rich and poor in northern Manhattan, in New York City, and in urban America more generally has continued to grow in the 1970s, while social peace has been maintained. If this is a tale of success, the term requires a very special definition.

PART THREE

Conclusion

CHAPTER 8

Social Theory, Urban Movements, and Social Change

In the early and middle 1960s, urban liberals and radicals were terribly optimistic about neighborhood and community politics. Armed with little more than Saul Alinsky's view of a world divided between "haves" and "have-nots," they embraced a politics of local action convinced, as Alinsky was, that the community provided a place where collective organization could overcome the malaise of the Eisenhower years and the sterility of the labor movement.[1] In the neighborhoods of urban America, genuinely radical movements for social change could be forged. With the collapse of the community-control efforts of the late 1960s and their envelopment by the public-policy responses of local authorities, most of the activists of the 1960s became considerably more skeptical as the expected promise of community action was not redeemed.

Today, however, a radical politics of the neighborhood is again in vogue. Underpinned this time by a much more sophisticated understanding of the connections between urban crisis and capitalist development than the one Alinsky provided, the prescriptive thrust is nevertheless the same: utilize community organization and community movements as vehicles of radical change. A remarkable consensus of activists is once again turning to the place of residence rather than to the place of work as the main locus of insurgent activity. In part this orientation is opportunistic. Many local self-help, consumer, environmental, and neighborhood organizations (many of which have discovered each other) have once again appeared on the scene.[2] In a period of declining union membership, growing attacks on the welfare state, and the growing capacity of conservative political philosophy to define

political choices, this mass activity provides the main possibilities for a creative politics of the Left, or at least so it seems. In part, too, this orientation is principled. It is grounded in the expansion of Marxist social theory beyond the narrowly economic and beyond simple versions of determinism that accord a uniquely privileged role to workplace relations.

The strategic and theoretical return to a politics of community makes an understanding of the politics of the urban crisis of the 1960s and early 1970s even more pressing. If this book makes no other argument, it surely insists that community-based strategies for social change in the United States cannot succeed unless they pay attention to the country's special pattern of class formation; to the split in the practical consciousness of American workers between the language and practice of a politics of work and those of a politics of community. If we do not self-consciously understand and address this key feature of our urban-class inheritance, we shall continue to play a losing game whose very rules will remain obscure.

Social theory, Arthur Stinchcombe reminds us, "ought to create the capacity to invent explanations."[3] And such explanations may or may not be useful in guiding how we think about and act in the world. The failure of political organizers to come to terms with the special American understandings of work and community reflects not merely a dogged obtuseness, or even the fact that they, like the rest of us, are deeply embedded in implicit cultural rules that produce conduct. This failure is also a theoretical one, and it is to this shortcoming that I wish to speak in this concluding chapter.

I

The development of the term "class" in the modern sense of hierarchical divisions with social implications, and not just as a general word for divisions in a system of classification, dates from the late-eighteenth and early-nineteenth centuries.[4] It became for all varieties of social description and theory an indispensable term for the mapping of the new social order, even if only to deny its importance in this or that realm of human affairs. Precisely because it has been so essential a tool of analysis, "class" has provided a battleground within and between theoretical traditions, especially the Marxist and the Weberian. Neither, however, has

dealt very well with the separation of work and community—the process, ironically, that has been at the very core of the capitalist industrialization and modernization they seek to explain. Ironically, too, both traditions have broadly agreed on how to think about this split; yet this very consensus has debilitated important features of their treatments of class.

The consensus about the modern split between work and home has two parts. The first treats the differentiation as a decisive break with a more holistic preindustrial, precapitalist past; the second treats each element of the pair, work and community, as if it were entirely independent or autonomous. This tendency takes the form of stressing the differentiation of society in Weberian social science, and the primacy of relations of production in Marxist analysis. These two parts of the consensus have been concretized in the two main traditions of community studies: portrayals of alternatives to the present that stress the wholeness of community, and an orientation that uses community as a label for a bounded system of social relations in a given geographic area.

Both Marx and Weber understood the expansion of market relationships as the central cause of the breakup of precapitalist holistic communities. The emergence of mercantile capitalism under the aegis of the absolutist state, Marx stressed, reinforced the solvent of local markets:

In the preliminary stages of bourgeois society, trade dominates industry. . . . Trade will naturally react back to varying degrees upon the communities between which it is carried on. It will subjugate production more and more to exchange value; push use value more and more into the background; in that it makes subsistence more dependent on the sale than on the immediate use of the product. Dissolves the old relations.[5]

It dissolves these relations by the substitution of money relations for traditional communal relations. As "the dimensions of exchange are drawn over the whole world," traditional communal units become, in the first instance, units of exchange: "Exchange begins not between the individuals within a community," in this formulation, "but rather at the point of contact between different communities."[6] In the second instance, these communities themselves are transformed from those of mutual interdependence and solidarity to congeries of isolated, indifferent individuals

pursuing their interests in the marketplace. "The social connection between persons is transformed into a social relation between things; personal capacity into objective wealth." As a consequence, "the individual carries his social power, as well as his bond with society, in his pocket."[7]

Weber stressed precisely these themes in his discussion of the market and its impact on traditional communities. "An emerging capitalist economy," he wrote, "the stronger it becomes, the greater will be its efforts to obtain the means of production and labor services in the market without limitations by sacred or status bonds, and to emancipate the opportunities to sell its products from the restrictions imposed by the sale monopolies of status groups." This market relationship, by penetrating and transforming those relations that stand in its way, creates a defining impersonal dynamic that is the context within which the personal subsequently must develop and reproduce:

The market economy as such is the most impersonal form of practical life into which humans can enter with one another. This is not due to that potentiality of struggle among the interested parties which is inherent in the market relationship. Any human relationship, even the most intimate, and even though it be marked by the most unqualified personal devotion, is in some sense relative and may involve a struggle with the partner, for instance, over the salvation of his soul. The reason for the impersonality of the market is its matter-of-factness, its orientation to the commodity and only to that. When the market is allowed to follow its own autonomous tendencies, its participants do not look toward the persons of each other but only toward the commodity; there are no obligations of brotherliness or reverence, and none of those spontaneous human relations that are sustained by personal unions.[8]

Marx and Weber also broadly concurred in their treatments of the differentiation of capitalist society. As Weber stressed in ways that are often ill understood, the process of capitalist development does not so much create three separate dimensions of stratification (class, status, power) as shape the experience of living in each of the spheres of work, community, and politics. As Marx's historical writings make clear, for him, too, each of these dimensions of social life patterns the connections between the dynamics of capital accumulation and what people think and do. Too frequently, the processes of the simplification of the social structure entailed in capitalist development (the main classes become those of capital and labor) and the process of differentiation (including

the split of work and community) are seen as competing explanations of the nature and place of class in the contemporary
world. To Marx's assertion that "the result of the process of
production and realization is above all the reproduction and new
production of the *relations of capital and labor itself, of capitalist and
worker*,"[9] much modern social science has counterposed Weber's
stratification arenas of class, status, and party. For example,
Raymond Aron has written that the conclusions Marx drew

were accurate but incomplete; he thought there was a constant and
fundamental tendency towards uniformity within the proletariat, he
thought that the elimination of independent workers would proceed to
its logical conclusion, he thought that as a result of industrial concentration alone the ruthless conflict required by his theory, between a tiny
minority of privileged persons and a vast mass of exploited workers,
would come into being. Today, with the experience of a century of
capitalism behind us, we know that this is not so. Against the law
of proletarianization and pauperization, I shall set what I call the law of
social differentiation.[10]

This position not only misunderstands the subtleties of Marx's
analysis; more important, it establishes a dichotomy that is terribly
misleading, for capitalist accumulation has been the source of
both the simplification *and* the differentiation of the class order.

This understanding, though shared by Marx and Weber and
by both social theoretical traditions that bear their names, has not
been a central feature of either tradition's approach to the
objective split between work and community. On the face of it,
Weberian social science has had much more to say about community relations. It has insisted on the importance and the
autonomy of community life; on the need to understand that
market relations between sellers and buyers of private goods,
including those between housing providers and tenants, must be
classified and mapped on their own terms; on the diversity of
incomes, ethnic configurations, and styles of life in different
residential areas; and on the importance of dealing with the
authoritative ties between governmental authorities, including
service bureaucrats, and community residents. Yet Weberian
approaches to the residence community take its differentiation
from the workplace as a relatively unproblematical given, so that
the community studies which they develop tend to float in a
historical and relational void.

Typically, they conceptualize a (or the) residence community

as an object to be studied in itself, and as a unit of comparative analysis. Social scientists study the community, as one textbook on the subject put it, "because it is almost a universal social form found wherever human beings live." When Lloyd Warner set out to study Yankee City, a New England shoe-manufacturing town, in the Great Depression, he took "community" as his unit of analysis. Having just returned from three years of field work with the aborigines of Australia, he explained that in both places he sought to understand "how men in all groups, regardless of place or time, solve the problems which confront them." The Australian case, he argued, was merely to be understood as a primitive laboratory for the exploration of issues identical to those of his American community study. Thus in the United States he searched for "a community sufficiently autonomous to have a separate life of its own," with an integrated social structure and a self-contained history.[11]

Out of historical and relational context, the search for the generic "community" and its functions has proved rather elusive and abstract. As a consequence, the term has become bloated with many meanings. In 1955 G. A. Hillery counted ninety-four definitions of community in the sociological literature alone.[12] Communities have been seen as power networks, sets of solidary institutions, distinctive social groups, psychic territories, loci of primary interactions, symbolic units, territories, marketplaces, and "natural" habitats among other things.[13] Much effort has been expended on such questions as whether territoriality or group solidarity is the touchstone of an adequate definition of community.[14] Though all of these issues and activities are important matters in real places and times, when approached in a search for a universally applicable definition of community they seem merely scholastic.

With very few exceptions, most twentieth-century American community studies share this bounded, presentist, and positivist orientation. In the atomistic treatment of the territories they examine, they reflect the growing complexity and compartmentalization of late-nineteenth- and early-twentieth-century America and the dominant perspectives of American social science. The differentiation of the professional enterprise of studying society was a part of the larger process of capitalist development. New forms of higher learning were created, including the professions of political science and sociology. In the United States they

developed as a part of the elective system of higher education introduced at Harvard in 1869, whose content, C. Wright Mills notes, was "increasingly scientific, utilitarian, and professional."[15] Integral to this organizational and curricular shift were the rise of graduate education (between 1880 and 1901, graduate schools were created at Columbia, Harvard, Wisconsin, and Princeton) and the specialization of research.

The fragmentation and professionalization of higher learning facilitated the segmented study of society, and societal differentiation defined the subject matter and orientations of the emerging disciplines. The subdivision of individuals into apparently separate roles and activities multiplied the number of potential bases of perceived interests in the society. The rapid reordering of the social structure also undercut traditional patterns of individual and group self-regulation. The availability of these mechanisms of social control declined precisely as social upheaval increased. Theodore Lowi has powerfully argued that these developments provided the basis for early-twentieth-century political science. Pluralism as political theory sought to account for a politics based on a multiplicity of roles, affiliations, and interests. And a science of public administration, seen as rationality applied to social control, became a centerpiece of the discipline.[16]

Sociology cast its net more widely to embrace all of society. But as the organizational principle of modern university sociology departments attests (the sociology of work, of religion, of politics, of art, of community, etc.), society as a whole was viewed atomistically, as the sum of its differentiated parts. The study of capitalist communities was part of this enterprise and was possible, of course, because it reflected the reality of the growing segmentation of community life. This orienting feature of community studies has contributed much to the tradition's achievements, especially to its ability to penetrate beyond such terms as "working-class community" in order to deal with the content of community culture on its own terms; but this starting point has also been its principal limitation.

Such an approach, nevertheless, has produced important contributions to our understanding of modern society. At their best, such studies provide outstanding treatments of the experiences of class, race, and ethnicity—of their sufferings and satisfactions. To read Zorbaugh on the Chicago of the 1920s, or Gans on the West End of Boston in the 1950s, is to penetrate and live a reality

pressed and hidden from view.[17] Such studies have also illuminated questions of space and of social control. Focusing on the patterning of space, the modern sociological tradition has stressed that communities are places, and thus it has brought the insights of land economists and geographers in contact with macrosociological analysis. In these places, matters of social cohesion come to the fore. Such issues are often dealt with only implicitly, in that all the fine descriptive community studies convey pictures of how community life is ordered and its social structure reproduced; and, on occasion, as in the work of the Chicago school of Lloyd Warner's *Jonesville* and *Yankee City*, the theme of cohesion is the centerpiece.[18]

But perhaps the most important contribution of this tradition of American community research is its failure, in its own terms, to restrict its frame of reference to the territories under study. In spite of Warner's quest for "a community sufficiently autonomous to have a separate life of its own," his work is about the ways in which class and associational life in Yankee City came to be defined by prevailing relationships in the United States as a whole. In order to explain community life, it proves necessary to comprehend how external social forces pattern and inform local events and behavior. Thus in the most self-conscious of such attempts, Robert and Helen Lynd organized their study of Muncie, Indiana, in the 1920s around a single axial question: how does the change in the ways residents make a living, as a result of the transformation of the city from a placid county seat in the 1890s to a manufacturing city, shape the other dimensions of social life? They answered, not by elaborating a systematic theory of the relation of the parts to the whole, but by providing dense descriptions of the patterning of social life to indicate the "long arm of the job."[19]

Marxist treatments of the residence community, with the exception of Engels's study of Manchester, have been most conspicuous by their absence. This omission has been due in part to a theoretical relegation of community to the superstructure, and in part to the teleological "class in itself–for itself" formulation, which has been more interested in what workers might do (act in revolutionary fashion to achieve their fundamental interests in socialism) than in what they actually do in all the facets of their lives. Since I think that the Weberian failure to treat the relationship of work and community is inherent in the limitations of the

social theory, but that the Marxist shortcomings are not, I propose to review some recent work on class in the Marxist tradition in order to suggest how it might deal with the split of work and community. This attempt requires distinguishing between four levels in the analysis of class that too frequently have either been inadequately distinguished or been wrongly treated as alternatives.

Of the many available Marxist *classifications* of the class structure of the active labor force, the most compelling that I know has been presented by sociologist Erik Olin Wright.[20] His schema requires three sets of distinctions: between the petty-bourgeois and capitalist modes of production; between workers and the bourgeoisie within capitalism; and between individuals who occupy unambiguous class positions and those who do not. In the petty-commodity mode direct producers own and control the means of production; in the capitalist mode they do not. Workers, in the latter, are defined by three negatives: they do not own or control the means of production; they do not control finance capital; and they do not control the labor power of others. Members of the bourgeoisie, by contrast, possess each of these attributes. In modern capitalist societies individuals may fall either into one of the three "pure" categories of worker, bourgeois, or petty bourgeois or into "contradictory locations" that share the attributes of two of the three pure categories, as in the case of the hierarchy of managers in the firm who are simultaneously bourgeois and proletarian, or of university professors, who are both in the petty bourgeoisie and the working class.

It is possible to elaborate on the classificatory merits as well as problems of this approach at some length. More to the point, however, I think it important to locate precisely the place of such a classification within the analysis of class and class formation more generally. Wright explicitly presents his schema as an alternative to that set forth by Nicos Poulantzas in *Classes in Contemporary Capitalism*.[21] He takes issue with, among other things, Poulantzas's restrictive definition of the proletariat as the group of productive workers in the technical Marxist sense of direct producers of surplus value. Instead of accepting the distinction between productive and unproductive labor as one capable of distinguishing between individual workers, Wright suggests that all workers perform unproductive and productive work (at least indirectly), so that the distinction has little force in a classification of the laboring population.

This debate between Wright and Poulantzas is in fact not a debate at all, since with respect to this issue they discuss class at two quite different levels. Both treat the term "capitalist economy" as if these distinguishable levels were one: first, the process of capitalist accumulation at the level of the mode of production (it is at this largely *heuristic* level that it is appropriate to distinguish between collective capital and collective labor and, more controversially to be sure, between productive and unproductive workers); and, second, the social relations of the labor market and the occupational order at work (here relations between classes are defined in actual experienced situations). At the first level (class$_1$), class is what Geertz, borrowing from psychoanalyst Hans Kohut, calls an "experience-distant" concept—one that specialists employ to further their scientific (or philosophical or practical) aims. Class$_1$ has no phenomenological referents. Class$_2$, by contrast, is "experience-near."[22] It refers to a pattern of social relations lived objectively by actual people in real social formations. The collapse of these two levels into the "economy" eliminates in one stroke a series of important questions about the causal connections between the trajectory of capitalist accumulation and its contradictory tendencies on the one hand, and the patterning of work on the other. By no means is it clear, for example, that different moments of capitalist development require particular configurations of labor markets or workplaces, or that economic factors alone determine the character of these relations. Rather, it would be more useful to try to sort out in comparative and historical analyses precisely what is generic and what is variable in the relationship between the economy and class understood at the first, more general and abstract level, and the economy and class at the second, more concrete and historically and spatially specific second level.

In orthodox "class in itself–for itself" Marxist theory, the class in itself is found at the level of class$_1$, which at some future, near or distant, moment, will become a revolutionary proletariat. In classifications like Wright's (or Carchedi's, the Ehrenreichs', and Baudelot's, among others),[23] the search for classes in themselves is at the level of class$_2$. Yet as in the more traditional approach, the analyst searches for the appropriate analysis of class structure in order to identify actors with the potential to achieve class consciousness, understood in terms of understanding and acting on fundamental class interests. Thus Wright insists that "class

structure is not intended as the end point of investigation, but as the starting point. The premise is that the structure of class relations establishes the basic parameters within which social struggle and change will take place. The purpose of studying class structure is to be able to understand the constraints and possibilities of transformation. Ultimately, for Marxists, this means understanding the conditions for the formation of a working class capable of generating revolutionary socialist change." He continues by insisting that alternative definitions of the working class are "alternative propositions about the structural basis for the formation of the working class as a class."[24]

As Wright also notes, one of the most fundamental consequences of alternative definitions based on the labor process at the level of class$_2$ concerns the size of the working class, ranging in possibility from the small group of the most restrictive definitions to the vast majority of the population if the working class is defined as all wage workers and their families. Wright claims that such definitions of size matter as "contending accounts of constraints on the process of class formation,"[25] but constraints in what meaningful sense? Perhaps they matter for various actors, especially political parties, as they make strategic assessments about how to act to form classes as constituents; and such classifications may help identify the subjects of studies of class formation, but surely no more, unless we are prepared to make a set of unwarranted teleological assumptions.

Furthermore, as soon as we move from the objective, logical, and heuristic treatments of class to the also objective but experiential level of class$_2$, a further question presses: *by what justification are the social relations of work given a special or privileged status with respect to other sets of social relations that are also structured in class ways,* including the social relations of community? If the differentiation of society is a key trait of capitalist development, why should work belong to the "base" and residence community to the "superstructure"? Whereas it may be compelling to grant "first causation" to patterns of accumulation (perhaps in association with state development), the special analytical position of work and the labor process in traditional Marxist scholarship has less obvious justification. What is clear is that workplace *and* residence-community relations are shaped (to a large but contingent degree) by the dynamics of capitalist accumulation, and that together with political relations they constitute the lived, experi-

enced world of capitalist societies (class$_2$, in full). This insight of Weberian social science is wholly compatible with Marxist class analysis at this second level. Indeed, at this level of analysis we badly need objective classifications of the social relations of residence communities of the kind that Wright has provided for the active labor force.

Orthodox "class in itself–for itself" Marxism moved from class$_1$ to the ultimate fashioning of revolutionary consciousness, as if the former implied the latter. What do we mean by "class formation" if not the generation of such a revolutionary proletariat prepared to act for socialism? One influential answer, which I take to be more satisfactory than that of the teleological view, has been provided by the great English historian Edward Thompson. He regards classes neither as heuristic constructs nor as members of this or that cell of a typology, but as formed groups sharing dispositions. "When we think of a class," he avers, "we are thinking of a very loosely defined body of people who share the same congeries of interests, social experiences, traditions and value system, who have a *disposition* to *behave* as a class, to define themselves in their actions and in their consciousness in relation to other groups of people in class ways." No other modern historian has contributed so much to the study of class at this level of analysis (class$_3$), of class "not as a thing" but as "a happening."[26]

In his polemical writings Thompson presents this perspective as an alternative both to logical-structural models of class structure and to objective classificatory schemes. "Class is not . . . a static category—so many people standing in this or that relation to the means of production—which can be measured in positivist or quantitative terms. Class, in the Marxist tradition, is (or ought to be) a *historical category*, describing *people in relationships over time*, and the ways in which they become conscious of their relationships, separate, unite, enter into struggle, form institutions and transmit values in class ways."[27] At issue is whether and how class will exist. As in the Althusserian formulation, class struggle is prior to class,[28] but this resemblance is only superficial. Insofar as all capitalist societies are members of a family of cases, Thompson is prepared to talk of a broadly shared "logic of process." He is quick to insist, however, that "history is not rule-governed, and it knows no sufficient causes. . . . For historical explanation discloses not how history *must* have eventuated but why it eventuated

in this way and not in other ways." The differentiations within the family of capitalist societies occur within the determinate fields of possibility, but it is the differentiations themselves that must be the central focus of the historian. Thus he understands class formation as a "process of self-making, although under conditions which are a 'given.' "[29]

This is a process with subjects—men and women "however baffled, and however limited their space for agency." Thompson's total and angry rejection of classificatory approaches to class structure is intimately bound up with his contempt for Althusserian analysis. Citing Balibar ("classes are *functions of the process of production as a whole.* They are not its subjects, on the contrary, they are determined by its form.")[30] he writes that this view of history without agents throws open the way "once again to all the rubbish of deducing classes, class fractions, class ideologies ('true and false') from their imaginary positioning—above, below, interpellatory, vestigial, slantwise—within a mode of production (or within its multiple contradictions, tortions, dislocations, etc. etc.)," and this mode of production is conceived as "something other than its eventuation in historical process, although in fact it exists only as a construction within a metaphysical oration."[31]

Strong words, indeed, but not wholly convincing ones. Thompson's insistence on a historical and contingent treatment of class formation is fundamental, especially as it asserts that the *making* of dispositions *consists in* a set of structured abilities and opportunities, which may contract or expand over time.[32] But Thompson's abhorrence of any objective classification of class relations leaves entirely opaque the question of *which* "givens" workers map as they are formed into a class at the level of disposition. Precisely because class is what Thompson calls a "junction-term,"[33] which lies at the intersection of structure and process, and of being and consciousness, it is impossible to analyze class$_3$ without some objective determination of class$_2$.

Thompson defines class formation as the making of a class that is capable of acting in class ways. This formulation, though a clear advance on teleological orthodoxy, is not adequate. It assumes that class formation is an all-or-nothing proposition (in this respect his view is bound up too tightly with the English example of the development in the early-nineteenth century of a society of "high-classness").[34] In addition, by failing to map the world of class$_2$, it falls short of providing a statement about the available alternatives

of class and group formation in different capitalist societies at structurally equivalent historical moments.

The connections between class as objectively structured and experienced at work, in communities, and in political life at different places and times (class₂) and the creation of dispositions of either a class or nonclass kind (class₃) constitute the process of class and group formation. It is only when they are formed that classes may be said to exist as potential historical groups. The precise character of class formation in a given society cannot be deduced from an analysis of class₁ or class₂. Class, which surely exists at these objective levels, may not exist at all at the third level of dispositions; or it may exist in different ways in different societies. Indeed, as I have put it elsewhere, "the character of the interplay between the second level of the social relations of class and a third level [produced by] class formation—in other terms the interplay between a set of givens produced principally by the historical and spatial logic of capitalist development on the one hand and class traditions and cultures on the other—is what is distinctive about the dynamics of class and class conflict in any single national society."[35]

If the process of class formation refers to the development in peoples' consciousness of ways to move between the experienced and the articulated, it cannot refer to that alone. Dispositions are tendencies. Much as language imposes areas of silence, so dispositions as cognitive structures define boundaries between the probable and improbable. Individuals who share in a set of class dispositions may do so in a variety of ways, but what they have in common is a motivational construction that may, *or may not*, produce common organization or action. It is in this sense that I referred to class₃ as a potential historical group, whose *potential* is realized only at the level of organization and action. That the ties between disposition and action are radically contingent can certainly no longer be considered a surprise.[36] When dispositions about work, community, and politics fashion a common-sense world that is concretized in institutions and customary practices, it is possible to talk of formed groups and classes that command a prescription for making sense of the experiences of living in society and for affecting society.[37] "What we have to study to understand history," Stinchcombe persuasively reminds us, "is how structural forces cause people to change their notions of what kind of situation they are in, and to sustain these new notions sufficiently long to build them into institutions that in turn sustain them."[38]

If I may summarize what, on reflection, are some rather obvious points, we need not—indeed must not—choose between the alternatives of structuralist formulations that claim (at least implicitly) that experience is ideology and culturalist stances (of the kind that are dominant in much of current linguistic and semiotic theory) "in which the epistemological wholly absorbs the ontological: it is only in the ways of knowing that we exist at all."[39] Class society exists even where it is not signified; but how and why it is signified in particular ways in particular places and times is the study of class formation.

Such a perspective reorients the ways in which we think about social control. In a recent article, Morris Janowitz has sought to reassert the distinctive meaning that "social control" had in the emerging discipline of American sociology at the turn of the century. In the work of E. A. Ross, Charles Horton Cooley, Robert Park, and other members of the Chicago school, social control referred, not to the array of mechanisms of imposed compliance, but to the ability of social groups to regulate themselves, and to the capacity of society as a whole "to regulate itself according to desired principles and values."[40] This tradition portrays matters of social control in terms of the clash between the thoughts and actions of free individuals and the imperative of social order at the level of society. As Georges Gurvich has noted, it sees order and social reality itself in accord with the classical liberal view "in a nominalistic way, as rather an assemblage of isolated individuals, whose connection and emergence in a whole stems from social control."[41]

Though this approach has permitted rich research at the "interface between micro- and macro-analysis," its assertion that "the *opposite* of social control can be thought of as coercive control"[42] clearly reveals its limitations as well; for such claim indicates the failure of this tradition to understand that a person's standing in society will decide whether he will be coerced or whether he will self-regulate. Lacking a convincing theory of the social structure of capitalist societies—or even of industrial societies more generally—and of the material bases of social and political behavior, the liberal tradition of social control has tended, normatively, to assert the paramount importance of order, and, scientifically, to reify society and leave unexamined the sources of threat to social cohesion. It reduces "social control" to one kind of technique of cohesion rather than making it an analytical tool for assessing the entire scope of means (including self-regulation)

for the fashioning of order in societies faced with the disjunction between the formal legal equality of citizenship and the franchise and the structural inequities produced by the routine operation of the political economy.

The obvious alternative is to link the analysis of social control to an analysis of social structure. In this view, as I have written elsewhere, stability in a capitalist society

does not imply the absence of structurally rooted conflicts, but reflects the operation of the social control mechanisms that shape and limit behavior. The state's function of social control consists in managing the consequences of making capitalism work, and can best be understood as an attempt to manage but not overcome the contradictions of the capitalist system.[43]

But even this formulation is insufficient. Its heuristic assumption that class and group conflict is "natural" is the mirror image of the liberal tradition's "natural" equilibrium. Although this assumption is rightly based in antagonisms inherent in productive and social relations, it begs a number of crucial issues. It does not easily allow for the friction between the institutional orders of class and the state. The state is not simply or exclusively the instrument of a dominant class or the carrier of the structural imperatives of capital. Because of the degree of autonomy the state has from the economy, and because members of the liberal state are citizens, political arrangements themselves may act as a constraint on the capacity of a dominant class to realize its interests. The triumph of urban reform at the turn of the century and beyond, for example, though promoted by the dominant classes, we have seen, itself facilitated the urban challenges of the 1960s. Furthermore, the radical tradition's assumptions make it difficult to discern the more dynamic or conflictual aspects of social control, and the analytical and real-world limits of the term itself. Gareth Stedman Jones has made this point well:

There is no political or ideological institution which could not in some way be interpreted as an agency of social control. There is no indication in the phrase of who the agents or instigators of social control may be; no indication of any common mechanism whereby social control is enforced; no constant criterion whereby we may judge whether social control has broken down—certainly not conflict, for this may ultimately, or even inherently, be a means of reinforcing conformity. Nor finally is there any fixed yardstick whereby we may know when social control

has been reimposed. Since capitalism is still with us, we can with impunity suppose, if we wish to, that at any time in the last three hundred years, the mechanisms of social control were operating effectively.[44]

By itself, in short, the term is too capacious and slack.

Lapses into nonexplanation may be avoided, however, and the term put to use, if "social control" is understood not in mechanically functional terms, but as referring to the specific coercive, institutional, and ideological *content* that defines the ways in which society is lived and perceived by real people in real places and times. Too often, the content of workers' cultures is interpreted almost exclusively in terms of what the dominant classes do to them, or, conversely, these cultures are described and celebrated as if they were whole cultures in the manner of isolated, primitive societies. Neither approach is satisfactory. For the interactions between the classes on the one hand, and between the classes and the state on the other, shape patterns of class and group formation that are of necessity distinctive from society to society. These patterns, reproduced over time, provide each society's main mechanisms of social control. Understood this way, "social control" refers to a crucible of interaction and struggle that has its own idiom, grammar, and expectations. The pattern of city trenches constructed before and after the Civil War in the United States was just such a crucible.

In short, in different places and in different times "there are degrees of class" in spite of the shared "logic of process" of the mode of production.[45] Conceptually there is a range from working classes who see themselves and act wholly on the bases of nonclass understandings to Marx's proletariat, which understands its world-historical mission and has the capacity (that is, is willing and able) to act in a revolutionary fashion. No national working class has been at either pole. Rather, history has been made in the more murky middle and has been shaped by the contingent connections between class at the level of the process of accumulation (where the heuristic classes of collective capital and collective labor collide); class at the level of objectively patterned experience (at work, in residence communities, and in political relations); class at the level of dispositions; and class at the level of organization.

II

Precisely this kind of attention to differences in national patterns is what is missing in recent Marxist and radical analyses of urban

movements and conflict. The starting point of such work has been focused rather more on the similarities between urban affairs across national boundaries. It must be apparent to every student of city life that the development of urban protest has been a major characteristic of political life throughout the West in the past quarter of a century. It is also clear that these movements belong to a family of cases. They have organized at the place of residence, not at work. The major themes of their protest have concerned the delivery of collective services by government and the impact of housing, transport, and social services on the built form of the city and on the quality of city life.

These similarities provide warrants for urban analysis that take up urban questions together as a structurally determined arena of advanced capitalism; and it is such cross-national analysis that has provided very recent community-organization strategists in the United States with their theoretical rationale for fashioning once again an intensely local politics. For this reason, it is worth briefly examining the limits of the urban-structural approach, whose most important intellectual figure is Manuel Castells.

In a series of energetic contributions, he has developed the most coherent analysis, Marxist or otherwise, of urban social movements. His approach, broadly located within the theoretical frame of structural Marxism, has posed two principal questions: What contradictions are *revealed* by the genesis and practice of urban movements? And, what are the potential *effects* of such movements—not simply in terms of discomfort, noise, or modest reform—for basic social transformation?

In reply to the first of these inquiries, he finds that "the development of urban movements is a general characteristic of advanced capitalism. They arise, on the one hand, from the urban crisis which derives from the socialization of consumption; and on the other hand, from the political crisis that results because state intervention in social life is being questioned."[46] This view is an aspect of his larger focus, which treats the city principally as the location of the reproduction of the work force and, hence, as a key location of individual and collective consumption (distinguished by whether the individual or the government organizes the distribution of goods and services). As the balance between the two shifts to the collective side, especially for specific groups of the population, urban movements *necessarily* develop, since they are the outcome or effects of the structural properties of

advanced capitalism. Thus Castells notes that in France, where urban movements initiated by political organizations of the dominated classes have been relatively meager, "we are willing to make the historical and theoretical wager that there will be a significant development of urban social movements as a means of changing social relations, and this will arise from urban contradictions."[47] There is, in short, a logic to the emergence of urban movements, broadly parallel to the "class in itself–for itself" formulation.

What are we to make of such claims? It is worth noting that they go beyond the intention to start with existing movements and see what features of social reality their existence illuminates. Instead, starting from a portrait of structured reality, Castells predicts a trajectory of organizational development. The concentration of capital concentrates the working population, which requires collective goods that the private market is unable to provide. Collective consumption organized by government underwrites the expansion of the private sector. There is a political logic to government intervention, which, on the one hand, creates new forms of inequality based on differential access to collective goods and services and which, on the other, politicizes urban issues. Quite obviously, I am in broad agreement with this presentation. Some features of advanced capitalism everywhere do make possible the emergence of urban movements; and where they have developed, their structural roots in capitalist urbanization may be identified.

But Castells's formulation makes the fashioning of urban movements too automatic, when in fact it is rather a contingent outcome. Not all structural possibilities find historical expression. There are ample reasons why individuals with grievances do not join organizations or act collectively. Furthermore, Castells's search for regularity misses important differences (which themselves must be explained) in both the frequency and the character of the development of urban movements in different national settings, even where the same structural causes exist. "History," Thompson writes, "knows no regular verbs . . . it knows no sufficient causes."[48] Pierre Vilar makes the same point when he insists that although the social scientist and the historian "must assimilate enough of the structuralist lesson to avoid conferring a historical meaning on what may only be a common inheritance; he knows that *differentiations* are still his domain. . . . The questions which interest the historian are *those to which structuralism has no*

answer."[49] In order for these differentiations to be understood, and thus for what is contingent in the creation of urban movements in specific places and times to be understood, questions of nationally distinctive working-class traditions, cultures, vocabularies, and practical consciousness—issues neglected by Castells— must come to the fore.

The effects of urban movements, he allows, do hinge importantly on the connections between these movements and other social forces. "One of my central hypotheses which must be recalled yet again, is that there is no qualitative transformation of the urban structure that is not produced by an articulation of the urban movements with other movements, in particular (in our societies) with the working class movement and with the political class struggle. In this sense I do not claim that urban movements are the only sources of urban change. I say rather that the mass movements (including urban movements) produce in the urban organization qualitative transformations, in the broad sense of the term, through a change, local or global, of the correlation of forces among the classes." Urban struggles in this view, even though they are about "secondary structural issues, that is to say, ones not directly challenging the production methods of society nor the political domination of the ruling classes," need not be relegated always to a peripheral or merely reformist role in the quest for social change. "Quite the reverse; their decisive importance in certain political conjunctures has been determined, for a structurally secondary issue can be a conjuncturally principal one." The importance of urban movements is thus an open, contingent matter, hinging principally on the "effects it has upon the power relations between social classes in concrete situations."[50] Obviously I am also broadly sympathetic to this view, but in the absence of a consideration of national patterns of working-class culture, it is incomplete in much the same way that his treatment of the genesis of urban movements is incomplete. If, for example, the ties between urban movements and trade unions are weak in the United States but strong (as they have in fact been) in Italy, these differences may well account for differences in effect, but the causal differences themselves need to be explained. Yet nowhere in Castells's emphasis on the connections between structure, practice, and effects are we given the analytical tools to do this task.[51]

It has been a central theme of this volume that working-class

understandings of the relationship between work and home in the early American industrial cities, reproduced mainly by political mechanisms over time, have become a *constitutive* element of the relationship between structure, practice, and effect. Once established as historical products, such cultural and organizational systems shape the making of history by providing guides to the recognition, interpretation, and categorization of experiences. These accumulated meanings provide implicit collective and historical theories. Political practice is not merely an effect of the objective structured relations selected. We need to know not only why urban movements are likely in advanced capitalism, but what the terms of such movements are in different societies whose working classes possess different selective traditions of class. Such cognitive and motivating systems cannot be derived directly from events.[52] Practice is shaped by the code of distinctions of the culture. Thus, unlike Castells, I have tried to marry a structural account of the urban crisis to the cultural inheritance of the American working class.

The major treatment of American social movements, Frances Fox Piven and Richard Cloward's *Poor People's Movements,* has a limitation that is precisely the opposite of the one that has characterized the work of Castells. In their thoughtful introductory chapter to their case studies of four mass movements of the 1930s and 1960s, they complement Castells's structural perspective by inquiring why social movements, including urban movements, choose this or that focus of attack. Whereas Castells emphasizes the growing importance of the tie between residence communities and state bureaucracies delivering collective services, Piven and Cloward stress the vantage point of movement participants:

People experience deprivation and oppression within a concrete setting, and not as the end product of large and abstract processes, and it is the concrete experience that molds their discontent into specific grievances against specific targets. Workers experience the factory, the speeding rhythm of the assembly line, the foreman, the spies and the guards, the owner and the paycheck. They do not experience monopoly capitalism. People on relief experience the shabby waiting rooms, the overseer or the caseworkers, and the dole. They do not experience American social welfare policy. Tenants experience the leaking ceilings and cold radiators, and they recognize the landlord. They do not recognize the banking, real estate, and construction systems. . . . In other words, it is the daily experience of people that shapes their grievances, establishes

the measure of their demands, and points out the targets of their anger.[53]

Institutional patterns, they furthermore stress, define the collectivity that is likely to act and the strategic possibilities of defiance.

This emphasis on experience is a compelling antidote to more structural views, but it too is incomplete. For experience does not yield meaning and behavior directly. If it did we could expect similarly situated groups in different societies (be they workers, tenants, welfare recipients, or whatever) to take identical action at moments when action was possible. But manifestly they do not. Once again we are forced onto the domain of class formation, where differences between societies are at least as compelling as their similarities. It is indeed just such an omission that impels Piven and Cloward to advance the general argument based on American experience that irregular action, not organization, is the key mechanism of movement gains. In the absence of enduring and regular working-class-party and union organizations that treat society in holistic class-defined terms, such a conclusion may be warranted, but only in this special, nationally specific situation.[54]

It is, in brief, crucial to avoid the temptation to study moments of crisis in isolation from the wider society and its history. In this book, it was only after I had accounted for the origins of the basic elements of the political culture of the American working class that I could make sense of the urban movements of the 1960s, the crisis of which they were a part, and its resolution. The social and political life of northern Manhattan could not be understood either in its own terms, or by an exclusively structural-institutional account of older American cities in advanced capitalism. The relationship of Washington Heights–Inwood to the wider society made its boundaries permeable; more important, the distinctive character of class formation in the United States provided widely shared rules for urban politics.

The current dilemmas of American capitalism and the collapse of neo-Keynesian nostrums for managing the economy present the American left with new challenges and opportunities. But given its cultural inheritance and the collapse of the organizational efforts of the 1960s, it does not have a rich stock of resources and strategies from which to choose. We have the ingredients but few utensils and no cookbook.

This book is hardly a compilation of recipes guaranteed to

bring change. But it does have an old moral. The past is constitutive of the present ("men make their own history but they do not make it just as they please"). The hard strategic questions can only be put if we understand and come to terms with the heritage of a split consciousness of work and community and with the special features of race and class in American cities. The failure to come this far in the 1960s exacted a high price, and an unreflective community politics in the 1980s is likely to have the same result. But, if I may challenge the master, the next time need not be farce.

Appendix

Notes

Index

Methodological Notes

In the early 1970s the Bureau of Applied Social Research conducted the "New York Neighborhood Study" in order to evaluate the city's programs of neighborhood government. As part of this effort, the bureau, assisted by the National Opinion Research Center at the University of Chicago, mounted three separate surveys, which I draw on in Chapters 5 and 6.

The first, which I refer to as the Public Survey, was the most ambitious of these efforts. Nathalie Friedman, who supervised this survey, summarized its sampling procedure:

The New York Neighborhood Study collected data from approximately 240 respondents on 24 blocks in seven Community Planning Districts in New York City. The prohibitive cost of probability sampling was a major factor in our decision to draw a block quota sample, using 1960 and 1970 census data to assure adequate representation of

men:	under 35
	35 and over
women:	employed
	not employed

Since we were well aware of the caveats with respect to quota sampling, we decided to draw a probability sample on six of the twenty-four blocks in each district. In this way we would be able to compare respondents obtained through each method in order to assess the bias of using one method rather than the other. The probability sample was one of households: selection of the respondent within the household was by quota, rather than probability. The completion rate for the probability sample was approximately two-thirds.

The "non-difference" between the two samples is rather striking. The probability sample yielded a somewhat larger proportion of white ethnics; persons of higher income, education, and age; widows, and unemployed persons. They seem to be slightly more satisfied with their neighborhoods, as indicated by the higher proportion who opt to remain and who feel that the area is a good place to live and a real home. None of these differences, however, is striking—in fact only a few yield Chi-squares which are significant at the .02 or .01 level.

Most interesting, perhaps, is the lack of difference in the proportion who report that they or a household member was a victim of a crime during the past year—an item we felt might strongly differentiate the two types of samples. These preliminary results suggest that the kind of probability sample it is practical to obtain in New York City these days—approximately a two-thirds completion rate—does not produce any notable differences from the much less expensive block quota method.

I have restricted myself to the northern Manhattan sample.

The second survey, which I refer to as the Block Survey, was conducted wholly within northern Manhattan. Michael Bucuvalas and Dale Nelson summarized the survey's process of selecting respondents this way:

The selection of respondents was a multi-stage sampling process. At the first stage, the blocks were selected to maximize ethnic concentration and similarity of socio-economic status: at the second stage, random samples of households on the blocks were chosen: at the third stage, respondents were selected within the households on the basis of quotas.

Blocks were selected which would facilitate the efficient study of variation between social units as the seats of ethnic subcultural patterns of political participation. The method of choosing blocks included the use of a number of different bases of selection: including, census-derived statistics, qualitative interviews with informants, the reverse telephone directory, enumeration of ethnic names on mailboxes, and personal observation of candidate blocks.

The census-derived statistics were used to insure comparability on such factors as age, number of dwelling units, population, persons per unit, persons per room, socio-economic status. The Shevky-Bell Index of Social Rank was used to select census tracts with similar socio-economic levels. In utilizing this census information there was the difficulty that the Five Blocks Study was dealing with "social" blocks, but census statistics were based on census blocks: some were not even available at the block level, but only at the tract level (median age, persons per room, and the Shevky-Bell Index). Therefore, some evaluations required adjustment on the basis of information from informants and personal observation.

Informants were selected from the Jewish, Irish, Hispanic, and Greek subcommunities on the basis of lists of leaders in CPD #12 compiled by the Leadership Study Component of the New York City Neighborhood Study. These informants were interviewed in an unstructured format for information about the geographic concentration of members of their respective ethnic groups. In addition, information was gathered regarding the areas of highest concentration on the age, income, occupation, and sense of community of the ethnics living in these areas. Interspersed in these interviews was a good deal of other information concerning life-styles and community history.

The candidate blocks arrived at through this process were checked against listings in a reverse telephone directory. This was done in order to validate the informants' perceptions of ethnic living patterns against the list of telephone subscribers. The reverse directory showed much lower concentrations of ethnics than the informants had estimated. The lack of correspondence between the informants' perceptions and the list of telephone subscribers could have been due to a number of factors: first, telephone subscription lists are invariably biased toward those with higher incomes and, therefore, might discriminate against certain ethnic groups; secondly, identifying the ethnicity of names can be tricky; thirdly, names may not be indicative of ethnicity in instances of mixed marriages. Therefore, it was decided to count the ethnically identifiable names on mailboxes on the candidate blocks, with the hope of, at least, getting a more complete listing of residents. This method tended to agree with the reverse directory in lowering the percentages of members of ethnic groups on blocks where they had been estimated as quite concentrated. (There were missing names on mailboxes just as there had been in the telephone directory.) However, where high concentrations of a particular ethnic group had been perceived by the informants, this ethnic group usually preserved a plurality vis à vis other groups as a result of both the telephone and mailbox counts. However, this plurality was almost invariably lower than that estimated by the informants.

These methods combined with observations and short conversations with residents on the blocks to yield five ethnically concentrated blocks, which seem to be as closely matched on other factors (particularly socio-economic status) as is possible in Washington Heights–Inwood.

Households to be interviewed were selected by drawing separate random samples on each block. Two samples of fifty households each were chosen by selecting a random starting point and using a skip interval. Replacement households were chosen by randomly ordering the remaining dwelling units. The refusal rate was relatively high, averaging about 30% for the blocks.

Within the dwelling unit, the interviewer selected the respondent on the basis of a quota. This quota was divided into four categories: men from eighteen to thirty-five years of age; men over thirty-five years of age; women over eighteen and working at least twenty hours a week; women over eighteen and unemployed. The number of individuals in each category was determined separately for each block on the basis of percentages for the respective categories present in the census tract according to the 1970 census.

One final instruction to the interviewers should be mentioned. The effort was made to match the interviewers to the respondents on the basis of ethnicity and race. They were assigned to blocks where they would "fit in" with the residents, and they were instructed never to interview across the racial boundaries established for this study (European, Hispanic, and Black). There were two exceptions to this rule: some interviewers of European background were assigned to the Dominican and Cuban blocks because of the difficulty in getting Spanish-speaking interviewers, and a few Hispanic respondents specifically requested to be interviewed by Europeans (a couple even threatened to refuse if an Hispanic interviewer were sent). The main reasoning behind matching interviewers and respondents was the feeling that certain of the questions regarding ethnicity and ethnic relations would be difficult to answer honestly if the interviewer were not identifiable as a member of the "in-group." Exceptions were made to this rule in those cases where either this hypothesis seemed to have been reversed or where there was just no practicable alternative.

Footnotes 2 and 37 of chapter 5, drawing on Block Survey data, estimate the class structure of northern Manhattan in 1972. In the face of limitations inherent in the survey data, Henry Wells and I devised the following class index, which he has summarized:

Coding the respondents to the Five Block Survey for class consisted of two separate steps: (1) Determination of the person whose occupation or relation to the productive system defines the class of the respondent; (2) Assignment of the appropriate class code to the respondent depending upon the occupation of the person whose role defines the class of the entire family.

The male member of the family possessing the highest occupational status defines the class position for all his relations living within the same household. However, the questionnaire provides occupational data only for respondents, the respondent's spouse, and, in some cases, the respondent's father. Therefore, the class code for respondent was determined by the occupation of respondent's husband, should there be such, except where respondent is divorced or separated from her husband; or where *any* member of the household receives AFDC or General Welfare Assistance. If this is the case, the respondent is coded according to the rules described below in the discussion of the Underclass. Where the husband is retired or deceased, the previous occupation of the husband is used, with the exceptions noted below for the coding of Underclass.

The class code for the respondent is determined by the occupation, past or present, of the respondent's *father*, if, (1) the respondent is female, under 25, unmarried, and not living with persons receiving either AFDC or General Welfare Assistance, or; (2) the respondent is female, unmarried, living in same household with father, but with no one else who receives AFDC or General Welfare; (3) the respondent is male, a full time student who has not yet completed four years of college. In all other cases, i.e., unmarried, divorced or separated over 25 females not in a household receiving the two kinds of public assistance mentioned above, and males not attending school full time *below* the graduate level, the class code for the respondent is determined by the respondent's own occupation.

After the definer of class for the respondent has been determined, the definer is assigned a class code, applied to the respondent, according to the following criteria:
(1) *Underclass.* The rules for determining members of the underclass are somewhat different from those for determining the members of other classes. First, a determination was made whether or not the respondent should be coded as a member of this class. If not, then the appropriate class code was assigned according to the rules set out above and below. Respondents were placed in the underclass if they met the following requirements: (a) lived in a household where someone received AFDC or General Welfare Assistance, but not Old Age Assistance, during the past year; (b) was employed at an unskilled occupation, was not a male undergraduate student, had been employed for less than one year, or had been employed for an indeterminate period, and had contributed to a family income of less than $4,000 for the past year; (c) was unemployed over the last year with a family income of less than $4,000. Persons were excluded from the underclass if those in the household receiving General Welfare or AFDC were over 60 *and* the family income was over $4,000 during the past year, or if they were unemployed, or sporadically

employed, but either widowed or retired with a family income above $2,000. In both cases, other class codes were assigned according to the occupation of the appropriate class definer.

(2) *Manual Working Class*. This class encompasses all those whose class status is defined by someone working in a nonmanagerial or nonprofessional capacity for someone else. The Manual Working Class includes those whose position is defined by being an employee doing physical labor, however skilled. In addition to the obvious cases, such as watchmakers and jewelers, this class also includes chauffeurs, bartenders, waiters and one country club steward.

(3) *Nonmanual Working Class*. This category encompasses all those whose class is defined by being a nonmanual, nonprofessional, or nonmanagerial employee. In addition to those holding clerical positions, this category includes salesmen and one Maitre d'Hotel.

(4) *Petit Bourgeois*. This category includes all those whose class position is determined by being in his own employ, but whose family income does not exceed $30,000 per year.

(5) *Professionals*. This includes all those whose position is determined by an occupation that *requires* training beyond the Bachelor's level. Thus, "professional" includes M.D.'s, lawyers, dentists, and those studying to be such, but not school teachers, nurses, accountants, or social workers, regardless of whether or not they actually possessed post-graduate degrees.

(6) *Managers*. This class includes all those whose position is defined *either* by being a non-manual employee with an income in excess of $20,000 for the past year, *or* being self-employed with an income in excess of $30,000 for the past year.

(7) *Upper-Class*. This class includes all those whose position is defined by living entirely from inherited wealth. This category did not appear among the respondents.

The third survey, the "Leadership Survey," was conducted in the seven Community Planning Board areas covered by the New York Neighborhood Study. A reputational method was used to select approximately fifty respondents in each community (the total N was 368) who were either general community leaders or influential in specific issue areas. There were obvious gaps in the procedure. Leadership was not rigorously defined; hence there is no basis for assuming that the results represent anything more than the views of the respondents themselves. Additionally, as in all reputational studies, there is the possibility of coming up with an incestuous sample, and a clear danger of racial and class bias.

There were also problems with the questionnaire itself. It was overly long and led many respondents to become impatient in the course of the interview. Many questions, moreover, while perfectly clear in the abstract, become extremely confusing when applied to a specific social setting. Finally, one especially unfortunate feature forced respondents to answer all subsequent questions in terms of the single issue area that they at one point named as the major focus of their community activity. In a number of cases in which the person interviewed had a wide range of experience on a variety of issues, the procedure generated distorted responses.

Nonetheless, the Leadership Survey did produce some useful results for Washington Heights. The list of respondents is definitely skewed away from the Hispanic community and toward the more affluent whites. Among the white leaders there are none who should not be included, and probably 40 percent would appear on any list of local leaders in CPD 12. Blacks were adequately represented in terms of numbers, although they tended to be black members of predominantly white organizations. More clearly black organizations, such as the Poverty Corporation, some of its delegate agencies, and the parents associations of the local public schools, seemed to be neglected.

I have tried to be very cautious in drawing inferences from the three surveys. The limited size of the relevant samples, especially the very small N in some important categories, compels such a prudent reading of results. Indeed, I treat

the survey findings as *suggestive* only, not as statistically significant or as high science. Read in conjunction with census materials and more qualitative data, however, the survey results help build a portrait of the community at a significant historical moment.

NOTES

Chapter 1. Introduction

[1] A recent, and lively, treatment of these themes is Godfrey Hodgson, *America in Our Times* (New York: Vintage Books, 1977).

[2] E. J. Hobsbawm, "From Social History to the History of Society," *Daedalus,* winter 1971, p. 34.

[3] Daniel Patrick Moynihan, *The Politics of a Guaranteed Income* (New York: Random House, 1973), pp. 102–3.

[4] Cf. James Q. Wilson, *Political Organizations* (New York: Basic Books, 1973); and Paul E. Peterson, "Incentive Theory and Group Influence" (Paper presented at the American Political Science Association Meetings, 1975).

[5] Aristide R. Zolberg, "Moments of Madness," *Politics and Society* 2 (winter 1972): 183–207.

[6] *New York Times,* 4 March 1978, p. 9.

[7] Daniel Bell and Virginia Held, "The Community Revolution," *The Public Interest,* no. 16 (summer 1969), p. 143.

[8] Lawrence Herson, "The Lost World of Municipal Government," *American Political Science Review 51* (June 1957); Robert T. Daland, "Political Science and the Study of Urbanism," ibid.

[9] Cf. James Rule, "The Problem with Social Problems," *Politics and Society* 2 (fall 1971).

[10] William Kornblum, *Blue Collar Community* (Chicago: University of Chicago Press, 1974).

[11] I owe this formulation to Steven Lukes, "Power and Structure," *Essays in Social Theory* (London: Macmillan, 1977).

[12] Johan Huizinga, *America* (New York: Harper & Row, 1972), p. 6.

[13] Werner Sombart, *Warum gibt es in den Vereinigten Staaten keinen Sozialismus?* (Tübingen: J. C. B. Mohr, 1906). The only full English translation is by Patricia M. Hocking and C. T. Husbands, *Why Is There No Socialism in the United States?* (White Plains, N.Y.: M. E. Sharpe, 1976).

[14] Ibid., p. 119 (italics deleted).

[15] E. P. Thompson, "The Peculiarities of the English," in Ralph Miliband and John Saville, eds., *The Socialist Register, 1965* (London: Merlin Press, 1965), p. 354.

[16] This list of three conventional explanations is by no means exhaustive; rather, these are the most frequently given explanations, each of which partially, but only partially, contributes to a convincing interpretation of American exceptionalism.

[17] Rowland Berthoff, "The American Social Order: A Conservative Hypothesis," *American Historical Review* 65 (April 1960): 499.

[18] Friedrich Engels, "No Large Socialist Party in America," cited in Arnold

Birenbaum and Edward Greer, "Toward a Structural Theory of Working Class Culture," *Ethnicity* 3 (March 1976): 4.

[19] Stanley Aronowitz, *False Promises: The Shaping of American Working Class Consciousness* (New York: McGraw-Hill, 1973), p. 140.

[20] Amy Bridges, "Ethnicity and Class Structure: Notes on United States Ethnic Studies," unpublished ms. Cf. John Evansohn, "Promises, Promises: A Critical Review of *False Promises*," *Radical History Review* 2 (summer 1975), for an expanded discussion of these themes.

[21] J. David Greenstone, "Ethnicity, Class, and Discontent," *Ethnicity* 2 (March 1974); and Donald von Eschen et al., "The Organizational Substructure of Disorderly Politics," *Social Forces* 49 (June 1971).

[22] Herbert G. Gutman, "Work, Culture and Society in Industrializing America," *American Historical Review* 78 (June 1973).

[23] Werner Sombart, "American Capitalism's Economic Rewards," in John Laslett and Seymour Martin Lipset, eds., *Failure of a Dream?* (Garden City, N.Y.: Doubleday Anchor, 1974), p. 599.

[24] Stephan Thernstrom, "Socialism and Social Mobility," in ibid., p. 551.

[25] Ibid., p. 519.

[26] Edward Greer, "Social Mobility in the U.S. Working Class," *Monthly Review* 26 (February 1975): 54.

[27] Seymour Martin Lipset, "Comment on Thernstrom," in Laslett and Lipset, eds., *Failure,* p. 528.

[28] Tom Rishøj, "Metropolitan Social Mobility, 1850–1950: The Case of Copenhagen," *Quality and Quantity* 5 (June 1971); Natalie Rogoff, *Recent Trends in Occupational Mobility* (New York: Free Press, 1963).

[29] Pitirim Sorokin, *Social and Cultural Mobility* (London: Collier-Macmillan, 1959).

[30] Cf. Frederick Jackson Turner, *The Frontier in American History* (New York: Henry Holt, 1920); Richard Hofstadter, *The American Political Tradition* (New York: Knopf, 1948); David M. Potter, *People of Plenty: Economic Abundance and the American Character* (Chicago: University of Chicago Press, 1954); Louis Hartz, *The Liberal Tradition in America* (New York: Harcourt, Brace, 1955); Daniel Boorstin, *The Americans,* 3 vols. (New York: Random House, 1958–1973); Michael Kammen, *People of Paradox* (New York: Vintage Books, 1973).

[31] See Bruce Wilkenfeld, "New York City Neighborhoods, 1730," *New York History* 57 (April 1976); Edward Pessen, "The Egalitarian Myth and the American Social Reality," *American Historical Review* 76 (October 1971); Douglas T. Miller, *Jacksonian Aristocracy* (New York: Oxford University Press, 1967).

[32] Hartz, *Liberal Tradition,* p. 20.

[33] Louis Hartz, "Comment," *Comparative Studies in Society and History* 5 (April 1963): 284.

[34] Cited from the New York *Labor Standard,* May 6, 1876, and from the Detroit *Labor Leaf,* September 30, 1885, in Gutman, "Work, Culture and Society," p. 568.

[35] Hartz, *Liberal Tradition,* p. 9.

[36] John H. Goldthorpe and David Lockwood, "Affluence and the British Class Structure," *Sociological Review* 11 (July 1963).

[37] Richard Hofstadter, *The Progressive Historians: Turner, Beard, Parrington* (New York: Vintage Books, 1970), p. 457.

[38] Still another school of American exceptionalism, identified with the work of Daniel Bell, argues that the reasons for the distinctive patterning of class in

America may be found, not in the conditions of the society, but in the actions of radicals and socialists themselves. Factors internal to the socialist movement—including ideological rigidity, leadership shortcomings, and tactical opportunism—account, in this view, for the failure to fashion a cohesive, conscious working class whose members understand their lives as shaped in all dimensions most fundamentally by capital. This kind of argument begs a number of important questions: Were the practices of American socialists really so different from those of their European counterparts? If so, in which ways? And even if so, why did they regularly act in ways that were not productive? Unless these questions are answered, this explanation cannot move beyond tautological claims. See Daniel Bell, *Marxian Socialism in the United States* (Princeton, N.J.: Princeton University Press, 1967).

[39] Antonio Gramsci, *Selections from the Prison Notebooks* (New York: International Publishers, 1971), p. 235.

[40] Clifford Geertz, *The Interpretation of Cultures* (New York: Basic Books, 1973), p. 22.

[41] Harry Eckstein, *Division and Cohesion in Democracy: A Study of Norway* (Princeton, N.J.: Princeton University Press, 1966).

PART ONE. AMERICAN PATTERNS OF URBANISM AND CLASS
Chapter 2. Community, Capitalist Development, and the Emergence of Class

[1] This point bears emphasis. The content and boundaries of a community are given by what people do in their place of residence at specific historical moments and by the relationship of these activities to other dimensions of their lives. Seen this way, both the historicist and positivist traditions have much raw material to contribute to our understanding of community. But seen this way, their attempts at definitions of community are doomed to mislead, since the meaning and place of community within a given social formation *necessarily* change over time, as the relationship of living space to other spheres of activity changes, and as patterns of production, consumption, political life, ideology, and everyday social interactions undergo change. As a locus of activity, not only the content and meaning of community may be transformed in historical time and space, but the functions its activities perform for the reproduction of the larger social whole may also undergo considerable and dramatic shifts.

[2] Henri Pirenne, "The Stages in the Social History of Capitalism," *American Historical Review* 19 (April 1914): 515, 495.

[3] Raymond Williams, *Keywords: A Vocabulary of Culture and Society* (New York: Oxford University Press, 1976), p. 66.

[4] Murray Bookchin, *The Limits of the City* (New York: Harper & Row, 1974), pp. 49, 50.

[5] See especially Lewis Mumford, *The City in History* (New York: Harcourt, Brace, 1961).

[6] Howard Saalman, *Medieval Cities* (New York: George Braziller, 1968), p. 32.

[7] Joseph Gies and Frances Gies, *Life in a Medieval City* (New York: Apollo Editions, 1969), p. 34.

[8] Ibid., p. 77.

[9] Mumford, *City in History*, p. 270.

[10] Ibid., p. 313.

[11] Ibid., p. 310.

[12] Fernand Braudel, *Capitalism and Material Life* (New York: Harper & Row, 1973), p. 399.

[13] M. M. Postan, *The Mediaeval Economy and Society: An Economic History of Britain in the Middle Ages* (London: Weidenfeld and Nicolson, 1972), p. 212.

[14] Taking this position, Paul Sweezy, in a celebrated debate with Maurice Dobb, argued that feudal cities were the "prime mover" in the transition from feudalism to capitalism because they constituted an "external" agent of dissolution within the embrace of the feudal mode of production. In his rejoinder Dobb did not disagree with the characterization of feudal towns as external agents, but rather insisted that the contradictory elements in feudalism could best be located within its agrarian economy. The relevant essays have been collected in Rodney Hilton, ed., *The Transition from Feudalism to Capitalism* (London: New Left Books, 1976).

[15] For a pointed critique of this position, see Raymond Williams, *The Country and the City* (New York: Oxford University Press, 1973), chap. 5.

[16] Marc Bloch, *Feudal Society* (London: Routledge & Kegan Paul, 1965), p. 444.

[17] Braudel, *Capitalism,* p. 398.

[18] Perry Anderson, *Passages from Antiquity to Feudalism* (London: New Left Books, 1974), p. 148.

[19] "Thus a *dynamic opposition* of town and country was alone possible in the feudal mode of production: opposition between an urban economy of increasing commodity exchange, controlled by merchants and organized in guilds and corporations, and a rural economy of natural exchange, controlled by nobles and organized in manors and strips, with communal and individual peasant enclaves. It goes without saying that the preponderance of the latter was enormous: the feudal mode of production was overwhelmingly agrarian. But its laws of motion . . . were *governed by the complex unity of its different regions, not by any simple predominance of the manor.*" Ibid., pp. 150–51 (italics added). See also pp. 11 and 422 for complementary discussions.

[20] Pirenne, "Stages," pp. 504–5.

[21] Ibid., pp. 508–9.

[22] A. B. Hibbert, "The Economic Policies of Towns," *Cambridge Economic History of Europe,* vol. 3 (Cambridge, Cambridge University Press, 1941), pp. 197–98.

[23] John Merrington, "Town and Country in the Transition to Capitalism," *New Left Review,* no. 93 (Sept.–Oct. 1975), p. 80.

[24] Ibid., p. 81.

[25] Anderson, *Passages from Antiquity,* p. 206.

[26] Moreover, Anderson observes, the urban sector of feudalism "had now developed to a point where it could decisively alter the outcome of the class struggle in the rural sector. The geographical location of the great peasant revolts of the later Middle Ages in the West tells its own story. In virtually every case they occurred in zones with powerful urban centres, which objectively acted as a ferment on these popular upheavals. . . . For the presence of major cities always meant a radiation of market relationships into the surrounding country-side: and in a transitional epoch, it was the strains of a semi-commercialized agriculture that proved most acute for the fabric of rural society." By now, however, the nobility could not shake its dependence on the towns for goods, including weapons, which only urban craftsmen could provide. Ibid., p. 205.

[27] Edward Nell, "Economic Relationships in the Decline of Feudalism: An Examination of Economic Interdependence and Social Change," *History and Theory* 6, no. 3 (1967): 317.

[28] Merrington, "Town and Country," p. 92.

[29] Cf. Immanuel Wallerstein, *The Modern World System: Capitalist Agriculture and the Origins of the European World Economy in the Sixteenth Century* (New York: Academic Press, 1974).

[30] Perry Anderson, *Lineages of the Absolutist State* (London: New Left Books, 1974), p. 19.

[31] Friedrich Engels, *Anti-Dühring* (Moscow: Progress Publishers, 1947), p. 126.

[32] Anderson, *Lineages*, p. 40.

[33] Wallerstein, *Modern World System*, p. 28.

[34] Ibid., p. 24.

[35] Mumford, *City in History*, p. 355.

[36] Ibid., p. 353.

[37] Ibid., p. 356.

[38] Ibid. For a complementary discussion, see Braudel, *Capitalism*, pp. 411–39.

[39] Mumford, *City in History*, p. 383. Also see Eli Zaretsky, "Capitalism, the Family, and Personal Life," *Socialist Revolution* 3 (March–April 1973).

[40] Mumford, *City in History*, p. 395.

[41] Ibid., p. 370 (italics added).

[42] Henry Fielding, *Inquiry into the Cause of the Late Increase of Robbers* (London, 1751); cited in Raymond Williams, *Country and City*, p. 145.

[43] Cf. Braudel, *Capitalism*, pp. 432ff.

[44] Williams, *Country and City*, p. 145 (italics added).

[45] Lynn Lees, "Metropolitan Types: London and Paris Compared," in H. J. Dyos and Michael Wolff, eds., *The Victorian City: Images and Realities*, vol. 1 (London: Routledge & Kegan Paul, 1973), p. 420.

[46] Ibid., p. 421. "For London was not, in the later sense, an industrial city. It was a capital centre of trades and of distribution: of skilled craftsmen in metals and in print; of clothing and furniture and fashion; of all the work connected with shipping and the market. . . . The new industrial city, when it came in the North, would be a creation of one or two kinds of work, and in its physical characteristics would reflect this singular emphasis. London, quite apart from its historical variety, was plural and various: not only in the sense of its hundreds of trades but in the sense that it was managing and directing so much of other people's business." Williams, *Country and City*, p. 147.

[47] Lees, "Metropolitan Types," p. 419.

[48] H. J. Dyos and D. A. Reeder, "Slums and Suburbs," in Dyos and Wolff, eds., *Victorian City*, p. 369.

[49] Lees, "Metropolitan Types," p. 419. See also Gareth Stedman Jones, *Outcast London: A Study in the Relationship Between Classes in Victorian Society* (London: Oxford University Press, 1971), esp. chaps. 7 and 8.

[50] David Harvey, *Social Justice and the City* (London: Edward Arnold, 1973), p. 259.

[51] Merrington, "Town and Country," p. 88.

[52] Friedrich Engels, *The Condition of the Working Class in England* (Stanford, Cal.: Stanford University Press, 1968), pp. 54–55.

[53] Steven Marcus, *Engels, Manchester, and the Working Class* (New York: Random House, 1974), p. 193.

[54] T. S. Ashton, *The Industrial Revolution, 1760–1830* (New York: Oxford University Press, 1964), pp. 76, 87.

[55] Max Weber, *Economy and Society* (New York: Bedminster Press, 1968), p. 379.

[56] Marx, *Grundrisse* (London: Penguin Books, 1973), pp. 293, 289, 403.

[57] With the emergence of class-differentiated residence spaces that are separated from workplaces, it is possible to shift much of our discussion to the present tense, since most contemporary urban communities in advanced capitalist societies, especially in the older cities, continue to share their basic contours. Although these spaces are not workplaces, from the vantage point of capitalist production, they are essentially places for the stockpiling and reproduction of the work force. But community life is not experienced in these functional terms. Rather, three sets of activities occur within their confines: individual and collective consumption; small-scale, face-to-face affective relationships; and political exchanges.

Each of the two most important modern social theorists of community development, Tönnies and Durkheim, emphasized only one of these processes. Tönnies contrasted the capitalist city with precapitalist villages and towns. For him, the crucial difference lay in the pervasive character of the market in the *Gesellschaft*, which he conceived to be an

artificial construction of an aggregate of human beings which superficially resembles the *Gemeinschaft* in so far as the individuals live and dwell together peacefully. However, in the *Gemeinschaft* they remain essentially united in spite of all separating factors, whereas in the *Gesellschaft* they are essentially separated in spite of all the uniting factors . . . everybody is by himself and isolated and there exists a condition of tension against all others . . . nobody wants to grant and produce anything for another individual, nor will he be inclined to give ungrudgingly to another individual, if it not be in exchange for a gift or labour equivalent that he considers at least equal to what he has given.

Durkheim's terminology to describe the new communities of capitalist cities was a mirror image of Tönnies's. Durkheim referred to communal transformations as movements from mechanical to organic solidarity, from relations of constraint to relations of shared values that produce authentic forms of cooperation. Society is thus the unity of different but complementary roles, at least partly organized in space. Yet one of the most striking features of the new communities has been the fusion of relations of exchange and affect; for this reason the apparently contradictory perspectives of Tönnies and Durkheim may both be correct, if only in truncated ways. See Ferdinand Tönnies, *Community and Association* (London: Routledge & Kegan Paul, 1955), pp. 64–65, 33–34; and Emile Durkheim, *The Division of Labor in Society* (New York: Free Press, 1964).

[58] Charles Tilly, "Major Forms of Collective Action in Western Europe, 1500–1975," *Theory and Society* 3 (fall 1976).

[59] John Foster, *Class Struggle and the Industrial Revolution: Early Capitalism in Three English Towns* (London: Weidenfeld & Nicolson, 1974), p. 25.

[60] Gareth Stedman Jones, "Class Struggle and the Industrial Revolution," *New Left Review*, no. 90 (March–April 1975), p. 50.

Chapter 3. City Trenches

[1] Raymond Williams, *Culture and Society* (New York: Columbia University Press, 1950).

[2] Remarkably, with the exception of Susan Hirsch, in her first-rate study of Newark, New Jersey, scholars have left these issues unexamined. Hirsch's work, moreover, for all its merits, is rather more descriptive of the split between work and community than analytical. Susan G. Hirsch, *Roots of the American Working Class* (Philadelphia: University of Pennsylvania Press, 1978).

[3] Richard Morris, *Government and Labor in Early America* (New York: Columbia University Press, 1946), p. 42; Howard P. Chudacoff, *The Evolution of American Urban Society* (Englewood Cliffs, N.J.: Prentice-Hall, 1975), p. 14; and Allan R. Pred, *The Spatial Dynamics of U.S. Urban-Industrial Growth, 1800–1914* (Cambridge, Mass.: MIT Press, 1966), chap. 4.

[4] Douglass C. North, *The Economic Growth of the United States, 1790–1860* (Englewood Cliffs, N.J.: Prentice-Hall, 1961); William N. Parker and Franklee Whartenby, "The Growth of Output Before 1840," Conference on Research in Income and Wealth, *Trends in the American Economy in the Nineteenth Century* (Princeton, N.J.: Princeton University Press, 1961); Stanley Lebergott, "Labor Force and Employment, 1800–1960," Conference on Research in Income and Wealth, *Output, Employment, and Productivity in the United States after 1800* (New York: Columbia University Press, 1966); Thomas C. Cochran, "The Business Revolution," *American Historical Review* 79 (December 1974); and J. R. T. Hughes and Nathan Rosenberg, "The United States Business Cycle Before 1860: Some Problems of Interpretation," *Economic History Review* 15, no. 3 (1963).

[5] North, *Economic Growth*; Walt W. Rostow, *The Stages of Economic Growth* (Cambridge: Cambridge University Press, 1961); Louis M. Hacker, *The Course of American Economic Growth and Development* (New York: Wiley, 1970); and Alfred Chandler, Jr., *The Visible Hand: The Managerial Revolution in American Business* (Cambridge, Mass.: Harvard University Press, 1977). On the impact of these changes on income and wealth, see Jeffrey Williamson and Peter Lindert, "Long Term Trends in American Wealth Inequality" (Discussion Paper given at the Institute for Research on Poverty, December, 1977).

[6] Allan R. Pred, *Urban Growth and the Circulation of Information: The United States System of Cities, 1790–1840* (Cambridge, Mass.: Harvard University Press, 1973), chap. 4.

[7] Jeffrey Williamson, "Antebellum Urbanization in the American Northeast," *Journal of Economic History* 25 (December 1965): 598–99.

[8] Pred, *Spatial Dynamics*, pp. 168, 176.

[9] Chandler, *Visible Hand*, pp. 15, 18, 27.

[10] Ibid., pp. 51, 57; Victor S. Clark, *History of Manufacturers in the United States*, 3 vols. (New York: Carnegie Institution, 1929).

[11] John Sawyer, "The Social Basis of the American System of Manufacturing," *Journal of Economic History* 14 (1954): 369.

[12] Raymond A. Mohl, "The Preindustrial American City," in Raymond A. Mohl and James F. Richardson, eds., *The Urban Experience: Themes in American History* (Belmont, Cal.: Wadsworth, 1973), p. 7.

[13] Pred, *Spatial Dynamics*, p. 183; see also Douglass C. North, "Location Theory and Regional Economic Growth," *Journal of Political Economy* 63 (June 1955).

[14] Williamson, "Antebellum Urbanization," pp. 603–4.

[15] David Montgomery, "The Working Classes of the Pre-Industrial American City, 1780–1830," *Labor History* 9 (winter 1968).

[16] Carl Abbott, "The Neighborhoods of New York, 1760–1775," *New York History* 55 (January 1974): 51.

[17] Ibid.; Sam Bass Warner, Jr., *The Private City: Philadelphia in Three Periods of Its Growth* (Philadelphia: University of Pennsylvania Press, 1968), pp. 2, 11.

[18] Ibid., p. 11.

[19] Ira Rosenwaike, *Population History of New York City* (Syracuse, N.Y.: Syracuse University Press, 1972), p. 16.

20. It is tempting to overstate the extent of change in the internal organization of city space that economic change entailed. As late as 1860, Warner cautions, most areas of Philadelphia were still "a jumble of occupations and classes, shops, homes, immigrants and native Americans." Yet the direction of change was unmistakable, and its degree quite dramatic. Warner, *Private City*, p. 50.

21. Ibid., pp. 58–59.

22. Ibid., p. 59.

23. Pred, *Spatial Dynamics*, p. 208.

24. Robert Ernst, *Immigrant Life in New York City* (New York: King's Crown Press, 1949), p. 38

25. For a brief comparative and theoretical discussion, see my "Working Class Formation in Europe and the United States: CES Research Group Report," *European Studies Newsletter* 9 (June 1980). See also the special issue on "Culture and Class," *Radical History Review*, no. 18 (fall 1978).

26. Asa Briggs, ed., *Chartist Studies* (London: Macmillan, 1959); John Foster, *Class Struggle and the Industrial Revolution* (London: Methuen, 1975); Trygve Tholfsen, *Working Class Radicalism in Mid-Victorian England* (New York: Columbia University Press, 1977); and E. P. Thompson, *The Making of the English Working Class* (London: Penguin Books, 1968).

27. Aristide R. Zolberg, "Belgium," in Raymond Grew, ed., *Crises of Political Development in Europe and the United States* (Princeton, N.J.: Princeton University Press, 1978).

28. Amy Bridges, "A City in the Republic: New York and the Origins of Machine Politics," Ph.D. diss., Department of Political Science, University of Chicago, December 1980, p. 48.

29. Martin Shefter, "Parties, Patronage and Political Change" (Paper presented to the Annual Meeting of the American Political Science Association, Chicago, September 1976).

30. Cf. Oscar Handlin, *Boston's Immigrants* (New York: Atheneum, 1976), esp. chap. 7.

31. Bridges, "City in the Republic," chap. 5.

32. Philip Foner, *History of the Labor Movement in the United States,* vol. 1 (New York: International Publishers, 1972), pp. 221, 223. See also John Commons et al., *History of Labor in the United States,* vol. 1 (New York: Macmillan, 1918), chap. 7.

33. Foner, *Labor Movement*, p. 224.

34. The best discussion is Amy Bridges, "The Working Classes in Ante-Bellum Urban Politics, New York City, 1828–1863," unpublished ms., June 1977.

35. Cf. Michael Wallace, "Changing Concepts of Party in the United States: New York, 1815–1828," *American Historical Review* 74 (December 1968).

36. Richard Hofstadter, *The Idea of a Party System* (Berkeley and Los Angeles: University of California Press, 1965), p. 211.

37. For a rich, if flawed, Beardian discussion of these issues, see Gabriel Almond, "Plutocracy and Politics in New York City" (Ph.D. diss., University of Chicago, Department of Political Science, 1938), esp. chap. 4.

38. Ronald P. Formisano, "Deferential-Participant Politics: The Early Republic's Political Culture, 1789–1840," *American Political Science Review* 68 (June 1974): 47; Martin Shefter, "Party Bureaucracy and Political Change in the United States," in Louis Maisel and Joseph Cooper, eds., *The Development of Political Parties: Patterns of Evolution and Decay*, Sage Electoral Studies Yearbook, vol. 4 (Beverly Hills, Cal.: Sage Publications, 1979).

[39] Ibid.; Matthew Crenson, *The Federal Machine: Beginnings of Bureaucracy in Jacksonian America* (Baltimore: Johns Hopkins University Press, 1975).

[40] Diane Ravitch, *The Great School Wars* (New York: Basic Books, 1974); David Rothman, *The Discovery of the Asylum* (Boston: Little, Brown, 1971); Wilbur R. Miller, *Cops and Bobbies: Police Authority in New York and London, 1830–1870* (Chicago: University of Chicago Press, 1977); Frank Goodnow, *Municipal Government* (New York: Century, 1909), pp. 234–324. Cf. Matthew Holden, "Ethnic Accommodation in a Historical Case," *Comparative Studies in Society and History* 8 (January 1966).

[41] Morris, *Government and Labor;* Gaston V. Rimlinger, "Labor and the Government: A Comparative Historical Perspective," *Journal of Economic History* 37 (March 1977): 213.

[42] Ibid., p. 219.

[43] Thompson, *English Working Class*, p. 550.

[44] Rimlinger, "Labor and Government," pp. 213–15.

[45] Foner, *Labor Movement*, pp. 163–64.

[46] Thompson, *English Working Class*, p. 570

[47] Foner, *Labor Movement*, p. 108.

[48] Douglas T. Miller, *Jacksonian Aristocracy: Class and Democracy in New York, 1830–1860* (New York: Oxford University Press, 1967), p. 48.

[49] Ibid., p. 49; see also Stephen Mayer, "People v. Fisher: The Shoemakers Strike of 1833," *The New York Historical Society Quarterly* 62 (January 1978).

[50] Miller, *Jacksonian Aristocracy*, pp. 146–48.

[51] Helen Sumner, "Citizenship," in John Commons, ed., *History of Labor in the United States*, vol. 1 (New York: Macmillan, 1926), p. 326.

[52] Reinhard Bendix, *Nation-Building and Citizenship* (Garden City, N.Y.: Doubleday Anchor, 1969), p. 119.

[53] This work is summarized in Richard Hofstadter, *The Progressive Historians* (New York: Vintage Books, 1968), pp. 280–84.

[54] Ibid., p. 282.

[55] Shefter, "Parties."

[56] J. P. Nettl, "The State as a Conceptual Variable," *World Politics* 20 (July 1968): 577–78 (italics added). See also Daniel Elazar, *The American Partnership* (Chicago: University of Chicago Press, 1962).

[57] Samuel P. Huntington, *Political Order in Changing Societies* (New Haven, Conn.: Yale University Press, 1968), p. 129.

[58] Hofstadter, *Party System.*

[59] Walter Dean Burnham, "Party Systems and the Political Process," in William Nisbet Chambers and Walter Dean Burnham, eds., *The American Party Systems* (New York: Oxford University Press, 1967), pp. 238–92; see also William Nisbet Chambers, "Party Development and Party Action: The American Origins," *History and Theory* 3, no. 1 (1963).

[60] Formisano, "Deferential-Participant Politics," p. 478.

[61] Richard P. McCormick, "Political Development and the Second Party System," in Chambers and Burnham, eds., *American Party Systems*, p. 110.

[62] The pioneering study of voting behavior in this period is Lee Benson, *The Concept of Jacksonian Democracy* (Princeton, N.J.: Princeton University Press, 1961). For a critique of this volume and for subsequent accounts in this tradition,

see Richard B. Latner and Peter Levine, "Perspectives on Antebellum Pietistic Politics," *Reviews in American History* 4 (March 1976). Two important case studies are Kathleen Neils Conzen, *Immigrant Milwaukee, 1836–1860* (Cambridge, Mass.: Harvard University Press, 1976); and Oscar Handlin, *Boston's Immigrants* (New York: Atheneum, 1974).

[63] Ravitch, *School Wars*; David Tyack, *The One Best System* (Cambridge, Mass.: Harvard University Press, 1974), pp. 84ff.

[64] Warner, *Private City*, p. 155; see also David Montgomery, "The Shuttle and the Cross: Weavers and Artisans in the Kensington Riots of 1844," *Journal of Social History* 5 (summer 1972).

[65] Richard Wade, "Urban Life in Western America, 1790–1830," *American Historical Review* 64 (October 1958); Robert O. Schultze, "The Bifurcation of Power in a Satellite City," in Morris Janowitz, ed., *Community Political Systems* (Glencoe, Ill.: Free Press, 1961).

[66] Robert Dahl, *Who Governs?* (New Haven, Conn.: Yale University Press, 1961).

[67] Caroline Golab, *Immigrant Destinations* (Philadelphia: Temple University Press, 1977), pp. 154, 156. Italics added.

[68] Allan Silver, "The Demand for Order in Civil Society: A Review of Some Themes in the History of Urban Crime, Police, and Riot," in David Bordua, ed., *The Police* (New York: Wiley, 1967), pp. 8, 12–13.

[69] M. J. Heale, "From City Fathers to Social Critics: Humanitarianism and Government in New York, 1790–1860," *Journal of American History* 63 (June 1976): 25, 29.

[70] Tyack, *One Best System*, p. 78.

[71] Martin Shefter, "The Emergence of the Political Machine: An Alternative View," in Willis Hawley, Michael Lipsky, et al., *Theoretical Perspectives on Urban Politics* (Englewood Cliffs, N.J.: Prentice-Hall, 1976), p. 34.

[72] M. Ostrogorski, *Democracy and the Organization of Political Parties*, vol. 2 (New York: Doubleday Anchor, 1964), p. 180.

[73] Werner Sombart, *Why Is There No Socialism in the United States?* (White Plains, N.Y.: Sharpe, 1976), p. 50.

[74] Ira Katznelson, *Black Men, White Cities: Race, Politics, and Migration in the United States, 1900–30, and Britain, 1948–68* (New York: Oxford University Press, 1973), p. 87.

[75] Douglas W. Rae, *The Political Consequences of Electoral Laws* (New Haven, Conn.: Yale University Press, 1967), p. 142; Gerhard Casper, "Social Differences and the Franchise," *Daedalus*, fall 1976, p. 108.

[76] Raymond Williams, *Politics and Letters* (London: New Left Books, 1979), p. 182.

[77] Cf. James Weinsten, *The Decline of Socialism in America* (New York, Vintage Books, 1969); Al Gedicks, "Ethnicity, Class Solidarity, and Labor Radicalism among Finnish Immigrants in Michigan Copper Country," *Politics and Society* 7, no. 2 (1977); Melvyn Dubofsky, "Success and Failure of Socialism in New York City, 1900–1918: A Case Study," *Labor History* 9 (fall 1968); Seymour Martin Lipset, "Why No Socialism in the United States," in Seweryn Bialer and Sophia Sluzar, eds., *Sources of Contemporary Radicalism* (New York: Westview Press, 1977); Charles Leineweber, "The American Socialist Party and 'New' Immigrants," *Science and Society* 32 (winter 1968); Henry F. Bedford, *Socialism and the Workers in Massachusetts, 1886–1912* (Amherst, Mass.: University of Massachusetts Press, 1966); and Stanley Buder, *Pullman* (New York: Oxford University Press, 1967).

Chapter 4. The Making of Northern Manhattan

[1] Lee A. Lendt, "A Social History of Washington Heights, New York City," unpublished ms., Columbia–Washington Heights Community Mental Health Project, February 1960; William Culver, "Recollections of Northern Manhattan," *New York Historical Society Quarterly* 32 (January 1948): 20–31.

[2] Richard Shephard, "Washington Heights—the Top of the Island," *New York Times*, 17 July 1976, p. c3.

[3] Pierre Vilar, "Marxist History, a History in the Making: Towards a Dialogue with Althusser," *New Left Review*, no. 80 (July–August 1973), p. 93.

[4] George Bird Grinnell, *Audubon Park* (New York: Hispanic Society of America, 1927).

[5] William B. Phillips, ed., *Washington Heights in the Past, in the Present, in the Future* (New York: The Washington Heights Taxpayers Association, 1889), pp. 14, 16.

[6] *West End and Washington Heights Gazette*, 1 May 1895, p. 4; 16 May 1895, p. 4.

[7] G. B. L. Arner, "Land Values in New York City," *Quarterly Journal of Economics* (August 1922), cited in Helena Dickinson, "Summary Report of Land Values in New York City Made by Dr. Arner in 1921–22," appendix 2, in Thomas Adams et al., *Population, Land Values and Government*, Regional Survey, vol. 2 (New York: Regional Plan of New York and Its Environs, 1929), pp. 187–88.

[8] *West End and Washington Heights Gazette*, 16 October 1895, p. 2.

[9] Peter Lee Abeles and Robert Weinberg, *Washington Heights Community Study* (Report to the New York City Planning Commission, March 1968), pp. 4–6.

[10] In the 1960s, as we shall see, each of these tracts had a distinctive ethnic cast: 239 was overwhelmingly black; 261, Dominican and Cuban; 273, Jewish; and 295, Irish. The block survey discussed in Chapter 6 is drawn from blocks either in or immediately contiguous with these four tracts.

[11] Each of the four tracts reached its measured population peak in the 1940 census and declined thereafter. Their rates of growth differed, however. If we thus give the 1940 population a percentage rating of 100, the trend for the four tracts is as follows:

	South Washington Heights (tract 239)	East Washington Heights (tract 261)	West Washington Heights (tract 273)	Inwood (tract 295)
1915	65	68	1	4
1920	80	79	15	17
1925	86	81	31	29
1930	96	90	62	58
1940	100	100	100	100

SOURCE: Walter Laidlaw, ed., *Population of the City of New York, 1890–1930* (New York: Cities Census Committee, 1932), pp. 53, 73. Department of Commerce, *U.S. Census*, 1940.

[12] According to census data in Laidlaw, the religious/ethnic distribution of the population, in 1920, was the following:

	South Washington Heights (tract 239) N = 3,213	East Washington Heights (tract 261) N = 11,792	West Washington Heights (tract 273) N = 1,138	Inwood (tract 295) N = 1,475
CATHOLIC	29.4%	26.9%	26.5%	26.1%
GREEK	0.1	0.2	0.1	0.1
JEWISH	20.0	33.3	19.4	20.3
PROTESTANT	49.5	39.6	54.0	54.5

SOURCE: Laidlaw, *Population,* p. 292.

[13] Lendt, "Social History"; Abeles and Weinberg, *Washington Heights Study.*

[14] In 1922 the area was described as "a rapidly growing section. It is entirely residential in character. It is the least congested section of Manhattan. The people are of moderate means and live in modern apartment houses. . . . There are comparatively few people of foreign birth. . . . The stores are all of a neighborhood character." Research Department, *New York Herald, New York Market* (New York, 1922), p. 79.

[15] Gerhart Saenger and Harvey M. Shulman, "A Study of the Intercultural Behavior and Attitudes among Residents of the Upper West Side" (Confidential report, City College, Department of Sociology, for the Washington Heights–Inwood Citizen's Committee for Youth, 1946), p. 1.

[16] Hulbert Footner, *New York, City of Cities* (Philadelphia: Lippincott, 1937), p. 271.

[17] Lendt, "Social History"; pp. 59ff.

[18] Abeles and Weinberg, *Washington Heights Study,* pp. 16–17.

[19] City of New York, *New Dwelling Units Completed 1921–1972 in New York City,* December 1973, p. 14.

[20] Yet they still did not have a fully urban "feel." A 1927 observer wrote, "The busy corner of Broadway and 181st Street, for example, looks like anything but modern New York. Rather it is the main business street of some little county-seat in the Middle West." Will Irwin, *Highlights of Manhattan* (New York: Century, 1927), p. 371.

[21] Daniel P. Moynihan, "The Irish," in Nathan Glazer and Daniel P. Moynihan, *Beyond the Melting Pot* (Cambridge, Mass.: MIT Press, 1963); Elmer Cornwell, "Bosses, Machines, and Ethnic Group," *The Annals of the American Academy of Political and Social Sciences* 353 (May 1964).

[22] Oliver MacDonagh, "The Irish Famine Emigration to the United States," *Perspectives in American History* 10 (1976): 373–74.

[23] Ibid., p. 377.

[24] Ibid., pp. 378–86.

[25] Cf. Moynihan, "Irish"; John Tracy Ellis, *American Catholicism* (Chicago: University of Chicago Press, 1956); Joseph H. Fichter, *Parochial School* (Notre Dame, Ind.: University of Notre Dame Press, 1958); idem, *Social Relations in the Urban Parish* (Chicago: University of Chicago Press, 1954); Andrew M. Greeley, *The Catholic Experience* (Garden City, N.Y.: Doubleday, 1967); Thomas T. McAvoy, *A History of the Catholic Church in the United States* (Notre Dame, Ind.: University of Notre Dame Press, 1969); and Gerald Shaughnessy, *Has the Immigrant Kept*

the Faith? A Study of Immigration and Catholic Growth in the United States, 1790–1920 (New York: Macmillan, 1925).

[26] Salo W. Baron, *Steeled by Adversity* (Philadelphia: Jewish Publication Society of America, 1971), esp. chap. 10; Zosa Szajkowski, "Emigration to America or Reconstruction in Europe," in Abraham J. Karp, ed., *The Jewish Experience in America: The Era of Immigration* (New York: Ktav Publishing, 1969); Simon Kuznets, "Immigration of Russian Jews to the United States: Background and Structure," *Perspectives in American History* 9 (1975).

[27] Ibid., p. 57.

[28] Cf. Abraham J. Karp, ed., *The Jewish Experience in America: At Home in America* (New York: Ktav Publishing, 1969); Marshall Sklare, ed., *The Jews: Social Patterns of an American Group* (New York: Free Press, 1958); Arthur Goren, *New York Jews and the Quest for Community* (New York: Columbia University Press, 1970).

[29] Neighborhood Action Program, "Community Organization and Service Directory for Washington Heights, Inwood, and Marble Hill," mimeographed, April 1972.

[30] Of the 30,295 residents of census tracts 261, 273, and 295 in 1940 (located in East Washington Heights, West Washington Heights, and Inwood, respectively), 6,459 were born outside the United States. Income data by census tract are not available for 1940. Saenger and Shulman's 1946 survey provides a rough surrogate. They reported the following family-income patterns for white residents:

	Catholics (%)	Jews (%)	Protestants (%)	All Whites (%)
FAMILY INCOME				
BELOW $1,600	14	11	12	12
$1,600–2,500	42	24	43	34
ABOVE $2,500	44	65	45	54
	(N = 79)	(N = 94)	(N = 35)	(N = 208)

SOURCE: Saenger and Shulman, "Intercultural Behavior," p. 5.

Rent patterns indicate that comparable shares of income were spent for housing by each group:

	Catholics (%)	Jews (%)	Protestants (%)	All Whites (%)
MONTHLY RENT				
BELOW $40	25	2	16	13
$40–50	33	34	44	35
ABOVE $50	42	64	40	52
	(N = 79)	(N = 94)	(N = 35)	(N = 208)

SOURCE: Ibid.

Census data on the area's housing further indicate the basic pattern of market homogeneity:

Tracts:	261 (%)	273 (%)	295 (%)	Manhattan (%)
TENANT OCCUPIED	97	87	96	88
VACANT	4	6	3	7
BLACK OCCUPIED	1	1	1	15
OVERCROWDED (MORE THAN 1.51 PERSONS/ROOM)	3	1	4	6
NEEDING MAJOR REPAIRS, AND/OR WITHOUT PRIVATE BATH	1	1	1	23

SOURCE: Computed from U.S. census data, 1940.

Under 3 percent of the housing in these tracts dated from before 1900. Eight of ten buildings in tract 261 were constructed before 1920; in tracts 273 and 295 most housings units were built in the 1920s, though about one in three was constructed during the Great Depression. For New York City most data in 1940 were compiled not by tract but by health area, defined as an "aggregation of contiguous census tracts with an average population of about 25,000." I have examined the three health areas that are larger than, but include, tracts 261, 273, and 295 (health areas nos. 4, 2.22, and 1.20, respectively). These data confirm Saenger and Shulman's findings on rent patterns (respective average rents were $45.74; $64.09; and $47.22). Approximately 99 percent of the residents possessed radios (compared to 94 percent for Manhattan as a whole); over 96 percent owned mechanical refrigerators (as opposed to iceboxes, still used by about 40 percent of Manhattan's population); and 99 percent lived in centrally heated apartments (compared to approximately 75 percent for the borough's population). Department of Commerce, Bureau of the Census, *Population and Housing: Statistics for Health Areas, New York City* (Washington: U.S. Government Printing Office, 1942), pp. 142, 148.

[31] Lendt, "Social History"; Saenger and Shulman, "Intercultural Behavior."

[32] *Washington Heights Neighbor*, 9 September 1940, 23 September 1940, and 30 September 1940; Lendt, "Social History"; Saenger and Shulman, "Intercultural Behavior"; Eric Hirshler, ed., *Jews from Germany in the United States* (New York: Farrar, Straus, 1955).

[33] Board of Elections, New York City, *Annual Reports*, 1920–1923, 1930–1933.

[34] Lendt, "Social History."

[35] Board of Elections, *Annual Reports*.

[36] M. G. Smith distinguished in a 1966 symposium on African plural societies between *differential* and *universalistic* incorporation of ethnic groups into the polity. Leo Kuper suggested a third possibility, that of *equivalent* incorporation, where the relevant groups are not structurally unequal in terms of access to material, social, and power resources. Leo Kuper and M. G. Smith, *Pluralism in Africa* (Berkeley and Los Angeles: University of California Press, 1969), p. 473.

[37] U.S. Census Reports, 1940, 1950.

[38] Reginald Pelham Bolton, *Washington Heights, Manhattan: Its Eventful Past* (New York: Dyckman Institute, 1936), p. 162.

[39] Cf. Gilbert Osofsky, *Harlem: The Making of a Ghetto* (New York: Harper & Row, 1963); Seth Scheiner, *Negro Mecca* (New York: NYU Press, 1965).

[40] Research Department, *New York Herald*, pp. 78–79.

[41] Saenger and Shulman, "Intercultural Behavior."

[42] Lendt, "Social History."

[43] Interview with Herman D. Farrell, 13 April 1974.

[44] Ibid.

PART TWO. THE CRISIS OF THE CITY
Chapter 5. The Remaking of Northern Manhattan

[1] In addition to using data generated by participant observation and governmental compilations (especially the census), the study of northern Manhattan in the 1960s and early 1970s utilizes the findings of three surveys conducted in 1972 and 1973 under the auspices of the New York Neighborhood Study of Columbia University's Bureau of Applied Social Research and the National Opinion Research Center at the University of Chicago. The first, referred to below as the Public Survey, collected data from approximately 240 respondents on twenty-four blocks in each of seven community planning districts in New York City. Although I draw for some limited comparative purposes on the survey as a whole, I have restricted myself largely to the Washington Heights–Inwood sample. The second, referred to as the Block Survey, was conducted wholly within northern Manhattan. Explicitly developed to concentrate on the links between ethnic groups and city agencies, the survey selected five blocks that maximized typical concentrations of distinctive ethnic and racial populations. The third, referred to as the Leadership Survey, interviewed community leaders identified by a reputational method in each of the community planning districts covered by the Public Survey. I draw exclusively on the Washington Heights–Inwood component. A methodological discussion of these surveys may be found in the Appendix.

[2] Using a class code we developed to analyze Block Survey data, Henry Wells and I constructed the following profile of the class structure of northern Manhattan in 1972:

	Men (N) (185)	Women (274)	Total (459)
UNDERCLASS[a]	9.2%	19.7%	15.7%
MANUAL WORKING CLASS	53.5	41.6	46.2
NONMANUAL WORKING CLASS	26.5	29.9	28.5
PETITS BOURGEOIS	5.4	5.5	5.4
PROFESSIONALS	3.2	2.9	3.1
MANAGERS	2.2	0.4	1.1

SOURCE: Block Survey.

[a] For an explication of these categories, see the Appendix.

LOCATION OF EMPLOYMENT (1972)

	White Ethnics[a] (N) (109)	Blacks (35)	Hispanics[b] (123)	Others[c] (7)	Total (279)
WASHINGTON HEIGHTS—INWOOD	20.1%	11.4%	8.9%	42.9%	15.3%
HARLEM	0.9	2.9	0.2	0.0	1.5
MANHATTAN SOUTH OF HARLEM	54.2	62.9	63.3	28.6	56.9
OUTSIDE MANHATTAN	24.8	22.8	27.6	28.6	26.3

SOURCE: Block Survey.

[a] Jews, Irish, Greeks, and other white ethnics.
[b] Cubans, Dominicans, Puerto Ricans, and other Hispanics.
[c] Asians and one American Indian.

ACTIVITIES IN NORTHERN MANHATTAN (1972)

	Jews (N) (62)	Irish (24)	Blacks (22)	Hispanics (73)	Others (57)	Total (238)
SHOPPING FOR GROCERIES	96.8%	81.0%	77.3%	80.8%	96.5%	91.2%
SHOPPING FOR CLOTHING	40.3	58.3	22.8	61.6	42.1	48.0
SHOPPING FOR HOUSE-HOLD GOODS	45.2	50.0	27.2	39.7	28.0	38.7
GOING TO PARK OR PLAYGROUND	77.4	66.7	54.6	72.6	70.2	71.4
VISITING DOCTOR OR CLINIC	75.8	79.1	63.6	76.7	61.4	72.7
ATTENDING RELIGIOUS SERVICES	75.8	87.5	54.5	78.0	70.2	75.2

SOURCE: Public Survey.

[5] Kenneth Fox, *Better City Government: Innovation in American Urban Politics, 1850–1937* (Philadelphia: Temple University Press, 1977), pp. 176–81.

[6] Frances Fox Piven, "The Social Structuring of Political Protest," *Politics and Society* 6, no. 3 (1976): 315. For further discussions, see James Q. Wilson, *Political Organizations* (New York: Basic Books, 1973); Mancur Olson, *The Logic of Collective Action* (Cambridge, Mass.: Harvard University Press, 1965); and Paul E. Peterson, *School Politics Chicago Style* (Chicago: University of Chicago Press, 1976).

[7] David Gordon, "Capitalism and the Roots of Urban Crisis," in Roger E. Alcalay and David Mermelstein, eds., *The Fiscal Crisis of American Cities* (New York: Vintage Books, 1976), pp. 109–12.

[8] Raymond Vernon, *The Changing Economic Function of the Central City* (New York: Committee for Economic Development, 1959), p. 40.

[9] Roger Friedland, "Class Power and the Central City" (Ph.D. diss., Department of Sociology, University of Wisconsin, Madison, 1976), p. 106.

[10] Friedland, "Class Power," p. 117.

[11] The performance of specific economic functions and uneven development are integrally related processes, as Coates, Johnston, and Knox point out: "The geography of well-being is primarily a reflection of the role played by (some would say allocated to) countries, regions and towns in the economic system. Our argument is then that the spatial distribution of social inequalities is a consequence of the spatially segregated functions within the dominant economic system." As a consequence, "the social livelihood of the individual (or any group of people) is in the first instance related to the economic function of the place in which he lives." Once established, moreover, the spatial arrangement of economic and social inequalities, and the dynamic of inequal development, is quite resistant to changes, as students of dependency in North-South relations on an international scale have often observed. B. E. Coates, R. J. Johnston, and P. L. Knox, *Geography and Inequality* (London: Oxford University Press, 1977), pp. 81, 90, 94–97. See also Michael Barratt-Brown, *The Economics of Imperialism* (London: Penguin Books, 1974); and G. K. Helleiner, *International Trade and Economic Development* (London: Penguin Books, 1972).

[12] These two distinctive matters have been confused in much of the discourse about older cities. A case in point is the lively debate started by two 1971 articles in *The Public Interest* that likened central cities to sandboxes or Indian reservations because of their lack of economic purpose. In a series of subsequent exchanges, Ganz and O'Brien stressed that although the cities' economic functions had changed, they were still economically significant. For evidence they pointed to the growth of white-collar employment and to an office-building boom. As I argue below, the protagonists were talking past each other.

[13] Kenneth Jackson, "Urban Deconcentration in the Nineteenth Century: A Statistical Inquiry," in Leo F. Schnore, ed., *The New Urban History* (Princeton, N.J.: Princeton University Press, 1975). Jackson's work has been controversial. Others date the decentralization of population and industry at the turn of the century. Cf. Vernon, *Changing Economic Function*.

[14] Barry Bluestone, "Economic Crisis and the Law of Uneven Development," *Politics and Society* 3 (1972): 65–82.

[15] Cf. Harry Braverman, *Labor and Monopoly Capital* (New York: Monthly Review Press, 1975), p. 246.

[16] For an excellent descriptive discussion, see Mark I. Gelfand, *Anatomy of Cities: The Federal Government and Urban America, 1933–1965* (New York: Oxford University Press, 1975); Jackson, "Urban Deconcentration," p. 118.

[17] The very rationality of the system that produced these results was also profoundly irrational, not only with respect to the outcomes for people's everyday lives, but with respect to the reproduction of the system of capitalist production itself. Clearly this is so in terms of the grossly inefficient ways that residential and job possibilities are separated from each other, in terms of the drains on capital required to maintain the "social expenses" of the welfare state, and in terms of the resulting problems of social cohesion. For the use of "social expenses," see James O'Connor, *The Fiscal Crisis of the State* (New York: St. Martin's Press, 1973), esp. chap. 6.

[18] The classic study is Robert Greenhalgh Albion, *The Rise of New York Port* (Hamden, Conn.: Archon Books, 1961).

[19] Daniel Bell, "The Three Faces of New York," *Dissent* 8 (summer 1961).

[20] Ibid., pp. 226, 230.

[21] Roy W. Bahl et al., *Taxes, Expenditures, and the Economic Base: Case Study of New York City* (New York: Praeger, 1974), pp. 2–3, 7, 15.

[22] Arthur Paris, "New York City Fiscal Crisis: The Hidden Dimension," unpublished ms. See also the trenchant discussion of the class situation of postwar blacks in William Julius Wilson, *The Declining Significance of Race* (Chicago: University of Chicago Press, 1978). A suggestive discussion of the role of minority labor may be found in Manuel Castells, "Immigrant Workers and Class Struggles in Advanced Capitalism: The Western European Experience," *Politics and Society* 5, no. 1 (1975), pp. 33–66.

[23] The data in this and the subsequent four paragraphs are compiled from U.S. Census data for 1950, 1960, and 1970.

[24] James S. Young, *The Washington Community, 1800–1823* (New York: Harcourt Brace Jovanovich, 1966), p. 64.

[25] The relevant census tracts were numbers 239, 241, 243.01, and 245.

[26] To the black middle class, " 'respectability' is the highest value, and respectability is obtained by carrying out in *public* behavior standard American bourgeois morality. Those who act correctly are middle class, while those who violate the moral code in public situations are relegated to lower class status." William Alan Muraskin, *Middle-Class Blacks in a White Society: Prince Hall Freemasonry in America* (Berkeley and Los Angeles: University of California Press, 1975), p. 13.

[27] Interview conducted by Arnold Zable, February 1973.

[28] The relevant census tracts were numbers 251, 249, 255, 253, 261, 263 (Highbridge), and 269, 277, 279, 283, and 271 (East Washington Heights).

[29] Paris, "Fiscal Crisis," has a good discussion, as does Glenn Hendricks, *The Dominican Diaspora* (New York: Teachers College Press, 1974), appendix A, pp. 149–57.

[30] The Cuban estimate, from which I started, is taken from Rafael J. Prohias and Lourdes Casal, *The Cuban Minority in the United States* (Cuban Minority Planning Study, Florida Atlantic University, August 1973).

[31] John Corry, "Neighborhoods: Changing Inwood Middle-Class," *New York Times*, 16 January 1972. Inwood census tracts were numbers 283, 285, 287, 289, 291, 293, 295, 297, 301, 303, and 307; the West Washington Heights tracts were numbers 265, 273, 275, and 281.

[32] Judy Goldstein, "The Inwood Community: Resistance to Ethnic Changeover," unpublished ms.

[33] Census tracts 273 and 295.

[34] Table, "Length of Residence in Northern Manhattan (1972)," p. 242.

[35] Table, "Selected Characteristics of Neighborhood Census Tracts (1970)," p. 243.

[36] For operational definitions of these categories, see the Appendix.

[37] Table, "Ethnicity, Race, and the Class Structure (1972)," p. 244.

[38] J. A. Barnes, "Class and Committees in a Norwegian Island Parish," *Human Relations* 7, no. 1 (1954): 43.

[39] For relevant discussions, see Elizabeth Bott, *Family and Social Network* (London: Tavistock Publications, 1972); and Richard Taub et al., "Urban Voluntary

LENGTH OF RESIDENCE IN NORTHERN MANHATTAN (1972)

YEARS IN NORTHERN MANHATTAN (N)	Jews (70)	Irish (57)	Other White Ethnics (55)	Blacks (63)	Cubans (80)	Dominicans (61)	Puerto Ricans (56)	Total (436)
LESS THAN 6 YEARS	15.7%	21.1%	25.5%	30.2%	52.5%	75.4%	52.0%	39.0%
6–10 YEARS	10.0	8.8	9.1	27.0	26.3	21.3	30.0	19.0
11–15 YEARS	2.9	8.8	7.3	14.3	11.3	1.6	2.0	7.1
16–20 YEARS	11.4	7.0	12.7	7.9	6.3	1.6	4.0	7.3
MORE THAN 20 YEARS	60.0	54.4	45.5	20.6	3.8	0.0	12.0	27.6

SOURCE: Block Survey.

SELECTED CHARACTERISTICS OF NEIGHBORHOOD CENSUS TRACTS (1970)

CHARACTERISTICS		#239 (South Washington Heights)	#261 (East Washington Heights)	#273 (West Washington Heights)	#295 (Inwood)
	(N)	(2,919)	(11,479)	(6,520)	(7,222)
AGE:					
0–15		21%	27%	10%	17%
16–64		63	65	68	65
OVER 65		16	9	29	24
	(N)	(2,140)	(6,784)	(5,185)	(5,273)
EDUCATION OF POPULATION OVER					
25: ELEM. SCH. ONLY		31%	49%	22%	30%
1–3 YRS. HIGH SCH.		26	24	15	17
COMPLETED HIGH SCH.		30	22	32	34
SOME EDUC. BEYOND HIGH SCH.		13	8	31	19
	(N)	(784)	(2,995)	(2,015)	(2,165)
INCOME OF FAMILIES:					
UNDER $4,000		25%	24%	13%	10%
$4,000–7,999		36	35	18	24
$8,000–14,999		27	31	35	40
OVER $15,000		12	10	34	26
	(N)	(714)	(1,124)	(1,268)	(1,150)
INCOME OF UNATTACHED INDIVIDUALS:					
UNDER $4,000		75%	59%	44%	49%
$4,000–7,999		19	33	39	27
$8,000–14,999		5	7	15	22
OVER $15,000		1	1	2	1

SOURCE: Department of Commerce, *U.S. Census*, 1970.

Associations, Locality Based and Externally Induced," *American Journal of Sociology* 83 (September 1977): 425–42.

[40] These thoughts were suggested by Arnold Zable.

[41] Table, "Family and Friendship Ties in Northern Manhattan (1972)," p. 245.

[42] E. E. Evans-Pritchard, *The Nuer: A Description of the Modes of Livelihood and Political Institutions of a Nilotic People* (London: Oxford University Press, 1940), chap. 3.

[43] For a discussion of a comparable value structure in nineteenth-century Kentish London, see Geoffrey Crossick, *An Artisan Elite in Victorian Society* (London: Croom Helm, 1978), esp. chap. 7.

[44] See note 34.

[45] In many respects the differences between the groups composing "new" northern Manhattan were formidable. Even within the Spanish-speaking population, the urban and Dominican residents were keenly aware of their dissimilarities—in their citizenship status, dominant political ideologies, and incomes,

ETHNICITY, RACE, AND THE CLASS STRUCTURE OF NORTHERN MANHATTAN (1972)

	Jews	Irish	Other White Ethnics	Blacks	Cubans	Dominicans	Other Hispanics	Others	Total
(N)	(71)	(58)	(55)	(63)	(78)	(61)	(67)	(13)	(466)
UNDERCLASS[a]	4.2%	5.2%	5.5%	39.5%	23.1%	24.5%	12.2%	23.1%	15.8%
MANUAL WORKER CLASS	22.6	46.6	43.6	46.2	55.2	59.1	49.2	38.4	46.4
NONMANUAL WORKING CLASS	39.4	46.6	40.0	12.7	17.9	13.1	31.3	23.1	28.4
PETITS BOURGEOIS	19.7	1.6	1.8	1.6	3.8	3.3	2.9	7.7	5.3
PROFESSIONALS	9.9	0.0	7.3	0.0	0.0	0.0	2.9	7.7	3.0
MANAGERS	4.2	0.0	1.8	0.0	0.0	0.0	1.5	0.0	1.1

SOURCE: Block Survey.
[a] For an explication of these categories, see the Appendix.

FAMILY AND FRIENDSHIP TIES IN NORTHERN MANHATTAN (1972)

	Jews	Irish	Other White Ethnics	Blacks	Cubans	Dominicans	Other Hispanics	Others	Total
(N)	(71)	(58)	(55)	(63)	(78)	(61)	(67)	(13)	(466)
RELATIVES ON HOME BLOCK	18.3%	32.8%	18.2%	23.8%	43.6%	23.0%	32.8%	38.5%	28.3%
RELATIVES IN NORTHERN MANHATTAN	57.4	39.6	40.5	42.9	56.3	49.1	34.3	10.0	46.2
FRIENDS ON HOME BLOCK	38.0	53.4	32.7	49.2	55.1	41.0	35.8	46.2	44.0
FRIENDS IN NORTHERN MANHATTAN	66.2	72.0	60.0	53.4	66.7	51.2	32.8	61.5	59.5
BEST FRIEND FROM RESPONDENT'S ETHNIC/RACIAL GROUP	66.2	73.2	NA	90.0	72.0	78.6	NA	NA	71.9 (331)

SOURCE: Block Survey.

among others. Yet by virtue of their compression into a shared territory, as well as their shared language, religion, political predicaments, internal group organization on patron-client lines, and their very recent arrival, they can for most purposes be considered collectively.

[46] Pierre Vilar, "Marxist History: A History in the Making: Towards a Dialogue with Althusser," *New Left Review*, no. 80 (July–August 1973), p. 94.

[47] Murray Edelman, "Space and Social Order" (University of Wisconsin, Institute for Research on Poverty Discussion Paper, August 1978).

[48] For Despres, the units of a plural society "may become politically functional only when individuals or groups make them so." Indeed, whether a society is merely culturally heterogeneous or plural depends not just on the diversity of group cultural patterns and on the degree of group enclosure, but also on the character of the institutional activity of political broker organizations:

With respect to each of these broker institutions, we may ask: Does the structure of the institutional activity reinforce the separate integration of similar local or minimal cultural sections at the national level of sociocultural integration? Or, does the structure of institutional activity serve to mediate relationships between different cultural groups, and thereby modify the expression of their different cultural values?

Leo Despres, *Cultural Pluralism and Nationalist Politics in British Guiana* (Chicago: Rand McNally, 1967), pp. 25, 28. For discussions of this contingent relationship, see Adam Przeworski and John Sprague, "A History of Western European Socialism," unpublished manuscript; and Amy Bridges, "A City in the Republic: New York and the Origins of Machine Politics" (Ph.D. diss., Department of Political Science, University of Chicago, 1980), chap. 1.

Chapter 6. Assaults on the Trenches

[1] Here I break with an interpretation I presented in "The Crisis of Capitalist City: Urban Politics and Social Control," in Willis Hawley and Michael Lipsky, eds., *Theoretical Perspectives on Urban Politics* (Englewood Cliffs, N.J.: Prentice-Hall, 1976).

[2] For welfare data, see James Dumpson, "Aiding the City's Poor," in Robert Connery and Demetrios Caraley, eds., *Governing the City* (New York: Praeger, 1969); and David Gordon, "Income and Welfare in New York City," *The Public Interest*, no. 16 (summer 1969).

[3] Ibid., p. 87. Piven and Cloward stress the noneconomic causes; Frances Fox Piven and Richard Cloward, *Regulating the Poor: The Functions of Public Welfare* (New York: Pantheon Books, 1971).

[4] Edward C. Banfield and James Q. Wilson, *City Politics* (New York: Vintage Books, 1963), p. 18.

[5] The phrase is Oliver Williams's, cited in James O'Connor, *The Fiscal Crisis of the State* (New York: St. Martin's Press, 1973), p. 87.

[6] Peter Berger and Thomas Luckmann, *The Social Construction of Reality* (Garden City, N.Y.: Doubleday Anchor, 1967), p. 64.

[7] Leonard Binder et al., *Crises and Sequences in Political Development* (Princeton, N.J.: Princeton University Press, 1972).

[8] Ibid., chaps. 4 and 5.

[9] Sidney Verba, "Sequences and Development," in ibid., p. 302. My treatment of this literature has been influenced by Mark Kesselman, "Order or Movement? The Literature of Political Development as Ideology," *World Politics* 26 (October 1973).

[10] S. N. Eisenstadt, "Bureaucracy and Political Development," in Joseph La-Palombara, ed., *Bureaucracy and Political Development* (Princeton: Princeton University Press, 1953), p. 105; Samuel P. Huntington, *Political Order in Changing Societies* (New Haven, Conn.: Yale University Press, 1968), p. 21.

[11] Martin Shefter, "The Emergence of the Political Machine: An Alternative View," in Willis Hawley and Michael Lipsky, eds., *Urban Politics*, p. 17.

[12] Andrew Nathan, "Clientalism in Politics: Introduction and Critique," unpublished ms.; Eric Nordlinger, *Conflict Regulation in Divided Societies* (Cambridge, Mass.: Center for International Affairs, Harvard University, 1972), pp. 79–132; see also Huntington, *Political Order*, p. 89.

[13] James Scott, "Corruption, Machine Politics, and Political Change," *American Political Science Review* 63 (1969): 1155; see also David Kurtzman, "Methods of Controlling Votes in Philadelphia" (Ph.D. diss., Department of Political Science, University of Pennsylvania, 1935).

[14] For a discussion of these themes, see Ira Katznelson, *Black Men, White Cities* (New York: Oxford, 1973), esp. chaps. 5–7; see also V. O. Key, Jr., "The Techniques of Political Graft in the United States" (Ph.D. diss., Department of Political Science, University of Chicago, 1934). Writing in the 1930s, Gosnell sought to construct a balance sheet of machine politics. In the midst of the century's major crisis of the capitalist order, he found that in Chicago the machine was a vital element in the maintenance of social cohesion:

From the standpoint of the business leaders, this function of parties has been very useful. Some of the submerged groups may not be so appreciative; but the fact remains that during the years 1930–1936 the city was comparatively free from violent labor disputes, hunger riots and class warfare. The decentralized, chaotic, and inadequate character of the governmental organization of the city has discouraged far-reaching demands upon local authorities.

Harold F. Gosnell, *Machine Politics* (Chicago: University of Chicago Press, 1968), p. 183.

[15] Katznelson, *Black Men*, esp. chaps. 5–7.

[16] Cf. Richard Taub et al., "Urban Voluntary Associations, Locality Based and Externally Induced," *American Journal of Sociology* 83 (September 1977).

[17] Piven and Cloward, *Regulating the Poor*, p. 227.

[18] Donald Von Eschen, Jerome Kirk, and Maurice Pinard, "The Organizational Substructure of Disorderly Politics," *Social Forces* 49 (June 1971): 529.

[19] For a superb discussion of these matters, see William J. Wilson, *The Declining Significance of Race: Blacks and Changing American Institutions* (Chicago: University of Chicago Press, 1978).

[20] See Lawrence Cremin, *The Transformation of the School* (New York: Knopf, 1961); Alice Felt Tyler, *Freedom's Ferment: Phases of American Social History to 1860* (Minneapolis: University of Minnesota Press, 1944); and Rush Welter, *Popular Education and Democratic Thought in America* (New York: Columbia University Press, 1963).

[21] Michael Katz, *The Irony of Early School Reform* (Boston: Beacon Press, 1968); Joel H. Spring, *Education and the Rise of the Corporate State* (Boston: Beacon Press, 1972).

[22] David B. Tyack, *The One Best System: A History of American Urban Education* (Cambridge, Mass.: Harvard University Press, 1974), p. 78.

[23] *Commentary* 37 (March 1964): 35.

[24] David Boesel, "An Analysis of the Ghetto Riots," in David Boesel and Peter

Rossi, eds., *Cities under Siege: An Anatomy of the Ghetto Riots* (New York: Basic Books, 1971), p. 413.

[25] Eric Hobsbawm, *Primitive Rebels* (New York: Norton, 1959), p. 118.

[26] Robert Blauner, "Whitewash over Watts," *Transaction* 3 (March/April 1966): 54.

[27] Robert Blauner, "Internal Colonialism and Ghetto Revolt," *Social Problems* 16 (spring 1969).

[28] Martin Shefter, "Party, Bureaucracy, and Political Change in the United States," in Louis Maisel and Joseph Cooper, eds., *The Development of Political Parties: Patterns of Evolution and Decay* (Beverly Hills, Cal.: Sage Publications, 1978, p. 226; see also Ari Hoogenboom, *Outlawing the Spoils: A History of the Civil Service Reform Movement, 1865–1883* (Urbana, Ill.: University of Illinois Press, 1961).

[29] Magali Sarfatti Larson, *The Rise of Professionalism: A Sociological Analysis* (Berkeley and Los Angeles: University of California Press, 1977), p. xvi.

[30] This discussion of professionalism relies mainly on Larson's work, which, in my view, is the most important discussion of these questions; ibid.

[31] Shefter, "Party," p. 230.

[32] Clifton K. Yearley, *The Money Machines: The Breakdown and Reform of Governmental and Party Finance in the North, 1860–1920* (Albany: State University of New York Press, 1972). See also Martin J. Schiesl, *The Politics of Efficiency: Municipal Administration and Reform in America, 1880–1920* (Berkeley and Los Angeles: University of California Press, 1977).

[33] Theodore J. Lowi, *At the Pleasure of the Mayor* (New York: Free Press, 1964), pp. 185–87; see also John D. Buekner, *Urban Liberalism and Progressive Reform* (New York: Scribners, 1973); J. David Greenstone and Paul Peterson, *Race and Authority in Urban Politics* (New York: Russell Sage Foundation, 1973), esp. chaps. 4 and 5; and Sheila Stern, "The American Labor Party, 1936–1944" (M.A. essay, Department of Political Science, University of Chicago, 1964).

[34] Lowi, *Mayor*, p. 190.

[35] Ibid., p. 207.

[36] For a discussion of a machine built from scratch with the largesse of the New Deal, see Bruce Stave, *The New Deal and the Last Hurrah: Pittsburgh Machine Politics* (Pittsburgh, University of Pittsburgh Press, 1970).

[37] Scott, "Corruption," pp. 1156–58; see also James Scott, *The Moral Economy of the Peasant* (New Haven, Conn.: Yale University Press, 1976), esp. chap. 6.

[38] Cited in Norman M. Adler and Blanche Davis Blank, *Political Clubs in New York* (New York: Praeger, 1975), p. 226.

[39] Roy V. Peel, *The Political Clubs of New York City* (New York: Putnam, 1935), p. 320.

[40] Adler and Blank, *Political Clubs*, pp. 32–37, 119–41.

[41] Interviews with Rose Turiello, club president, and John Hart, member of the State Liquor Commission, February 1973.

[42] Interview with Arlene Stringer, female leader, Seventy-third Assembly District, Part A, March 1973; Hart interview.

[43] Michael Byowitz, "An Analysis of Two Local Political Organizations and Theoretical Considerations Arising from the Data," unpublished ms. The tangible costs to the club of this contraction proved to be considerable. Zaretzki, long thought by club members to be unbeatable, was defeated for renomination by a nonclub challenger in the September 1974 primary election.

The relative decline of such party organizations as the Progressive Democrats needs to be interpreted cautiously. For however weak they had become, compared to their capacity in the past, and however vulnerable they now were to the challenges of independent political entrepreneurs, the local party continued to have virtually no organizational competitors in white-ethnic neighborhoods for the performance of its traditional electoral, patronage, and symbolic functions. As a result, the party clubs of northern Manhattan continued to be the most important broker institutions in the community in the 1960s and early 1970s. Other community brokers, including most notably the local Community Board, which had advisory jurisdiction over land use and capital expenditures, were frequently organized on the basis of party affiliations and strength. Thus of the forty-seven members of the board in the early 1970s at least thirty-eight were appointed by the borough president on the recommendation of the party organizations; the largest contingent (eleven) belonged to the Progressive Democrats. We return to a discussion of the Community Board in Chapter 7 but for now we should note that this basis for selection made the board largely an extention of the institutional capacity of "old" Washington Heights.

[44] Table, "Welfare State Assistance (1972)," p. 250.

[45] Block Survey.

[46]

PUBLIC, PRIVATE, AND PAROCHIAL ELEMENTARY EDUCATION IN FOUR NORTHERN MANHATTAN CENSUS TRACTS (1970)

Elementary School Type	(N)	#239 (South Washington Heights) (217)	#211 (Highbridge–East Washington Heights) (1641)	#273 (West Washington Heights) (344)	#295 (Inwood) (555)
PUBLIC SCHOOL		82.9%	75.5%	47.3%	33.6%
PRIVATE SCHOOL		9.6	0.9	13.7	63.2
PAROCHIAL SCHOOL		7.4	23.6	39.0	3.2

SOURCE: U.S. Census.

[47] Michael Lipsky, *Street-Level Bureaucracy: Dilemmas of the Individual in Public Services* (New York: Russell Sage Foundation, 1980).

[48] By comparison, only 1 percent of the Jews and 3 percent of the Irish were not U.S. citizens.

[49] Public Survey and Block Survey. Relevant discussions include Julio Cesar Rojas, "Clientalism in Washington Heights and Its Ability to Adapt to Changes in the Community's Composition and Needs," unpublished ms.; Luis Recolons Arquer, "Spanish Speaking People and Participation in Washington Heights," unpublished ms.; Lourdes Casal, "Cuban Immigrants and U.S. Politics," unpublished ms.; and Glenn Hendricks, *The Dominican Diaspora* (New York: Teachers College Press, 1974), chaps. 5 and 7.

[50] Tables, "Support for Ethnic Political Action (1972)," and "Support for Militant Ethnic Tactics (1972)," pp. 251–52.

[51] Block Survey.

[52] This count may not be precise, since it is based in some instances on the extrapolation of ethnicity from surnames.

WELFARE STATE ASSISTANCE IN THE PAST YEAR (1972)

	Jews (71)	Irish (58)	Other White Ethnics (55)	Blacks (63)	Cubans (78)	Dominicans (61)	Other Hispanics (67)	Others (17)	Total (466)
(N)									
UNEMPLOYMENT COMPENSATION	5.6%	1.7%	5.5%	6.3%	10.3%	19.7%	7.4%	0.0%	7.9%
SOCIAL SECURITY	31.0	25.9	18.2	7.9	0.0	1.6	0.1	0.0	11.6
OLD AGE ASSISTANCE	1.4	0.0	0.0	4.8	2.6	0.0	0.0	0.0	1.3
AID TO FAMILIES WITH DEPENDENT CHILDREN (AFDC) AND/OR GENERAL WELFARE ASSISTANCE	2.8	1.7	5.5	20.0	21.8	18.0	11.9	15.4	11.8
NONE	59.2	70.7	70.9	63.5	65.4	60.7	79.1	84.6	67.4

SOURCE: Block Survey.

SUPPORT FOR ETHNIC POLITICAL ACTION (1972)

(N)	Jews (71)	Irish (58)	Other White Ethnics (55)	Blacks (63)	Cubans (78)	Dominicans (61)	Other Hispanics (67)	Others (13)	Total (466)
AGREE STRONGLY	35.2%	22.4%	10.9%	71.4%	43.6%	47.5%	58.2%	38.5%	42.1%
AGREE SOMEWHAT	28.2	31.0	18.2	15.9	26.9	27.9	20.8	23.1	24.2
MIXED FEELINGS	16.9	22.4	9.1	3.2	3.8	4.9	7.5	7.7	9.4
DISAGREE SOMEWHAT	2.8	3.4	25.5	4.8	14.1	9.8	4.5	7.7	9.0
DISAGREE STRONGLY	6.0	17.2	27.3	3.2	6.4	8.2	8.9	7.7	10.7
DON'T KNOW/OTHER	8.4	3.4	9.0	0.2	5.1	1.6	0.0	15.3	4.5

SOURCE: Block Survey.

SUPPORT FOR MILITANT ETHNIC TACTICS (1972)

(N)	Jews (71)	Irish (58)	Other White Ethnics (55)	Blacks (63)	Cubans (78)	Dominicans (61)	Other Hispanics (67)	Others (13)	Total (466)
AGREE STRONGLY	11.3%	8.6%	1.8%	33.3%	15.4%	31.1%	11.9%	7.7%	16.2%
AGREE SOMEWHAT	11.3	6.9	5.5	15.9	14.1	18.0	28.3	23.1	14.8
MIXED FEELINGS	15.5	17.2	3.6	14.3	9.0	11.5	3.0	7.7	10.5
DISAGREE SOMEWHAT	18.3	13.8	21.8	19.0	19.2	6.6	17.9	15.4	16.7
DISAGREE STRONGLY	35.2	51.7	61.8	15.9	32.1	29.5	38.9	30.8	36.9
DON'T KNOW/ OTHER	8.5	1.7	5.5	1.6	10.3	3.3	0.0	15.4	4.9

SOURCE: Block Survey.

53

**PUBLIC AND PRIVATE SECTOR EMPLOYMENT FOR RESIDENTS OF FOUR
NORTHERN MANHATTAN CENSUS TRACTS (1970)**

Employment Chars.	#239 (South Washington Heights) No.	%	#261 (Highbridge– East Washington Heights) No.	%	#273 (West Washington Heights) No.	%	#295 (Inwood) No.	%
LABOR FORCE 16–65 YRS. OLD	1,302	100	4,715	100	3,213	100	3,485	100
LOCAL GOVERNMENT EMPLOYEE	145	11.2	314	6.6	370	11.5	271	7.8
STATE GOVERNMENT EMPLOYEE	32	2.5	76	1.6	39	1.2	51	1.5
FEDERAL GOVERNMENT EMPLOYEE	92	7.0	144	3.1	75	2.4	82	2.3
TOTAL PUBLIC SECTOR	269	20.7	534	11.3	484	15.1	404	11.6
PRIVATE SECTOR EMPLOYMENT	1,033	79.3	4,181	88.7	2,729	84.9	3,081	88.4

[54] Piven and Cloward, *Regulating the Poor,* p. 311.

Chapter 7. Innovation and Reform, 1969–1974

[1] "The hallmark of the Great Society programs was the direct relationship between the national government and the ghettoes, a relationship in which both the state and local governments were undercut." These programs, Piven and Cloward perceptively note, were attempts to structure and manage the discontent of a volatile and politically rebellious population by creating discrete institutional structures outside of the usual political arrangements:

Although the federal government did not fully anticipate and could not fully manage all of the varied activities it had set into motion, it nevertheless shaped the overall course of these events, and in very traditional directions. If civil rights workers often turned federal dollars to their own purposes in the short run, in the longer run they became model-cities directors, or community-action executives—that is, they became government employees or contractors subject to the constraints of federal funding and federal guidelines. In many cities the Great Society agencies became the base for new black political organizations whose rhetoric may have been thunderous but whose activities came to consist mainly of vying for position and patronage within the urban political system. . . .

Over a period of time, in other words, federal intervention had the effect of absorbing and directing many of the agitational elements in the black population. . . . those who regard these federal actions as unintended, as a mistake, will have to account for the reason the mistake was repeated and enlarged from one legislative program to another as the decade wore on.

Peter Rossi, an acute but less critical observer, has captured the same basic point:

The new poverty and related agencies provided positions for black leaders. In the urban ghettoes of the North, the quasi-public offices of community action programs, Model Cities Agencies, Urban Coalition Committees, and the like provided positions with

sufficient visibility that black leaders could become better known to their own communities and to the city officials. Just as the political machine provided opportunities for the newly arrived ethnic groups on their way up, so the health, welfare and education industries are providing similar opportunities for blacks. New types of urban "machines" are being constructed. . . .

Frances Fox Piven and Richard Cloward, *Regulating the Poor: The Functions of Public Welfare* (New York: Pantheon Books, 1971), pp. 274–77; Peter Rossi, "Urban Revolt and the Future of American Cities," in David Boesel and Peter Rossi, eds., *Cities under Siege: An Anatomy of the Ghetto Riots* (New York: Basic Books, 1971), p. 421. For discussions of the progress of decentralization in other American cities, see George J. Washnis, *Municipal Decentralization and Neighborhood Resources* (New York: Praeger, 1973).

[2] Theodor Geiger, *Die Masse und ihre Aktion* (Stuttgart: 1926), p. 59.

[3] Arno Mayer, *Dynamics of Counterrevolution in Europe* (New York: Harper & Row, 1971), p. 45.

[4] Mayor John V. Lindsay, "A Plan for Neighborhood Government for New York City," June 1970.

[5] John V. Lindsay, *The City* (New York: Bantam Books, 1970), p. 118 (italics added). Actually, as a 1969 evaluation study carried out for the mayor's Office of Administration indicated, the city's neighborhood city halls lacked adequate filing systems, received only sporadic cooperation from the city's bureaucracies, hardly got any help from the program's citywide coordinators, and relied for results (as had more traditional party machines) on personal contacts with friendly bureaucrats and landlords. But as Lindsay indicated, substantive performance counted for less, at least in the short run, than did mass perceptions of effectiveness and responsiveness. Office of the Mayor, Office of Administration, "A Study of the Complaint-Receiving Mechanisms of the Mayor's Action Center, the Urban Action Task Force, and the Neighborhood City Halls," October 1969.

[6] Barry Gottehrer, *The Mayor's Man* (Garden City, N.Y.: Doubleday, 1975), p. 4.

[7] Ibid., p. 34.

[8] Lindsay, *City*, pp. 87, 95.

[9] Gottehrer, *Mayor's Man*, p. 38.

[10] Ibid., p. 50.

[11] City of New York, Office of the Mayor, Executive Order no. 73, "Establishment of the Urban Action Task Force," 22 April 1968.

[12] Ibid.

[13] Lindsay, *City*, p. 101.

[14] *Report of the National Advisory Commission on Civil Disorders* (New York: Bantam Books, 1968), p. 290.

[15] E. S. Savas, letter to community groups calling for an initial meeting of the Washington Heights–Inwood Urban Action Task Force, 20 May 1969; cf. Douglas Yates, "Decentralization in Cities: Initiatives and Impacts" (Working paper for the Institution for Social Policy Studies, Yale University, May 1972).

[16] Washington Heights–Inwood Urban Action Task Force, "Minutes," 4 June 1969.

[17] Communicated to Lewis Feldstein, chairman of the Mayor's Urban Action Task Force, 22 July 1970.

[18] "The Citizens Union Program for Community Planning," *The Searchlight* 37 (July 1947).

[19] City of New York, President of the Borough of Manhattan, "Community Planning Districts," 23 July 1951.

[20] Brigitte Doring-Bradley, "The Community Board: An Agent of Change or Legitimation?" (M.A. essay, Department of Sociology, Columbia University, 1972).

[21] City of New York, Local Law 39, July 1969.

[22] Doring-Bradley, "Community Board."

[23] E. S. Savas, "Pilot Program for Neighborhood Government in Washington Heights–Inwood," August 1970.

[24] Interview with Jules Cooper, member and former chairman of Community Board No. 12, August 1973.

[25] Negotiating session, 28 January 1971.

[26] The draft agreement setting up this structure was dated 1 March 1971.

[27] Jordan Linfield, "Report to the Community," January 1972; idem, letters to community groups, 24 June 1971 and 29 June 1971.

[28] By contrast, the Leadership Survey found that NAP was quite visible. Only 23 percent had not heard of the organization, and about half knew that it was led by Jordan Linfield.

[29] Meeting of the Community Board, 9 November 1971 (verbatim notes).

[30] Subsequent budgets were very similar in their programmatic emphases to the first.

[31] The discussion in this and subsequent paragraphs is drawn from Henry C. Wells, Paul A. Ballard, Ira Katznelson, and E. Sharman Mather, "The Office of Neighborhood Government and Community Leaders," Bureau of Applied Social Research, Columbia University, October 1973.

[32] *Heights–Inwood,* May 24, 1973, p. 1.

[33] *Heights–Inwood,* March 20, 1975, p. 1.

[34] "Desegregating the Public Schools of New York City," report prepared for the Board of Education of the City of New York by the State Education Commissioner's Advisory Committee on Human Relations and Community Tensions (the Allen Report), 12 May 1964.

[35] Diane Ravitch, *The Great School Wars: New York City, 1805–1973* (New York: Basic Books, 1974), p. 294. See also Carolyn Eisenberg, "The Parents Movement at IS 201: From Integration to Black Power, 1958–1966" (Ph.D. diss., Teachers College, Columbia University, 1971).

[36] Preston Wilcox, "One View and a Proposal," *Urban Review,* July 1966, pp. 12–16.

[37] For useful but antagonistic treatments, see Maurice Berube and Marilyn Gittell, eds., *Confrontation at Ocean Hill–Brownsville: The New York School Strikes of 1968* (New York: Praeger, 1969); and Martin Mayer, *The Teachers Strike: New York, 1968* (New York: Harper & Row, 1969).

[38] A major concern of those involved at the time were the activities of Dr. Thomas Matthews, head of NEGRO and later a prominent supporter of the Nixon administration, who was attempting to sponsor his own elections for a school board in District Six. Strauss and many other parents-association leaders were anxious to forestall what they regarded as an illegitimate attempt to claim the mantle of representativeness. Eventually, the associations and Matthews met and worked out common guidelines for the anticipated elections, but this agreement was made moot by the passage of the Decentralization Act of 1969.

[39] In addition to Ravitch, *School Wars*, see Mario Fantini, Marilyn Gittell, and Richard Magat, *Community Control and the Urban School* (New York: Praeger, 1970); and Marilyn Gittell and Alan G. Hevesi, eds., *The Politics of Urban Education* (New York: Praeger, 1969).

[40] In addition to the usual electorate, the act provided for a new category of parent voters. Parents of public-school children who were aliens or were too young to ordinarily qualify could register for school-board elections.

[41] The voters cast a preferential, transferable ballot, writing "1" next to their first choice, "2" next to the second, and so on, for as many candidates as they wish. To be elected, a candidate must get a "quota" of votes, determined by the following formula: total number of votes cast/number of seats − 1, plus 1; or, in other words, a tenth plus one of the votes cast in the district for the nine-member board. In the tallying, first preferences are counted first. Candidates over the quota are declared elected. Surplus votes are then allocated to second choices, and so on until a nine-member board is chosen.

[42] Especially the United Bronx Parents.

[43] Ravitch, *School Wars*, p. 389.

[44] Fully 90 percent of Cashin's vote surplus on the first count was distributed to Ayala and Halloran.

[45] Interview with Richard Cashin, 1 April 1974.

[46] For this observation I am indebted to Mark Glasser.

[47] "Minutes," Community School Board, District Six, 28 July 1970.

[48] "Minutes," Community School Board, District Six, 24 September 1970.

[49] Henry C. Wells, "Notes for the Analysis of School Politics in Washington Heights," unpublished ms.

[50] Michael Krasner, "Neighborhood Groups and Urban Education: The Politics of Two New York City School Districts in the Period Following Decentralization," Ph.D. diss., Columbia University, Department of Political Science, 1977.

[51] Seventy-two people were employed in the bilingual education program in the fall of 1971.

[52] Interview with Leonard Strauss, 19 May 1974.

[53] "Minutes," Community School Board, District Six, 9 June 1971.

[54] See Paul E. Peterson, "Forms of Representation: Participation of the Poor in the Community Action Program," *American Political Science Review* 64 (June 1970); and V. O. Key, *Southern Politics* (New York: Knopf, 1950).

[55] "Minutes," Community School Board, District Six, 21 March 1974.

[56] Ibid.

[57] Strauss interview.

[58] "Minutes," Community School Board, District Twelve, 15 November 1973.

[59] Ibid.

[60] E. P. Thompson, "Eighteenth Century English Society: Class Struggle Without Class?" *Social History* 3 (May 1978): 151.

[61] Ibid.

[62] Irving Kristol, "Decentralization for What?" *The Public Interest*, no. 11 (spring 1968), p. 19; Daniel Bell and Virginia Held, "The Community Revolution," *The Public Interest*, no. 16 (summer 1969), pp. 152–53.

[63] Milton Kotler, *Neighborhood Government* (Indianapolis: Bobbs-Merrill, 1969), pp. 26, xii.

[64] Alan Altshuler, *Community Control: The Black Demand for Participation in Large American Cities* (New York: Pegasus, 1970), p. 203.

[65] Ibid., p. 195.

[66] Ibid., pp. 30, 55.

[67] Ibid., pp. 113, 197.

[68] Ibid., pp. 112–13, 199.

[69] Cf. Michael Lipsky and David J. Olson, "The Processing of Racial Crisis in America," *Politics and Society* 6, no. 1 (1976).

[70] Frances Fox Piven, "The Urban Crisis: Who Got What and Why," in Robert Paul Wolff, ed., *1984 Revisited: Prospects for American Politics* (New York: Knopf, 1973), p. 183.

[71] Piven and Cloward, *Regulating the Poor.*

[72] Piven, "Urban Crisis."

[73] Frances Fox Piven and Richard Cloward, *Poor People's Movements: Why They Succeed, How They Fail* (New York: Pantheon Books, 1977).

[74] I am indebted for these observations to Paul A. Ballard and Deborah Socolow Katznelson, who spent considerable time observing meetings of the Community Board.

[75] Ravitch, *School Wars.*

[76] See David Rodgers, *110 Livingston Street: Politics and Bureaucracy in the New York City School System* (New York: Random House, 1968).

[77] The rhetoric of local authorities sounded as if it had been borrowed from Samuel P. Huntington, *Political Order in Changing Societies* (New Haven, Conn.: Yale University Press, 1968).

[78] Mark Kesselman, "Overinstitutionalization and Political Constraint: The Case of France," *Comparative Politics* 3 (October 1970): 24–25.

[79] Cf. "Disillusioned Incumbents Tell Why They're Leaving After Years of Battles on Community School Boards," *New York Times*, 2 May 1977, p. 35.

[80] *New York Times*, 18 May 1977.

[81] Frank J. Macchiarola, "Political Decentralization in New York City: A Progress Report," unpublished manuscript, September 1973.

[82] Adam Przeworski, "Social Democracy as a Historical Phenomenon," *New Left Review*, no. 122 (July–August 1980), pp. 28–32.

[83] Piven and Cloward, *Poor People's Movements*, pp. 29–36.

PART THREE. CONCLUSION
Chapter 8. Social Theory, Urban Movements, and Social Change

[1] Saul D. Alinsky, *Reveille for Radicals* (Chicago: University of Chicago Press, 1942); idem, *Citizen Participation and Community Organization in Planning and Urban Renewal* (Chicago: Industrial Areas Foundations, 1962); Margaret Levi, "Poor People Against the State," *Review of Radical Political Economics* 6 (spring 1974).

[2] A good guide to this new mood and to the seductiveness of community-organization strategies is the special issue on "Organizing Neighborhoods" of *Social Policy* 10 (September/October 1979). Especially useful and revealing are Harry Boyte, "A Democratic Awakening"; John Mollenkopf, "Neighborhood Politics for the 1980's"; Janice Perlman, "Grassroots Empowerment and Government Response"; Gar Alperowitz and Jeff Faux, "Neighborhoods for a

Democratic Society"; and the concluding "Profile of Some Neighborhood and Community Organizations."

[3] Arthur C. Stinchcombe, *Constructing Social Theories* (New York: Harcourt, Brace & World, 1968), p. 3.

[4] Asa Briggs, "The Language of 'Class' in Early Nineteenth Century England," in Asa Briggs and John Saville, eds., *Essays in Labour History* (London: Macmillan, 1967); Raymond Williams, *Keywords: A Vocabulary of Culture and Society* (New York: Oxford University Press, 1976), pp. 51–58.

[5] Marx, *Grundrisse* (London: Penguin Books, 1973), p. 858.

[6] Max Weber, *Economy and Society* (New York, Bedminster Press, 1968), p. 637.

[7] Marx, *Grundrisse*, p. 157.

[8] Weber, *Economy*, p. 636.

[9] Marx, *Grundrisse*, p. 458.

[10] Raymond Aron, "Social Structure and the Ruling Class," *British Journal of Sociology* 1 (March 1950): 4–5.

[11] W. Lloyd Warner and Paul S. Lunt, *The Social Life of a Modern Community* (New Haven, Conn.: Yale University Press, 1941), pp. 3, 5.

[12] G. A. Hillery, "Definitions of Community," *Rural Sociology* 20 (June 1955): 111–23.

[13] For a review of the literature, see Marcia Pelly Effrat, "Approaches to Community: Conflicts and Complementarities," in Effrat, ed., *The Community: Approaches and Applications* (New York: Free Press, 1974).

[14] Cf. Charles Tilly, "Do Communities Act?" in ibid.

[15] C. Wright Mills, *Sociology and Pragmatism: The Higher Learning in America* (New York: Paine-Whitman, 1964), p. 40.

[16] Theodore J. Lowi, *The End of Liberalism* (New York: Norton, 1969), esp. chaps. 1–3.

[17] Harvey W. Zorbaugh, *The Gold Coast and the Slum* (Chicago: University of Chicago Press, 1929); Herbert J. Gans, *The Urban Villagers* (New York: Free Press, 1962).

[18] W. Lloyd Warner, *Democracy in Jonesville: A Study of Quality and Inequality* (New York: Harper, 1949); The Yankee City Series, published in six volumes, studies a New England manufacturing town. Warner and Lunt, *Social Life,* inaugurated the series.

[19] Robert S. Lynd and Helen Merrell Lynd, *Middletown: A Study in American Culture* (New York: Harcourt, Brace, 1928). "The Long Arm of the Job" is the title of chap. 7. The theme of "penetration" recurs in virtually all the best community studies. Patterns of racism are embedded in the content of St. Clair Drake and Horace Cayton's *Black Metropolis* (New York: Harcourt, Brace, 1945). Dominant-value patterns about consumption and acceptable styles of life shape the communal patterns of John Seeley's *Crestwood Heights* (with R. Alexander Sim and E. W. Loosley; New York: Basic Books, 1956); and Herbert Gans's *Levittowners* (New York: Vintage Books, 1967). Arthur Vidich and Joseph Bensman's *Small Town in Mass Society* (Princeton, N.J.: Princeton University Press, 1958) resonates to a self-image largely fashioned by a picture of expectations internalized from the wider society. The spatial patterns of interaction in the Chicago school's portraits of the 1920s (and 1960s) are heavily shaped by larger spatial and cultural articulations. And, as in the redevelopment of Gans's West Side of Boston (*Urban Villagers*), communities may meet their end by the planning decisions of outsiders.

[20] Erik Olin Wright, "The Class Structure in Advanced Capitalist Societies," in Wright, *Class, Crisis and the State* (London: New Left Books, 1978) pp. 30–110; and Wright, "Varieties of Marxist Conceptions of Class Structure," *Politics and Society* 9, no. 3 (1980).

[21] Nicos Poulantzas, *Classes in Contemporary Capitalism* (London: New Left Books, 1975).

[22] Clifford Geertz, "On the Nature of Anthropological Understanding," *American Scientist* 63 (January–February 1975): 47–48.

[23] G. Carchedi, *On the Economic Identification of Social Classes* (London: Routledge & Kegan Paul, 1977); Christian Baudelot, Roger Establet, and Jacques Malemort, *La Petite bourgeoisie en France* (Paris: Maspero, 1974); Barbara Ehrenreich and John Ehrenreich, "The Professional-Managerial Class," *Radical America* 11, no. 2 (1977).

[24] Wright, "Varieties," p. 53 (ms.)

[25] Ibid.

[26] E. P. Thompson, "The Peculiarities of the English," in Ralph Miliband and John Saville, eds., *The Socialist Register, 1965* (New York: Monthly Review Press, 1966), p. 357.

[27] E. P. Thompson, "Folklore, Anthropology, and Social History," *Indian Historical Review* 3 (January 1977): 264.

[28] For an important discussion, see Adam Przeworski, "Proletariat into a Class: The Process of Class Formation from Karl Kautsky's *The Class Struggle* to Recent Controversies," *Politics and Society* 7, no. 4 (1977).

[29] E. P. Thompson, "The Poverty of Theory," *The Poverty of Theory and Other Essays* (London: Merlin Press, 1978), pp. 351, 242, 299.

[30] Etienne Balibar, "The Basic Concepts of Historical Materialism," in Louis Althusser and Etienne Balibar, *Reading Capital* (London: New Left Books, 1972), p. 267.

[31] Thompson, "Poverty," p. 299.

[32] This formulation is suggested by Steven Lukes, "Power and Structure," *Essays in Social Theory* (London: Macmillan, 1977).

[33] Thompson, "Poverty," p. 302.

[34] The term is E. J. Hobsbawm's; see his "From Social History to the History of Society," in M. W. Flinn and T. C. Snout, *Essays in Social History* (London: Oxford University Press, 1974).

[35] Ira Katznelson, "Considerations on Social Democracy in the United States," *Comparative Politics* 11 (October 1978): 85.

[36] Cf. Mancur Olson, *The Logic of Collective Action* (New York: Schocken Books, 1968); James Q. Wilson, *Political Organizations* (New York: Basic Books, 1973); Paul E. Peterson, "Incentive Theory and Group Influence" (Paper presented at the American Political Science Association Meetings, 1975); and Stephen E. Cornell, "American Indian Political Resurgence" (Ph.D. diss., Department of Sociology, University of Chicago, in progress).

[37] In order to refer to durable dispositions and practices, Bourdieu developed the concept *habitus*; Pierre Bourdieu, *Outline of a Theory of Practice* (Cambridge: Cambridge University Press, 1977), esp. pp. 78–87.

[38] Arthur L. Stinchcombe, *Theoretical Methods in Social History* (New York: Academic Press, 1978), p. 117.

[39] Raymond Williams, *Politics and Letters: Interviews with New Left Review* (London: New Left Books, 1979), p. 167. Williams, of course, is critical of this position.

[40] Morris Janowitz, "Sociological Theory and Social Control," *American Journal of Sociology* 81 (July 1975): 82.

[41] Georges Gurvich, "Social Control," in Georges Gurvich and Wilbert Moore, eds., *Twentieth Century Sociology* (New York: Philosophical Library, 1945), p. 272.

[42] Janowitz, "Sociological Theory," pp. 87, 84.

[43] Ira Katznelson, "The Crisis of the Capitalist City: Urban Politics and Social Control," in Willis Hawley, Michael Lipsky, et al., *Theoretical Perspectives on Urban Politics* (Englewood Cliffs, N.J.: Prentice-Hall, 1976), p. 220.

[44] Gareth Stedman Jones, "Class Expression versus Social Control: A Critique of Recent Trends in the Social History of 'Leisure,' " *History Workshop* 4 (autumn 1977): 164.

[45] Hobsbawm, "Social History," p. 15; Thompson, "Poverty," p. 242.

[46] Manuel Castells, "Urban Social Movements and the Struggle for Democracy: The Citizens' Movement in Madrid," *International Journal of Urban and Regional Research* 2 (March 1978): 133–34.

[47] Manuel Castells, "The Social Prerequisites for the Upheavals of Urban Social Movements: An Exploratory Study of the Paris Metropolitan Area, 1968–72," in Castells, *City, Class and Power* (London: Macmillan, 1978), pp. 126–27.

[48] Thompson, "Poverty," p. 238.

[49] Pierre Vilar, "Marxist History, A History in the Making: Towards a Dialogue with Althusser," *New Left Review,* no. 80 (July–August 1973), p. 97.

[50] Manuel Castells, *The Urban Question: A Marxist Approach* (London: Edward Arnold, 1977), p. 377.

[51] This "silence" is hardly Castells's alone; it is perhaps the most important "silence" in Marx's work.

[52] See Marshall Sahlins, *Culture and Practical Reason* (Chicago: University of Chicago Press, 1976), pp. 65–66, 123. Indeed, the language that movement participants use to talk about and to make sense of their experience reveals the character of their selective tradition as it shapes the possibilities of their action. When workers who talk about their situation as a class situation at work go home and act politically as Croatians or Poles, their language in use not only reveals the character of their dispositions, it also shapes possibilities of practice, and thus indirectly the nature of the social structure. The situationally specific language that workers use locates themselves, others, and the meaning of situations. The culture, expressed in speech, is a motivational currency. For a discussion of these issues, see A. D. Edwards, *Language in Culture and Class* (London: Heinemann Educational Books, 1976).

[53] Frances Fox Piven and Richard Cloward, *Poor People's Movements: Why They Succeed, How They Fail* (New York: Pantheon Books, 1977), pp. 20–21.

[54] Consider briefly the urban situation in Italy, compared to that of the United States. There, as in the U.S., the structural situation analyzed by Castells has been disposed toward the development of urban movements. There, as in the U.S., the concrete institutional experiences of urban residents stressed by Piven and Cloward impelled them to act in their communities against the regime. But here the similarities stop and the differences impose themselves. There, but not in the U.S., urban struggles have been organized by the PCI and the trade unions as an aspect of a larger, global class movement. Their aim, at least since the Second World War, has been to "create a movement that was not confined to the limits of the workplace. . . . From the first post-war years the unions had tried to throw themselves into society, fearing the risks involved in a politics concentrated entirely within the factory." The massive urban movements of

Italy after 1969, in this view of Piero Della Seta's, had their origins in the factory and the party. Endorsing this strategic orientation, he writes that

it is the main merit of the Italian workers' movement to have known how to harness the impulse coming from this multitude of movements and to link it to the institutions: to have kept the first tied to the second, to have utilized their propulsive force—unifying a multiplicity of particular and diverse issues and preventing them from exhausting their charges within the limits of the local institutions from whence they came and extracting the *political* from the purely *social,* applying them to the modification and the transformation of other areas. In this way the workers' movement has given to those struggles an historical perspective and a national breadth, transforming them into a "movement."

How different—in spite of shared structural causes and manifest experiences—the American case of the urban crisis and its resolution! Piero Della Seta, "Notes on Urban Struggles in Italy," *International Journal of Urban and Regional Research* 2 (June 1978): 325; see Richard M. Merelman, "On Interventionist Behavioralism: An Essay in the Sociology of Knowledge," *Politics and Society* 6, no. 1 (1976): 65–66. See also David J. Elkins and Richard E. B. Simeon, "A Cause in Search of Its Effect, or What Does Political Culture Explain?" *Comparative Politics* 11 (January 1979). I would add, albeit without the necessary argumentation here, that recent trends in the social sciences toward interpretive, hermeneutic approaches cannot be substitutes for more structural and historical methodologies. Yet in their place such quests for meaning are indispensable. For a sympathetic selection and commentary, see Paul Rabinow and William M. Sullivan, eds., *Interpretive Social Science: A Reader* (Berkeley and Los Angeles: University of California Press, 1979).

INDEX

Abbott, Carl, 49
absolutism, rise of, 32–3, 39
Academy of the Sacred Heart, 173, 174–6
Advisory Panel on School Decentralization, 155
Alianza, La, 131
Alinsky, Saul, 193
Allen, James, 154–5
Altshuler, Alan, 178–9
"American exceptionalism," 7–10; and ethnicity, 10–12; and national character tradition, 14–17; and social mobility, 12–14
American Federation of Labor, 67
American Labor Party, 124
Anderson, Perry, 29–30, 32, 33, 227 nn. 19, 26
Aron, Raymond, 197
artisans: in early cities, 26, 27, 35, 36, 37, 39; in U.S., 45, 48, 49, 52, 61, 66; and workingmen's parties, 53, 54
Ayala, Emma, 159

Bailey, Joseph, 160, 161, 162, 166
Baldwin, James, 118
Balibar, Étienne, 205
Baltimore, Md., 46–7, 60
Banfield, Edward C., 110
Barnes, John, 103
Beame, Abraham, 153
Bell, Daniel, 95–6, 225 n.38
Berger, Peter, 111
Berthoff, Rowland, 10
Birmingham, England, 39
Black Power, 120
blacks, 11, 12, 66, 137; employment, 96; and internal colonialism, 118–21; and political parties, 111, 112–15, 120; and school issues, 115–18

blacks, in Washington Heights–Inwood, 81, 89, 90, 98–100, 103, 106–7; and decentralization programs, 137, 140, 147, 176–80; in political bloc, 130–4; and school politics, 154, 155, 156–7, 159, 161, 164, 166, 168, 170, 171–2, 175; schools, enrollment in, 129; and welfare programs, 129
Blauner, Robert, 120
Bloch, Marc, 28–9
Boesel, David, 119
Bookchin, Murray, 26
Boorstin, Daniel, 14, 16, 17
Boston, 45, 46–7, 94; social mobility in, 12, 13
Braudel, Fernand, 28, 29, 30
Bridges, Amy, 18, 54
Bundy, McGeorge, 155
Burnham, Walter Dean, 64

capitalism, 7, 9, 71, 93; differentiation of, 194–201; and education, 116–17; and industrialization, 39–44; and party organization, 65–6; preindustrial, 31; and professionals, 122; and social control, 91–2, 207–9; and social mobility, 12–14; and urban movements, 209–15. *See also* cities; social class
Caro, David, 172
Cashin, Richard, 159
Castells, Manuel, 210–13
Catholic Church: and Irish immigrants, 80–1; and medieval towns, 26; and school politics in upper Manhattan, 157, 159–60, 161, 165, 166, 167, 169, 172
Chandler, Alfred, 46, 47
Chern, Gideon, 167

262

ABOUT THE AUTHOR

Ira Katznelson is professor and chairman of the department of political science at the University of Chicago. He is the author of *Black Men, White Cities*, and co-author of *The Politics of Power: A Critical Introduction to American Government*.